PUTTING DEMOCRACY TO WORK

PUTTING DEMOCRACY TO WORK

A Practical Guide for Starting
Worker-Owned Businesses

Frank T. Adams   Gary B. Hansen

HULOGOS'I   EUGENE
1987

A Yew Book
Published by Hulogos'i Communications, Inc.

Library of Congress Cataloging-in-Publication Data
Adams, Frank T.
Putting democracy to work.
Includes index.
1. Employee ownership. 2. Cooperation.
I. Hansen, Gary B. II. Title.
HD5650.A3   1987   658.1'147   87-4246

ISBN 0-938493-03-05

First Edition

Printed in the United States of America
By Thomson-Shore, Inc., Dexter, MI
Text typeset by Precision Graphics, Eugene OR
12 point Times Roman
Charts and Tables produced by Hulogos'i Communications
10 point Helvetica Laserprint

Hulogos'i Communications, Inc.
P.O. Box 1188
Eugene, OR 97440

ACKNOWLEDGEMENTS

We are indebted to the women and men who, over the years, have struggled in their workplaces to put democracy to work. They are the principle sources of our inspiration. They have given history theory and practice, teaching chiefly that there is something new to learn about workplace democracy every day.

We are particularly grateful to Steven Dawson, David Ellerman, Peter Pitegoff and Jan Saglio of the Industrial Cooperative Association, to Rick Surpin of the Community Service Society, to Keith Bridger of the Northeastern Research and Development Group, and Christopher Meek of Brigham Young University, who gave us the benefit of their experience and wisdom by reading the manuscript, offering suggestions for improvement, and for bearing with our frequent innocence. They are not responsible for the content, however. Tom Biesinger, who helped develop the tables for the sample business plan, and Janet Hansen, who typed the manuscript, also deserve acknowledgement and our thanks.

Frank T. Adams   Gary B. Hansen
Quincy, Massachusetts   Logan, Utah

CONTENTS

LIST OF CHARTS

PUTTING DEMOCRACY TO WORK

INTRODUCTION

What is Worker-Ownership?   *1*

This handbook is for women and men who want to own their labor. It is about creating good jobs, bringing democracy to the workplace, and promoting labor entrepreneurship. In a nutshell, it is about worker-ownership.

The concept of worker-ownership is easily understood, almost self-defining. In practice, however, the ownership of capital by labor and labor's resulting management of capital pose thorny problems, chiefly because we, as workers, regardless of where we work, have had virtually no experience in owning or managing our working lives, much less applying the principles of democracy in the workplace.

Specifically, this book is about worker-owned cooperatives, for-profit businesses owned by those who work to make them prosper, and controlled by those same persons on the democratic principle of one person, one vote. All workers, including managers, become members after a trial period and the payment of a membership fee. No person outside the firm can be an owner. Profits earned by the business (or losses) are allocated to member-owners according to hours worked or gross pay. Wages vary according to skill and seniority, but usually the range of wages nurtures widespread well-being rather than making a few persons very well-off.

Worker-ownership is a third way to organize work. The term means what it says—a form of ownership where the employees in a for-profit business directly own and control the enterprise. It is not a guise for government ownership of the means of production, nor does it describe workers who own a few shares of stock in a company where the bosses, not the state, tell them what to do.

The idea that workers could own, govern, and manage the means of production was put forward first in the 1840s as an alternative to the domination of labor by either capital or the state. Today it is experiencing a surge of interest, or resurgence, especially in the United States and Europe. Around the world, hundreds of firms are owned by the persons who work in them. They manufacture a wide variety of products, including books, bicycle locks, stoves, and satellite parts. Others offer vital services, including health care, food service, and transportation.

Anyone can start a worker-owned and managed business, and thousands of working women and men have. Unions have organized them, too. These businesses operate prudently for profit while putting democracy to work.

A worker-owned business requires sound organization, skilled management, adequate financing, careful business planning and profitable markets like any successful business. But in a worker-owned business, the worker-owners elect a board of directors who hire the management, then hold them accountable for the corporate success. In turn, the board of directors is accountable to the worker-owners. In some few places, workers have extended democratic practice from the board room to the shop floor itself, directly governing their jobs.

While worker-owned and managed firms cross national boundries, ignoring race, religion, sex, age, and political persuasion, and are growing daily, they remain an infinitesimal part of the world economy. Nevertheless, because they demonstrate unique opportunities for work reorganization, democratic management structures, economic self-governance, even a redefinition of work and property, the idea is spreading from the bottom up. Worker-ownership offers a vision of what ought to be.

There are no definite formulas for establishing these democratic firms. The suggestions we offer derive from experience, both of workers themselves and of their supporters; the ideas here have been tested over time. They are tempered by our work as teachers who had the good fortune to collaborate with workers who knew what they needed to know, and asked us to help them learn. We offer the handbook for four groups:

☐ Workers, union members or the unorganized, in firms whose owners, for whatever reason, are willing to change from traditional ownership to worker-ownership.

☐ The unemployed who dream of starting their own business.

☐ Individuals or organizations who would use the workplace to foster human and capital growth.

☐ Rank-and-file union members and their leaders as they search for new roles for unions in a rapidly changing economy.

Why Worker-Ownership?

Why would a group of people want to organize a worker-owned business? Historically, there have been three main reasons:

First, people have been dissatisfied with the inability of private enterprise or government to provide good jobs—even enough work—for all people who wanted work.

Second, workers, especially those joining labor unions, have long sought more control over working conditions as well as an equitable share in the fruits of their labor.

Third, workers have sought to make work creatively useful, not drudgery which is endured to put bread on the table. They have wanted, in the words of E. F. Schumacher, work which will "enable workers to produce necessary and socially useful goods and services; enable each of us to use and perfect our skills; and to do so in service and in cooperation with others." (1)

Usually, employers have considered labor to be a variable cost and have treated workers as a "factor" or "units" of production to be hired, paid as little as possible, and managed in conformity with the demands of the production system. Workers, and sometimes their unions, have sought alternative ways of organizing work which provided more jobs, stabilized employment, eliminated the adversarial or paternal employer-employee relationship, or modified the traditional

3

role of managers.

Ideally, worker-ownership will alter the role of managers, no less than it reverses the traditional relationship between capital and labor. When workers control capital, managers are accountable to labor through a democratic, representational process. Worker-ownership treats management as one among many important skills which each business must employ, but one that does not denote special rank or privilege.

Western industrialized nations faced with plant closings or the threat of capital relocation, along with workers and their unions, have looked at various worker-ownership schemes to see if they offer alternatives to the destructive economic, social, and psychological effects shutdowns and layoffs impose on workers and their communities. Converging economic and political forces have produced serious declines in productivity, major structural changes in economies, stiffer foreign and domestic competition in traditional markets, high levels of inflation, rapid transfers of capital among nations, widespread unemployment, and a decline in industrial competitiveness. These economic problems have caused a dramatic rise in plant closings and the displacement of veteran blue-collar workers in basic industries.

In the United States and Canada, the principal source of our experience, workers and their unions have responded to potential shutdowns and layoffs by becoming directly, though sometimes reluctantly, involved in highly publicized efforts to save jobs. Noteworthy among these efforts were worker buyouts of large and small business enterprises such as South Bend Lathe in Indiana, Rath Packing in Iowa, Weirton Steel in West Virginia, Hyatt-Clark Industries in New Jersey, Canadian International Paper (Tembec) in Quebec, Canada West Shoe in Winnipeg, Northern Breweries Ltd. of Sault Ste. Marie, and many others. Workers in North Carolina, Florida and Oregon have started their own firms rather than accept welfare. Even unsuccessful attempts to found profitable worker-owned companies spark interest and further experimentation.

In Western Europe there have been similar responses. In Britain in 1975 workers bought out Meridian Motorcycle Works, Scottish Daily News, and Kirby Manufacturing and Engineering. Three years later, a national Cooperative Development Agency was created and local counterparts in many cities and regions, each charged with the responsibility of promoting worker-ownership. In France, since the mid-1970s, the creation of job-saving worker-owned cooper-atives expanded from one every few years to roughly 30 co-ops annually under the auspices of the Confederation Generale des Sociétés Coopératives Ouvrierés de Production (SCOP). In Wales the Trades Union Congress explored the creation of an industrial cooperative-based economic develop-ment program to ease chronically high unemployment due to the declining steel and coal industries. (2)

Gradually, in the United States, worker-owned businesses are becoming an important mechanism for economic develop-ment. They are a natural means for small towns or cities to promote job growth without resorting to government owner-ship or absentee owners. Jobs created by local residents themselves create profits that stay within the community. Fostering worker-ownership becomes a way to reduce costly unemployment benefits and capricious capital mobility while stabilizing tax bases. Worker-ownership offers ordinary citizens and workers the opportunity to become entrepreneurs, to join with other like-minded individuals and participate in the challenge, excitement, frustration, and sometimes heart-break of starting or operating a new form of business enterprise.

For unions, faced with fewer and fewer traditional labor agreements to administer, worker-ownership offers an oppor-tunity to carve a new, dynamic role which could add members by using tested skills in negotiation, grievance handling, and job design, to say nothing of their considerable human and capital resources, which, particularly in sizeable worker-owned firms, will be called on repeatedly. Even in small firms like Busy Needle Sewing Company in North Carolina, workers see the value of unions. At Busy Needle, once their firm got going, workers chose to become union members, and they willingly pay dues in return for engineering help furnished by the union, health and medical insurance obtained through group policies, and, importantly, solidarity with other workers.

Is Worker-Ownership Successful?

Worker-ownership is not a panacea, nor is it for everyone. Not all worker-owned businesses succeed. Not all forms of employee ownership promote democracy in the workplace. But evidence available from American and Canadian ex-perience concludes that employee ownership companies, in-

5

cluding worker-owned cooperatives, have done better than their rivals. They grew faster, were more profitable, generated more jobs, experienced higher productivity growth, and were more desirable to work for. (3)

A recent critical review of all forms of employee ownership in Britain and the United States by two internationally respected scholars, Keith Bradley of London University and Alan Gelb of the World Bank, arrived at three main conclusions:

☐ First, that the case for employee share ownership stands up well to critical analysis. It *is* a better alternative than traditional collective bargaining at arm's length, even if it is no panacea for bad industrial relations. The evidence is in our view strong enough to justify moves to spread employee ownership as rapidly as possible.

6

☐ Secondly, that employee ownership through buy-outs, admittedly more clearly in American than British experience, is a far more effective way of rescuing ailing companies and saving jobs than has been generally realized. We should not be put off by the failures of Meriden, Kirby and Scottish Daily News cooperatives. Buy-outs are generally a better bet than bail-outs.

☐ Thirdly, that despite the desirability of more employee share . . . (holding as a form of ownership) we should be cautious about tax incentives. Over-generous tax concessions (such as those provided by the federal government to Employee Stock Ownership Plans in the United States) will lead to abuse. . . . (4)

These same scholars reviewed the experience of the Basque worker-owned cooperatives in Spain during the last recession, and found that while they were not unscathed by the recent economic downturn, their adjustment was more flexible and less costly in terms of jobs. The cooperatives chose to trim pay over the 1980-83 period. Correspondingly, employment held up far better than the rest of Spanish industry. Had the Basque cooperative's membership paralleled employment throughout the entire Basque region of Spain over the 1979-83 period, the cooperatives would have ended the period with only 80 percent of their actual number of members. But through labor reallocation between enterprises and across occupations, unemployment was held to negligible levels. And while the rate of capital formation was slowed during this period, the cooperative's generous pension plan remained fully funded, unlike certain firms in difficulty in the United States which have sought to divert such assets. (5)

What the Basque experience suggests is that during their growth phases worker-owned cooperatives can promote regional development and create jobs. In their stabilization phases they offer some evidence that "internalizing adjustment within relatively small groups and communities and abolishing the capital/labour distinction can increase flexibility and reduce job loss." (6)

The most successful North American example of worker cooperatives contributing to job creation and workplace democracy is in Quebec. Starting worker-owned cooperatives became an important component of economic development and revitalization in the province, which experienced a poor economic situation in the late 1970s. In the period from 1979 to 1986, worker co-ops in Quebec grew at an annual rate of 12 percent, numbering over 265 today with 10,000 worker-owners. The growth of worker-owned cooperatives was promoted by the provincial government, which established two new interrelated programs and expanded a third one: the "Groupe Conseils" (GC) (advisory groups) and the "Coopératives de developement regional" (CDR) (regional development co-ops), and the "Société de Development Coopératif" (SDC) (cooperative development society). (7)

A staff of 40 provincial Department of Cooperatives development officers were hired to work with the GCs, helping workers interested in creating a worker cooperative. They are involved from the planning stage through to the first few months of operation, helping with feasibility studies, financial projections, aid requests, and development of internal structures. Through their efforts 53 new worker cooperatives were started and conversions of 14 conventional enterprises to worker cooperatives completed between 1983 and 1985. (8)

Eleven CDRs were established in the province from 1983 to 1985, and funded with about $2 million (Canadian) per year. They help identify the most promising prospects for worker co-op development and to match them with people who have the resources and potential to make them successful. Where the GCs provide the technical assistance, the CDRs, "like godfathers, try to ensure that a maximum of human and financial resources are available in their region" to facilitate worker cooperative growth. The CDRs serve as "resource banks", bringing together existing worker cooperatives, other

7

cooperatives, educational institutions, unions, and social and economic development agencies. They are partially financed by the government and partially by their member organizations. (9)

The third component of the successful Quebec worker cooperative movement is the SDC, which provides financial assistance to cooperatives. Established in 1979 to finance cooperative development, the SDC has invested nearly $7 million in more than 100 worker co-op proposals. Recently, the provincial government gave it new authority to foster worker cooperatives by guaranteeing loans, and assuming part or all of the interest on loans, that cooperatives can negotiate through financial institutions. (10)

Putting Democracy to Work

During the past 20 years there has been an extension of political democracy to new groups and individuals in America as a result of the 1964 Civil Rights Act and other legislation. The extension of the one person/one vote principle to formerly disenfranchised individuals and groups has broadened the base of democracy. More recently, there has been a movement to provide new forms of participation and extend greater democracy to employees in the workplace. This movement, sometimes called worker participation, employee involvement, or quality of work life, is proceeding apace, not only in America, but throughout Western Europe and Asia. Unfortunately, many companies have participated in these efforts only out of an interest in increasing productivity and profits, and have ignored employee rights. These companies have encouraged workers to take on new roles and responsibilities, but are reluctant to give them the management rights or "prerogatives" that go with the expanded roles.

To help clarify what workplace democracy means in this new environment of pervasive workplace innovations, it is important to understand the possible range of involvement and participation open to employees. Chart 1 lists five potential areas of employee involvement, three areas of decision-making, the sharing of material rewards, and ownership. (11) This handbook is designed for workers who want to become directly involved in increasing employee rights in all five types of workplace democracy in their places of employment. That is what worker-ownership is all about.

Chart 1

THE POTENTIAL RANGE OF WORKPLACE DEMOCRACY

Extent of Employee Rights	*None*	*Partial*	*Complete*
Shop Floor/Work Group Decision Making	☐	☐	☐
Management Level Decision Making	☐	☐	☐
Board Room Decision Making	☐	☐	☐
Profit/Surplus/Gain Sharing	☐	☐	☐
Ownership of Equity or Stock	☐	☐	☐

Within the worker-owned firm itself, democracy encourages leadership and skill development. Workers—often for the first time in their working lives—have an opportunity to participate in a broad array of economic and managerial responsibilities. From shop floor to the board room, workers can be their own bosses. This handbook is organized so that any interested person can learn the basics about worker-ownership, then proceed through the steps required to actually start a worker-owned cooperative. We focus on starting a business from scratch, and on a worker buyout of an existing business. Each has differing requirements, and differing dynamics. An argument can be made that the steps outlined could be used to target businesses within one industry for conversion to worker-ownership one by one until a significant market was controlled by worker-owners.

A sample business plan for The Worker-Owned Cooperative, its articles of incorporation, and a set of model by-laws are included. It is a fictional company, but one which represents a size in which democracy could flourish inside, while inspiring others outside. Sources of additional reading are included at the end of the book for those interested in following up some of the concepts and information presented. Finally, we include generally available sources of free information, or relatively inexpensive technical assistance for those who want to go beyond reading and are ready to put democracy to work.

9

1 HISTORY OF THE IDEA

THE ROCHDALE PIONEERS
WORKER COOPERATIVES IN THE UNITED STATES
WORKER COOPERATIVES IN EUROPE

Who came up with these ideas? The practice of workplace democracy and worker-ownership has been traced to antiquity. However, its present or modern form was sparked by critical reaction to industrial capitalism and the excesses of the industrial revolution. The formation of worker-owned and managed firms first appeared in Chatham and Woolwich, England, beginning in 1760. Artisans liked the idea because it permitted them to control their jobs, rather than merely carrying out orders. Intellectuals were drawn to the idea too, especially in England and France. By the early 1800s, dozens of consumer cooperatives were operating, as were several worker-owned production factories and mills. Dr. William King, a Brighton, England, medical doctor active in the cooperative movement, wrote on August 1, 1828, in the **Co-operator**, a monthly paper he edited:

> The working classes have the strongest possible motives *for opening shops for themselves* (italics his). The sum of money, which the working classes spend in the course of a year, is enormous. It amounts to many millions. The profit upon this sum, would of itself be sufficient to establish many manufactories. It is not the want of *power*, but the want of knowledge, which prevents their setting up to work and making a beginning. *Shopping for themselves*, and *working for themselves*, will give them profit, and therefore, *capital*, and therefore *independence*. (1)

The Welsh-born social reformer Robert Owen, a prosperous cotton mill owner in New Lanark, Scotland, promoted cooperation by setting up four communities, including one in New Harmony, Indiana, where work was to be self-managed. All of them failed. Owen's ideals were not sufficient glue to bind them together. In France, Charles Fourier was advocating the formation of phalanxes or associations as a way to fight pauperism. Pierre-Joseph Proudhon called for revision of property rights, including an end to inheritance of factories, the creation of workers' associations for artisans, and industrial associations for larger-scale production firms. He encouraged the idea of mutual aid. Dozens of clubs bearing that name sprang up in Europe and America.

Another French activist, Philippe Buchez, published on December 17, 1831, the basic principles of a producers' cooperative, ideas which have since been tested repeatedly throughout the world. Democratic control was uppermost in Buchez's mind. He wrote: (2)

> Associates would establish themselves as contractors; for this purpose they will elect from among themselves one or two representatives who would have the signature of the firm (meaning, in today's terms, be its managers. Ed. note.)

He fashioned a way to pay worker-members in proportion to the labor they contributed; a formula which while primitive, paralleled the patronage dividend of the consumer cooperative.

> Each person would continue to receive his salary according to practices in use in his profession, that is either by the day, or for the work done, and according to individual skill. A sum equal to that deducted from each day's work by intermediate contractors would be put aside; at the end of the year this sum, representing the net profit, will be divided into two parts: twenty percent of it would constitute and increase the registered capital and the rest would be devoted to assistance or distributed among the associates proportional to their work.

To protect against a minority of the worker-members seeking to sell the firm, Buchez proposed a third principle which can be stated as the principle of disinterested transfer of the net assets: in case a worker-owned firm dissolved the cooperators should donate the net assets to another producer cooperative, to a philanthropy, or to the state.

Finally, to insure that there would be no division within the workforce between those who contributed labor only or those who provided both labor and capital, Buchez proposed a fourth principle:

> The association would not be allowed to employ non-affiliated labour to its account for more than one year; at the end of this time admission of as many new workers as the increase of activity would necessitate, would become compulsory.

His ideas proved beneficial to the enterprises which tested them. At the time, workers and their allies everywhere in Europe and North America were actively seeking alternatives to the emergence of industrial capitalism.

13

The Rochdale Pioneers

Cooperative ideas coalesced in Rochdale, England, when twenty-four willing but jobless weavers formed the Society of Equitable Pioneers on October 24, 1844. They had spent a year discussing among themselves how to make life a bit better. They knew of Robert Owen and tried in vain to secure his personal help. They believed what Dr. King said in his newspaper. They agreed to contribute two pence weekly to a fund to buy enough supplies to open a consumer cooperative. Because they knew many of these stores failed, they hammered out some guidelines that they felt would make their store prosper. The Rochdale weavers set forth eight principles:

1) There would be democratic control, every member would have one vote.

2) A person could join or quit or rejoin the cooperative without prejudice.

3) The Society would pay limited interest on capital.

4) Any profits, or surplus, would be distributed among members according to the value of their purchases over a year.

5) All sales would be for cash.

6) The products sold were to be pure and measured in full.

7) Funds would be set aside from any surplus for membership education.

8) Any person, regardless of religious faith or political belief, could belong, but the cooperative would remain politically neutral.

The tiny shop they opened on Toad Lane flourished. Soon they expanded into a second room, and then secured the second floor for a library and classroom. Today, hundreds of cooperatives emulate the Rochdale Pioneers, using essentially the same principles in consumer cooperation.

However, the twenty-four Pioneers, as they came to be called, learned over time that the Rochdale principles were inadequate when applied to production. After successfully managing a corn mill, they founded the Rochdale Cooperative Manufacturing Society in 1850. Today the firm would be called a joint partnership. Whether they worked in the factory or not, shareholders subscribed capital. Any person could buy two shares but not more than twenty. In accord with the principle of voluntarism, workers could buy shares or not, as they saw fit. Most did, and they constituted the majority of stockholders. By 1859, the firm needed additional capital to expand. Shares were sold to persons whose only interest was getting a return on their investment. Under their sway, the firm became a traditionally managed joint stock company in 1862.

For years the failure of the mill as a worker-owned cooperative was felt as a blow by supporters of the idea of workplace democracy. Consumer cooperatives continued to grow, as did cooperatives in agriculture and the crafts. But the idea of industrial democracy in the workplace languished, at least in France and England.

Worker-Owned Cooperatives in the United States

In the United States, the impact of the industrial revolution was first felt in the late 1790s, pushing workers to look for alternatives to the way their work lives went. The first significant experiment in worker self-management started in 1806 when journeymen cordwainers in Philadelphia decided during a strike to become their own bosses. They opened a warehouse to market shoes and boots made by members at wholesale and retail prices. While their business prospered, it did not prompt imitation until the 1830s.

In that decade enthusiasm for labor-managed enterprises swept the nation's workingmen's associations, predecessors to today's unions, as a reaction to the rapid advance of the factory system. The National Trades Union resolved in October 1836 to raise a fund to help start cooperatives and insure them against loss "until a system of Cooperation is adapted by which the producers of wealth may also be its possessors, and consequently enjoy its benefits, that the great burden of the evils of which we so justly complain will ever be removed."

Cabinetmakers opened their own furniture stores. Weavers opened mills, while tailors, bootmakers and saddlers started self-managed firms. The panic of 1837 and the ensuing economic downturn closed many of these promising experiments. However, efforts to organize worker-owned cooperatives continued, and in 1866 the first National Labor Congress adopted this resolution:

> ...in cooperation we recognize a sure and lasting remedy for the abuses of the present industrial system, and hail with delight the organization of cooperative stores and workshops in this country, and would urge their promotion in every section of the country and in every branch of business. (3)

Encouraged by such backing, workers in nearly all the leading trades within two years started self-managed businesses: bakers, foundrymen, nailers, coal miners, shipwrights, machinists and blacksmiths, hatters, printers, women in the needle trades, laundries, and others. The Molders' International Union formed 11 cooperative stores and factories between 1866 and 1868. The Knights of St. Crispin, a shoemaker's union, declared in 1869, "The present demand

15

of the Crispin is steady employment and fair wages, but his future is self-employment." (4)

Among farmers, the Patrons of Husbandry had great success starting up cooperatives, including a bank. William H. Earle, inspired by achievements in agriculture, started the National Council of the Order of Sovereigns of Industry in 1874 and declared it's purpose was:

> . . .to establish a better system of economical exchanges and to promote, on a basis of equality and liberty, mutual fellowship and cooperative action among the producers and consumers of wealth throughout the world. (5)

Earle and his followers sold stock to anyone interested in the few businesses they opened. This was the Order's undoing; the lessons of Rochdale were ignored. Stockholders had little direct financial interest at stake, especially in the consumer stores.

Perhaps the most significant, sustained drive to widen the practice of worker-ownership in the United States was undertaken by the Knights of Labor. Beginning in 1878 the union took over the defunct Industrial Brotherhood, a group which had called for "the establishment of cooperative institutions, productive and distributive." The Knights invited skilled and unskilled workers to join their organization and seek better conditions for all. The formation of worker cooperatives became a central plank in their reformist platform which was designed to cope with the evils of unbridled capitalism and the insecurities of wage labor. Terrence V. Powderly, president of the Knights, declared two years later, "There is no good reason why labor cannot, through cooperatives, own and operate mines, factories and railroads." (6)

Powderly ordered the union's "best minds" to give "their precious thought to this system." Within a year a cooperative fund was started to help finance new businesses. Each month every male member of the Knights paid 10 cents into the kitty and every female member paid five cents. In return, stock certificates were issued assuring each holder an equal share of all profits from the investment. A Cooperative Board of Five was formed to oversee formation of businesses through local union chapters. The Knights wanted "all kinds of productive enterprises" started along decentralized lines, free of their central control. They issued a model constitution, a set of by-laws which could be adapted to local situations, and published pamphlets on "how to organize cooperative societies" and on the "dangers and pitfalls in cooperative ventures." Locally, Knights were urged to think carefully about these problems:

☐ That in establishing our cooperative institutions we must not forget that men reared under the conditions of wage-service cannot jump at once to the much higher level of cooperation...Therefore, it seems that in our institutions we must preserve that feature of the wage-system which calls upon the man to put forth his best exertions, and to put them forth harmoniously, or be stricken from the payroll.

☐ That individual incentive must be provided. It seems that although the desire for social honor may be a motive force with many, yet, after all, the material benefits are the most generally desired, and that, therefore, gradations of wages must be retained.

17

☐ That the executive officers be amply endowed with authority to select the men best adapted to the work in hand. (7)

The Knights of Labor opened 135 cooperatives of various sorts, more than half of them mines, cooperages, shoe and clothing factories, foundries, even soap works. Most were small; the average investment was $10,000. The union's effort reached a zenith by 1886 when the union, under attack by the more conservative craft-dominated American Federation of Labor and tainted by the Haymarket riot in Chicago, began a rapid decline. The Knights lost nearly 600,000 members between 1886 and 1890 and ceased to be a viable labor organization by the end of the century.

Many lessons come from the experience of the Knights. By attempting to practice cooperation on one hand and collective bargaining on the other they were, as one labor historian noted, driving teams of horses "in opposite directions." (8) Adding to their difficulties were forces beyond their control. Merchants organized boycotts and refused to furnish the factories with needed raw materials. Banks refused financing. Some cooperatives failed because members did not work harmoniously. Nationally, the economy was in a depression. Only the strongest cooperatives survived.

By the turn of the century, under the leadership of Samuel

Gompers and the American Federation of Labor, organized labor discarded the principles of cooperation and opted for a policy of "business unionism" which accepted the capitalist system of ownership and advocated collective bargaining as the means to obtain a share in the fruits of production for workers. Although a few attempts were made by more radical groups such as the Industrial Workers of the World to develop alternative approaches to organizing the means of production, by the end of World War I capitalism was the dominant and largely unchallenged form of business ownership in America.

It was not until the Great Depression and the Roosevelt Administration in the 1930s that interest was renewed in worker-owned cooperatives. Government planners saw the formation of these firms as a strategic means to shore up the economy, especially in agriculture. Several hundred self-help production cooperatives (defined as democratic associations of unemployed or underemployed workers who organized to obtain the necessities of life through their own production of goods) were organized in states like California, Washington, and Utah where they were engaged in a broad range of activities including gardening, baking, canning, lumbering and soap making. Lack of capital, unstable and heterogeneous labor, untrained management, and shifting government policies plagued the cooperatives. Most of them disappeared by the outbreak of World War II. But they had employed large numbers of previously unemployed workers and performed a valuable service during the depths of the depression. (9)

Worker-Owned Cooperatives in Europe

In Europe and elsewhere, the drive for worker control took many forms, and continued relentlessly without regard for national borders. During the first days of the October 1917 revolution in Russia, workers' soviets were created to run the machinery of production, only to be crushed by an emerging bureaucracy. Workers' Councils were organized in Germany in 1918. Before the Spanish Civil War, peasants and industrial workers, inspired by the International Workingmen's Association's advocacy of self-management, ran countless factories and farms. Following World War I, the kibbutz movement in Israel expanded and the national experiment in self-management in Yugoslavia commenced after World War II. Beginning with a tiny stove factory in 1956 in the community of Mondragon, Basques of northern Spain established a network of more than 80 worker-managed cooperatives, all linked to a bank which they owned and controlled. In the doing, they sharpened thinking about worker-ownership.

For all their foresightedness, the Rochdale Pioneers did not give much consideration to the duality of a worker-member. Unlike the situation in a consumer cooperative, in the industrial setting each worker is a member or beneficiary of the cooperative's benefits, and each is an owner. Traditionally, membership was confined to a participant role in the firm's decision-making processes. However, the Basques recognized that ownership carried with it responsibilities beyond mere participation.

Accordingly, the Basques created the doctrine of labor-entrepreneurship which, in addition to participation, includes risk-taking, enterprise building or growth, husbandry of productivity, and the search for new opportunities. Ana Gutierrez-Johnson, a student of the Basque accomplishments, has argued the distinction is important.

19

> The difference in labor-entrepreneurship lies in the active role assumed by the associated workers, the collective decision-making process and the labor-based vision of development. Labor- entrepreneurship transformed the traditional concept of the cooperative as a private, closed, corporation into a concept of broader social enterprise. (10)

Additionally, the Basques devised what is sometimes called the individual or internal membership account—as the firm prospers, it provides a major source of its own financing. Basque worker-owners credit each member's account with between fifty to seventy percent of net income on the basis of the number of hours worked and the rate of pay received. Interest is paid on each individual member's account in proportion to the balance in all accounts. What is not set aside in the internal accounts once interest is paid will then be divided among the workers as a dividend in proportion to the labor contributed by each. When members leave the firm for whatever reason, membership in the cooperative is terminated. Their membership shares are returned to the cooperative, and the remaining balance is paid out to them over a number of years.

The percentage of net earnings not set aside in this manner is usually divided into two parts: a large part goes for the development of new cooperatives, and part is used to educate worker-owners or for education in the surrounding community.

To answer the question posed at the outset of this chapter, the idea for and fundamental principles of worker-owned cooperatives evolved from the determination of many women and men to possess their own labor.

2 THE FUNDAMENTALS OF WORKPLACE DEMOCRACY

Organizing a worker-owned business is not easy, nor is it easy to convert a conventionally managed company to worker-ownership. There is no single set of rules to guide either process, but there are basic principles which characterize prosperous worker-owned firms, making money while enlarging democracy. These principles represent current knowledge and thinking about worker-ownership in North America. However, this is a dynamic, growing social movement. Every day that workers open the doors of the factories or stores they own and manage, some new knowledge is created.

A worker-owned firm is a business enterprise that makes a product to sell or offers a service—for profit. Some worker-owned firms employ as many as 8,000 persons, others as few as three persons. The workers themselves own and manage the business, hire any needed capital, determine the use of the firm's assets, set objectives, hire managers and delegate authority. They make the entrepreneurial decisions through a process of representational democracy. Ideally, every worker should be an investor. Each worker's equity investment or membership fee must be no greater or smaller than any other worker's. Investment and one's labor give the worker the right to vote, to share equally in any profit or loss, and to the ownership of one share of stock. No person outside the firm may obtain all these rights. Wages vary according to skill and seniority and may be raised or lowered in good times or bad. (1)

Such a business has also been called an industrial cooperative, a worker-owned cooperative, a labor-managed enterprise, or a cooperative labor-enterprise. The terms "industrial cooperative" and "worker-owned cooperative" have been loosely applied to several different types of cooperatives which are quite different in their objectives or operations and do not encompass all the fundamentals of a worker-owned firm. There are basically three types of cooperatives: consumer, producer or marketing, and worker-owned which also have been called industrial or labor-managed cooperatives.

Consumer Cooperatives

Usually consumer cooperatives are set up to provide goods or services to their members, and possibly non-members, at reasonable prices. Food buying clubs, co-op grocery stores, co-op bookstores, credit unions, or housing cooperatives are examples of this form of cooperative. If consumer co-ops make a profit, the "net savings," as profits are called, are usually returned to members and customers in the form of "patronage dividends" or distributions. These are made in proportion to the amount of business the member did with the co-op.

Producer or Marketing Cooperatives

Producer cooperatives are organized by individuals who independently produce a common product like turkeys, milk, or grain and then band together to process and/or market their products collectively. Sometimes independent producers form cooperatives to collectively buy goods—seeds, fertilizer, and feed—or services used to produce their primary products. The function of purchasing or supply co-ops is quite similar to that of consumer co-ops. Producer cooperatives also distribute profits in much the same way as consumer co-ops. Profits are periodically returned to the members in proportion to the amount of business each one has done with the co-op.

Worker-owned Cooperatives

Worker-owned cooperatives, industrial cooperatives, or labor-managed cooperative enterprises are the specific focus of this guide. They are business enterprises established to provide employment and economic reward to worker-owners.

The two most fundamental principles of a worker-owned enterprise are: (1) that ownership and control of the enterprise are derived from working in it, not just from capital investment; and (2) the concept of labor-entrepreneurship is adopted. Labor-entrepreneurship means that the workforce or a group within it assumes the responsibilities of searching for profitable business opportunities, of obtaining productive resources, while engaging in risk-taking and organization building.

In worker-owned companies, management control derives from employment and membership. In consumer cooperatives, control derives from patronage and shareholding in the ownership of the enterprise. In producer and marketing cooperatives ownership and control rest with the members who are independent growers or suppliers of the crops and raw materials produced and made available for processing and/or marketing. In most consumer or producer co-ops the workers are employees, not owners. Producer and consumer cooperatives are owned and controlled by member-patrons. Only industrial and worker cooperatives are owned and controlled by the employees.

23

Other Forms of Employee-Ownership

Worker-ownership differs from traditional corporate forms of business where control is directly related to stock ownership. Some firms give their employees stock or allow them to buy it at reduced cost, but in many instances this is limited to high level executives. In most cases, workers, either individually or collectively, can never buy enough stock to exercise any significant degree of ownership and control. The terms profit sharing, stock options, employee bonus plans, workers' capitalism, and Employee Stock Ownership Plans (ESOPs) describe these forms of employee stock ownership which do not normally include any significant worker control. Appendix D provides a systematic comparison between the conventional corporation and the "pure" form of worker-owned cooperative.

During the past decade ESOPs have become an increasingly popular way for American workers to buy out their company in attempts to prevent plant closings. Sometimes owners, wishing to retire, have sold their firm to workers; in other situations management has enlisted the help of workers to prevent outsiders from taking over the business. An ESOP is a legal device created in the 1950s which became popular as a result of changes in the tax laws in 1974. It enables employees to obtain stock in their employer's business without having to pay taxes on the stock until they retire or leave the company.

The ESOP is a specialized type of stock ownership plan. Assets must be invested primarily in employer securities. The company may borrow money to buy employer stock, and the employer is permitted to guarantee such loans. The company pays for stock out of earnings or money saved by employee wage concessions. Each year the company pays money into an Employee Stock Ownership Trust (ESOT), which, in turn pays off the loan. As the loan is repaid, stock usually passes into accounts for individual workers based on their wage levels or seniority. Unlike conventional financing, an ESOP permits a company to repay both loan principal and interest in pre-tax dollars, and thus save the company taxes. If all goes well, the workers will eventually own a substantial share or perhaps all of the company. The stock allocated to employees is tax free until the employees leave or retire, which is when they actually receive their shares from the trust. Cash dividends are taxable when paid to employees.

ESOPs are promoted as a form of worker-ownership, but unfortunately there are some problems. In some cases a small group of managers or investors use ESOPs to accomplish a "leveraged buyout" of a firm without any real concern or interest in the workers other than to use them and their money to make the deal. (2) In most ESOP buyouts to date, very little worker control is included with the employee stock ownership. Only rarely has there been an immediate "pass-through" of voting rights so the worker-owners can vote their shares of stock, elect directors, and exert influence on the management. While workers are beneficiaries of the ESOP, a trust actually owns and votes the stock. In most cases, the bankers who loan workers and management money to buy the firm choose the ESOT trustees. The workers have no say in managing the business until the loan is paid off—usually in five to ten years. Another problem with ESOPs is cost; they are expensive to install, making them uneconomical for small firms.

There are ways ESOPs can be organized in a democratic manner. Seymour Specialty Wire in Connecticut is one such firm. (3) Changes incorporated in the 1986 Tax Reform Act make it easier to use a cooperative system of democratic governance and take advantage of the ESOP financial and tax benefits. But it should not be forgotten that while ESOPs have

24

HOW A LEVERAGED ESOP WORKS

THE INITIAL SETUP...

1. Bank lends money to ESOP. **2**. ESOP passes loan to company...
3. in return for an equivalent amount of company stock, which is held
in trust for employees.

...AND THE WAY IT OPERATES

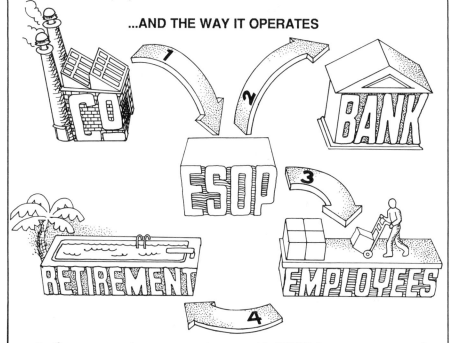

1. Company makes an annual payment to ESOP from revenues and
deducts the full amount from taxable income. **2.** ESOP uses company
contribution to pay off loan. Bank pays taxes on only 50% of interest
income. **3**. Stock is allocated to each employee's ESOP account as
loan is paid off. **4**. When employees quit or retire, they withdraw their
stock or sell it, often back to ESOP. New employees join the plan and
begin accumulating stock.

been evaluated "as a tool of corporate finance, a means to motivate employees and improve corporate performance, and a way to make business more democratic," their basic purpose "was and is to broaden the ownership of wealth" and not to extend workers' control. (4) Consequently, democratic ESOPs are few and far between.

Foundation of Self-Management

Over the years workers have figured out seven universally applicable cooperative principles which seem vital to profitable, democratic self-management. When set in policy through company by-laws, they become the principles of governance and decision-making, guides for both organizational and individual behavior, as well as the norms operating in the workplace. (5) Modern social scientists have found imbedded in them the values and essential ingredients for building and sustaining successful worker-owned enterprises. (6)

The Democratic Principle. The workforce controls management, policies, and the use of capital on the basis of one person/one vote or, in other words, representational democracy.

The Equity Principle—I. After a trial period of employment, all workers must become members. Each member pays an equal membership fee.

The Equity Principle—II. Any surplus, profit, or loss, belongs to the members and must be equitably distributed among them so that no member gains at the expense of another.

The Voluntary Principle. Within the employment needs of a worker-owned firm, participation in the workforce is voluntary and open to anyone willing to accept the responsibilities of self-management. There should be no restrictions based on sex, religious affiliation, race, national origin, or political beliefs.

The Openness Principle. All meetings and records are open to all fully vested members. Mutual aid is to be promoted at all levels through education of members, officers, managers, the general public, and other cooperatives.

The Limited Returns Principle. Where labor employs capital, a clear distinction must be made between reward for labor (wages based upon skill and seniority), and capital (retained earnings, dividends) which is limited.

The Evolution (Dissolution) Principle. The firm cannot be sold or dissolved without the consent of the workforce through a vote, and then its assets must be distributed to the members in accordance with the organizational charter and by-laws.

The values underlying worker-ownership are:

☐ While labor is of greater value than capital, corporate interests can be balanced with human ones.

☐ Democracy can be extended to the workplace.

☐ Workers can and will take responsibility for entrepreneurial decisions.

☐ Cooperation and participation yield greater productivity and returns on the investment of both labor and capital than does hierarchy and coercion.

☐ Rewards for labor expended can be equitable and just.

☐ Workers are capable of contributing to enterprise development, and want to, if given the opportunity.

☐ Problem-solving can shift profitably from individualism to representational group solutions.

These may appear to be abstractions, having little to do with the practical matters of day-to-day life in a business. However, if rooted in corporate by-laws and evolving traditions and attitudes, they insure each worker a direct say in workplace governance.

Membership Rights and Ownership Rights

Another way to understand the rights and responsibilities of worker-ownership is to compare them with political democracy. Economist David Ellerman suggests that political democracy embodies certain essential principles that are

27

necessary if one is to establish true workplace democracy.

In a traditional investor-owned corporation, ownership rights include: (1) voting rights; (2) profits or net income rights; and (3) rights to the net book value of the corporate assets. All three of these are transferable property rights. In a conventional non-democratic employee-owned corporation, including most ESOPs, there is no restructuring of conventional ownership rights. Traditional ownership rights are owned as property rights by company employees. Both voting rights and profit rights are attached to the capital shares. Additionally, in the case of the ESOP, an intervening trustee exercises the rights for the "beneficial" owners, the workers, until the loans used to buy the company stock are paid off.

Applying the basic principle of political democracy to the workplace leads to a different configuration of ownership rights and responsibilities according to Ellerman. Democracy is founded upon the idea of one person, one vote. Consequently, workplace democracy should embody that fundamental rule.

> Democracy is a method for people to govern themselves, not a method for property owners to govern their property. Democracy must be people-based, not property-based or capital-based. Hence in a democratic workplace, the people hire the capital, not vice-versa. And if labor hires capital, then the residual net income after all costs (including interest on capital) is a return to labor, not a return to capital.

> The voting and other citizenship rights in a democratic polity are personal or human rights, not property rights which may be bought or sold. Property rights are marketable so they can become highly concentrated in huge accumulations of wealth and power. Personal or human rights cannot be "bought" or "sold"; they are automatically distributed on a one-per-person basis. Hence if any democracy, political or industrial, is to endure, the basic citizenship or membership rights should be assigned as personal or human rights, not as marketable property rights. (7)

Voting and profit rights in a worker-owned cooperative constitute "membership rights." An enterprise is a worker cooperative if the membership rights are personal rights attached to the personal role of working in the company, and if each worker-member gets one and only one vote. The net income of the enterprise is assigned to the worker-members on the basis of their labor contribution which is usually measured in hours, by pay, or both. In a worker cooperative the right to the capital assets (net book value) of the enterprise remains a property right held by the worker-members of the cooperative through appropriate legal mechanisms which are sometimes called individual or internal membership accounts.

Ellerman sees the worker cooperative as "labor-ist" rather than "capital-ist." Labor is the hiring factor, therefore the voting and profit rights are assigned to the people who do the work and not to capital, even though the worker-members supply capital through membership fees and retained earnings. The member-supplied capital is recorded in the internal capital accounts, and receives a fixed interest-like return. Any profit or loss after normal operating expenses is assigned to members on the basis of their labor contribution. (8)

There are significant differences between ends and means between firms where capital controls labor, or firms where the state controls both labor and capital. Worker-ownership has been described as "a third way." These distinctions are easily seen when measured by essential elements of commerce: purpose, organization, ownership, control, sources of capital, distribution of profits, dividends, operational practices, and tax treatment. Chart 2-1 compares the commercial elements of capitalism, socialism, and cooperative worker-ownership.

29

Chart 2-1

MAJOR COMMERCIAL CHARACTERISTICS
OF CAPITALISM, SOCIALISM, AND COOPERATION

Commercial Criteria	Capitalism	Socialism	Workers' Cooperation
Purpose	a) To earn profit for owner, to increase value of shares.	a) To provide goods and services for citizens.	a) To maximize net and real worth of all owners.
Organization	a) Organized and and controlled by investors.	a) Organized and controlled by state.	a) Organized & controlled by worker-members.

	b) Incorporated under state corporation laws: no federal incorporation laws.	b) Chartered by state/ central government.	b) Incorporated under state corporation laws; no federal incorporation laws.
	c) Except for closely held companies anyone may buy stock.	c) No stock.	c) Only worker-members may own stock, one one share per member.
	d) Stock may be traded in the public market.	d) n/a	d) No public sale of stock.
Ownership	a) Stockholders.	a) State.	a) Worker-members.
Control	a) By investors.	a) By state.	a) By worker-members.
	b) Policies set by stockholders or board of directors.	b) Policy set by govern-ment planners.	b) Policy set directors elected by worker-members.
	c) Voting on basis of shares held.	c) n/a	c) One person, one vote.
	d) Proxy voting permitted.	d) n/a	d) Proxy votes seldom allowed.
Sources of Capital	a) Investors, banks pension funds, the public.	a) The state.	a) By members or lenders who have no equity or vote.

30

	b) From profitable subsidiaries or by retaining all or part of the profits.		b) From net earnings, a portion of which are set aside for reinvestment.
Distribution of Net Margin	a) To stockholders on the basis of number of shares owned.	a) To the State.	a) To members after funds are set aside for reserves and allocated to a collective account.
Capital Dividends	a) No limit, amount set by owner or Board of Directors.	a) n/a	a) Limited to an interest-like percent set by policy.
Operating Practices	a) Owners or managers order production schedules and set wages and hours, sometimes with union participation.	a) State controlled.	a) Workers set production schedules through elected boards and and appointed managers.
	b) Except in union shops, workers' rights depend on unilateral decisions of bosses.		b) Social Audit Council or union and dialogue between members and managers.
Tax Treatment	a) Subject to state and federal taxes.	a) n/a	a) Special tax treatment under federal and in some states.

31

The essential differences among capitalism, socialism and workers' cooperation pertain to the way workers control capital, and the way earnings are distributed. The narrow ends of a capitalist firm and the output quotas set by socialist planners for state-owned firms stand in contrast to the ends presently considered essential to genuine worker-ownership and workplace democracy.

Employment Security in a Worker-Owned Cooperative

Another major difference between conventional businesses and the worker-owned cooperative is the principle of employment security—and the resulting treatment of direct labor as a fixed cost. In conventional businesses indirect labor (e.g., supervisors, administrative labor, managers and support staff) are treated as fixed costs. Direct labor, however, is treated as a variable cost. Workers directly involved in the production of goods and services are assumed to be expendable—to be hired and fired as demand warrants. While some businesses such as IBM and Hewlett-Packard may provide employment security for their employees, and the system is embodied in the lifetime employment programs in certain Japanese industrial firms including some operating in the U.S., this concept is not widely accepted in North America, nor is it normally built into the logical structure of conventional managerial accounting. (9)

Direct labor is not counted by a conventional business as an externally given quantity. It is normally treated as an internally determined variable: product sales, together with desired levels of inventory investment, determine production. Production determines the direct labor requirements (for example, 2 hours per unit of production). (10)

In a worker-owned cooperative, these relationships are reversed. Labor (i.e., the number of workers and hours of labor available) determines production (for example, 1/2 unit per hour), rather than vice versa. The cooperative membership of direct workers is a given for short-term planning (e.g., annual business plans). Within certain limits, the worker-owned cooperative membership of direct workers determines the level of production for the enterprise. Production together with sales determines the level of inventory investment—which may or may not be the desired level. This leads to what David Ellerman has called "the matching problem." (11)

Since the equation is: Inventory Investment = Production minus Sales, any two of these three quantities determines the third. In conventional businesses, sales and desired inventory investment (normally about ten percent of the next month's sales) determine production which, in turn, determines direct labor. In a worker-owned cooperative direct labor—and thus production—are, within certain limits, given independently of sales. The three quantities of production, sales, and desired inventory investment might not match up to satisfy the equation. That is the matching problem. How is it solved? The short answer is: with careful planning and several adjustment mechanisms. Charts 2-2 and 2-3 illustrate the matching problem.

Chart 2-2

**PRODUCTION PLANNING
FOR A CONVENTIONAL BUSINESS**

Sales forecast *(5000 units)* + inventory investment *(500 units)*
= production *(5500)* units

Direct labor required *(2 hours per unit)*
= *5500 x 2 = 11000* hours

11000 hours divided by *2,000* *= *5.3* person years

**40 hr. week x 50 weeks = 2,000 hours.*

Chart 2-3

**PRODUCTION PLANNING
FOR A WORKER-OWNED COOPERATIVE**

Worker-members available for direct labor
= *6* person years

Direct hours of labor available
= *6 x 2000* = *12,000* hours

Production possibilities
= *1/2* unit per hour x *12,000* hours = *6000* units

Sales forecast *(5000* units)

Production *(6000* units) - Sales *(5000* units)
= Inventory *(1000* units)

In this example if the company has 6 workers on the payroll, one worker will have be to laid off or fired after 6 months of work in order to bring the direct labor costs down to the planned 5.5 person years needed to produce the projected output.

If production for inventory in the worker-cooperative is considered excessive at 25 percent of projected sales, prices may have to be reduced (with corresponding reduction in revenues and profits), or other cost savings achieved to sell the additional units of production. Alternatively, workers may have to share a period of reduced wages or short-time to resolve the matching problem.

In a worker-owned cooperative, after a limited probationary period, all workers are either accepted into membership or rejected from membership and terminated. Thus all permanent workers are members. They must be fit into the equation. Worker-owned cooperatives try not to terminate worker-members for short-term economic reasons such as periodic decreases in demand. Reduction in membership normally comes through retirement or voluntary departures. But brisk and stable demand for products may lead to the need for more direct labor—and hence the hiring and admission of new members in the short run. Thus, the membership of direct workers in a worker-owned cooperative is somewhat fixed downward, but not normally fixed upwards.

Where labor is a fixed cost and the membership level is fixed, working hours are not. This means that the worker-members may experience "overtime" and its opposite, "undertime," or "short-time" during business fluctuations. And, since the workers are member-owners and thus residual claimants on the profits earned by the cooperative, their income is, in part, determined by the uncertain fortunes of the firm. Bad times could lead to reductions in paid-out income as well as short-time.

While short-time and reductions in pay are possibilities, the annual and longer-term business plans can and should be used to minimize the likelihood of such drastic measures. Treating labor as a fixed cost increases the importance of the planning process. In conventional business enterprises, poor planning results in the direct labor workers paying the price by periodic layoffs and firing. Direct labor is the principal escape valve. But when the membership of direct labor workers in a worker-owned cooperative is made a constraint and a philosophy of employment security is adopted, management planning does not have the same easy out.

In the Basque cooperatives, when faced with a drop in demand for their products, managers cut price rather than production to preserve jobs. They attempt to compensate for the fixity of labor, and thus of production, by making sales more variable, more under the control of management's price-cutting and sales efforts. What this means is that the worker-owned cooperative must place greater emphasis on marketing. Instead of treating sales as strictly a market determined variable, management should maximize the cooperative's control over the volume of sales to offset the short-term fixity of labor.

If the imbalance in production and sales persists over an extended period of time, the Basque cooperatives seek to innovate and introduce new products or reduce the labor surplus by finding new jobs in other cooperatives for excess workers.

How Worker-Owner-Members are Selected and Paid

Three important concepts form the basis of membership in a worker-owned and controlled enterprise: acceptance based on objective screening criteria, voluntarism, and proportionality.

Nearly every organization screens prospective members by some set of criteria. Worker-owned cooperatives are no exception. It should be recognized that not everyone can or should join a worker-owned cooperative. At the very least, hiring levels must be set to provide an efficient basis for operating the business. Conventional business firms, in addition to screening for obedience and regularity, may also take into account variables not strictly related to the job for which the worker is being hired. Japanese firms screen new workers according to group acceptability.

Screening to enter a worker-owned cooperative must include at least two kinds: social and financial. The group must establish some criteria to insure that the potential entrant is the kind of person who can be integrated into the workplace and into the cooperative. In the Basque cooperatives, the criterion of integration carries considerable weight in assessing candidates.

> Once a person is inside he makes demands so we have to be very careful just who we select. Not only professional qualifications but morals are closely looked at.

We concern ourselves about how the person behaves in the community. If he is bad, we put him on trial before allowing him to join our cooperative. (12)

Following initial acceptance a worker undergoes a six-month trial period during which the immediate supervisor assesses his or her social acceptability. Once in the cooperative the members are exposed to an extensive socialization process which includes educational courses in the cooperative ethic.

Monetary screening of the potential entrant into a Basque cooperative is accomplished by requiring the individual to purchase a membership share— which equals approximately one year's earnings at the lowest level of employment. Additionally, part of future accumulated profits may be forfeited if the new worker-member departs prematurely. This policy curbs adventurers.

The importance of a screening process is illustrated by the hard won experience of Space Builders, a worker-owned North Carolina construction firm. Several times in their early years they hired people impulsively, either because of a desperate need for help or personal association. In a few months they were forced to fire them because it became evident that these workers lacked the motivation and did not accept the group's norms or expectations.

Once they have been screened in accordance with the established criteria, and an opening exists, workers are free to join or leave, as they see fit.

In a labor-managed cooperative the determination of pay rates should be guided by principles of proportionality, external solidarity and internal solidarity. There are no wages *per se*, since workers are members, and not employees, of the cooperative. The net value accruing to workers is the value of their product minus non-labor costs. Some of that value is paid out during the year (which might be compared with wages), some is paid out at the year's end (bonuses), and some is retained in the cooperative (in internal accounts). Since net profit is not known until the end of the fiscal year, the amount paid out during the year is an advance or an anticipation of the worker-members' income.

The principle of external solidarity means that the advances for the lower pay rates will be geared at or near the wages of comparable work in other firms in the geographic area, and will be paid on a similar basis.

The principle of internal solidarity means that the top to bottom pay ratio in a cooperative will not be excessive. Most worker-owned cooperatives do not have pay ratios greater than 5 to 1. Under certain circumstances, there might be special bonuses. This contrasts with many conventional North American business corporations where these ratios may exceed 30 to 1, or even higher. The Basque cooperatives originally established the top to bottom pay ratio at 3 to 1. However, because these pay ratios made it difficult to recruit experienced executives from outside the movement, a ratio of 4.5 to 1 was adopted in 1983. In 1985, the Solar Center in San Francisco adopted a 5 to 1 ratio to facilitate the recruitment of persons with specialized skills.

Individual pay rates within the cooperative are determined by the labor index attached to the various jobs, from the bottom to the top. Each job is evaluated using one of several standardized job evaluation techniques (ranking, point system, factor comparison, Position Analysis Questionnaire, etc.). For example, characteristics such as necessary training and experience, decision-making responsibility, social skills, physical and mental demands, and special hardship factors (danger, noise, etc.) can be used to rate a job. On the basis of the points obtained through the evaluations, each job is assigned a labor index on a 1 to 5 scale. The labor indices can then be published in a single manual that covers all blue- and white-collar workers from operatives to the chief executive.

Characteristics of Successful Employee-Owned Businesses

Recent studies of employee-owned businesses—including worker-owned cooperatives—have found that making employee ownership succeed is "not that complicated."

You don't have to be big or small; you don't have to be capital intensive or labor intensive; your line of business isn't important; the presence or absence of unions is not a critical factor. A poorly educated workforce makes communicating the employee ownership plan harder, but not impossible; otherwise, workforce characteristics do not seem crucial. A company that consistently loses money, or has very flat earnings, will have a tougher time, but frankly, these companies are not going to stay around for long anyway. (13)

37

According to researchers, what does matter is pretty straightforward:

☐ The business must make regular, substantial contributions (e.g., stock and dividends) to the workers *as owners.*

☐ Employees must be involved in decision-making.

☐ Workers should be treated like owners, not employees.

☐ Repeated and careful efforts must be made to make sure employees know what their ownership means. (14)

Ingredients of a Successful Labor-Managed Enterprise

These principles are an important part of the basic ingredients needed to start a successful worker-owned enterprise. Creating a business enterprise which incorporates them into its organization, structure, and operations are fundamental steps, but three additional ingredients are also necessary. They are: entrepreneurial characteristics, a business concept, and access to capital. These, together with the principles of democratic worker-ownership and worker control constitute what we call the labor-entrepreneurship window of opportunity. Chart 2-4 illustrates this concept.

Organizers of successful worker-owned cooperative businesses possess to some degree or another the elements in Chart 2-4.

A Commitment to Worker-Ownership

First, the organizing group must understand and accept the principles of worker-ownership. These principles are the framework upon which successful labor-managed cooperative enterprises are constructed. Without a thorough understanding of these principles and a willingness to practice them from the outset, serious problems can arise.

A Viable Business Concept

The second essential component of a successful worker-owned business is that each member of the group have a shared, viable business concept. An idea for a business must be carefully considered, researched, and put through the analytical processes outlined below. Timeliness is important.

Chart 2-4
LABOR-ENTREPRENEURSHIP WINDOW OF OPPORTUNITY

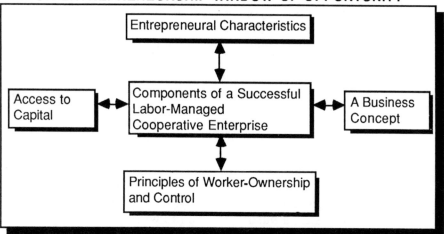

Changing technology, economic conditions, or an impending plant closing are just a few of many forces imposing time constraints.

39

Access to Capital

Third, there must be access to adequate capital. Capital comes in many forms and from many sources. It may include the time and labor of the worker-owners, credit extended by landlords, lawyers, accountants, or suppliers. Of course, there is a need for cash. This can be provided by membership subscriptions, friends, relatives, or public and private sources. Sources of capital are also constrained by time or place, and may be harder to come by during a recession or easier to obtain in a particular community or state. For example, New York, Michigan, Oregon, and Massachusetts, now have legislation and mechanisms to provide financial assistance for starting worker-owned businesses.

Entrepreneurial Skills and Knowledge

Fourth, there is usually one and often several individuals in the organizing group who think like entrepreneurs. They will have gained sufficient experience and business skill needed to season them for the struggle necessary to start a cooperative worker-owned enterprise.

Worker-owned firms have yet to gain much attention from business management researchers. No one has defined the personality traits possessed by successful entrepreneurs in worker-owned firms. But worker-owned firms, like any other businesses, require management leaders and directors who, singly or in a group, guide the business. Research on conventional entrepreneurs suggests that such individuals differ from the general population. They have specific personality characteristics, follow an identifiable career path, and operate under the influence of elements which are critical to the birth and growth of their business.

Entrepreneurs are willing to assume responsibility and accept accountability. Characteristics possessed by most successful entrepreneurs include good health, self-confidence, a sense of urgency, and a comprehensive awareness of what is going on around them. They are realistic, have above average conceptual abilities, a low need for status, the ability to be objective, emotional stability, and are attracted to challenges, not unnecessary risks. Additionally, they usually want to start a business, have the willingness to invest their time and energy to obtain knowledge and experience about business and marketing, and to develop a business concept, not just a bright idea. (15)

Entrepreneurial skills and characteristics cannot be neatly packaged, then given to an individual or group. Some skills can be learned through formal education; others can be gained through work experience or through union or community work. Some of the more important elements of the entrepreneurial characteristics are: a high energy level—the ability to get up early and work hard all day; a positive self-image—faith in oneself to succeed; communication skills—the oral and written skills to sell one's product or service; the ability to analyze the potential success of a product/service/idea; flexibility and resiliency—the ability to adjust to the rewards and pitfalls of the marketplace; decision-making skills; interest in learning; the ability to marshal resources; and a sense of adventure—the feeling of wanting to try something new and the courage to take a chance. (16)

Function of Cooperative Labor-Entrepreneurship

What do labor-entrepreneurs do? They practice innovation, using the same tools used by all successful entrepreneurs. Innovation is not a thing, but an action—"what an entrepreneur does to impart value to a resource." (17) Peter Drucker, a management teacher and writer, has said that "innovation is not mysterious, it doesn't depend on inspiration, it isn't an activity confined to a special class of geniuses." Just as systematic research can result in the "invention" of a new product, Drucker argues that there can be—needs to be—purposeful pursuit of opportunities for innovation. And "purposeful innovation," he says, means monitoring seven sources of opportunity: (18)

☐ The unexpected—unexpected successes, failures, or outside events.

☐ The incongruous—differences between the world as it is and as it "ought to be".

☐ A process need—a better way to do a familiar job.

☐ Unpredicted changes in an industry or market structure.

☐ Demographics—population changes.

☐ Changes in perception, mood, meaning.

☐ New knowledge.

Drucker asserts that anyone or any organization can be an entrepreneur—individual, small business, worker-owned cooperative, big business, or government institution. 'The rules are pretty much the same, the things that work and those that don't are pretty much the same, and so are the kinds of innovation and where to look for them." (19)

Review Checklists

Should you and some fellow workers be thinking about starting a worker-owned enterprise, Chart 2-5 is a basic checklist summarizing the principles outlined. The more "yes" responses you and your fellow workers give to these questions, the better prepared you are to undertake the challenging task of organizing. If the firm you work for is considering changing to a worker-owned and controlled structure, the chart provides a way to measure the principles which should be considered by all concerned. The list is not exclusive; other, related principles can be added.

41

Chart 2-5

CHECKLIST OF THE FUNDAMENTALS OF LABOR ENTREPRENEURSHIP

Basic Principles	*Yes*	*No*	*Other*
1) Each worker has one vote in all elections; and more than two groups of workers may contest in any election).	☐	☐	☐
2) Each worker must become a member and pay an equity fee.	☐	☐	☐
3) Only persons employed by the firm may become members.	☐	☐	☐
4) Jobs are not restricted on the basis of sex, religion, race, national origin, or political beliefs.	☐	☐	☐
5) All meetings and records are open to fully-vested members.	☐	☐	☐
6) Profits, or losses, are shared equitably by worker-members.	☐	☐	☐
7) A minority of worker-members cannot sell or close the firm for their own benefit.	☐	☐	☐
8) An elected group, or a social audit board, or union exists or will be created to handle grievances and provide another means of internal communication.	☐	☐	☐
9) Work may be rotated, and training provided to help workers learn new skills and competencies.	☐	☐	☐
10) There is a willingness to actively search for suitable business opportunities, obtain productive resources, and engage in risk-taking and organization building.	☐	☐	☐

11) A philosophy of employment security will be adopted; business planning and other appropriate techniques will be used to ensure the greatest possible degree of job security to worker-members. ☐ ☐ ☐

12) The princples of entrepreneurship and innovation are known and accepted, or will be learned by the worker-members. ☐ ☐ ☐

Chart 2-6 is a checklist of some of the traits that relate to success in business. Read through the list and check the traits that you think apply to you, or if they characterize several persons in your group. (19)

Chart 2-6

CHECKLIST OF TRAITS RELATING TO SUCCESS IN BUSINESS

☐ I am a self starter. Nobody has to tell me to get going.

☐ I like people and can get along with just about anybody.

☐ I can work with a group, sharing ideas, clarifying thinking, reaching consensus, and supporting group decisions.

☐ I can lead others. Most people will go along with me when I start something.

☐ I am a good organizer. I like to have a plan before I start.

☐ I am a good worker. I can keep going as long as I need to. I don't mind working hard for something I want.

☐ I like to take charge of things and I can make decisions.

☐ People can trust what I say.

☐ I can stick with something even when the going gets tough.

☐ If I make up my mind to do something, I finish it.

☐ I am in good health and have lots of energy to do what I want to do.

☐ I am willing to work long hours to succeed.

☐ I can be patient. I am willing to wait longer than I wish for somethings to happen.

☐ I can tolerate taking a risk. While I like security, I am willing to gamble to some extent on my future.

☐ I am creative and often can see new ways to approach problems.

44

☐ I have a support group behind me that may include family, friends, or other potential worker-member-owners.

Count the checks you made on the checklist. The more checks you have, the more you are like successful business people. If you are lacking several traits that are important to a labor-managed enterprise, develop a plan for adding this expertise to your business.

A Time to Vote

Having come this far, and considered these factors, do you want to go on? This is a good time to vote. The question is—do we want to take the next steps?

3 MAKING A PRELIMINARY ASSESSMENT

There is no single tried-and-true formula to assure the successful creation of a worker-owned business. There are too many variables, human and otherwise. Some businesses start easily in a short time; others experience months, even years of difficulties before opening. Typically, labor-managed enterprises have been started when:

☐ An existing business or plant shuts down, throwing workers out of jobs and leaving them wondering how to make a living.

☐ An individual or group decides to start a business where human values and democracy are of equal importance to productivity and profits.

☐ An owner wants to retire, or shareholders want to put their capital to other uses so the firm's assets are sold or given to employees.

☐ A large firm divests a subsidiary or smaller unit by selling it to the employees.

☐ A union or, in the case of some communities, states and in some European nations, a governmental agency promotes or sponsors the creation of worker-owned businesses to boost employment or save jobs.

These are the common situations, but others exist; each

has its own peculiarities. Each industry or worksite has its own history with unique social relationships. No two situations are the same. No matter what the circumstances, workers have used preliminary, inexpensive feasibility studies to lower the risks they face and to give some order to the bewildering array of facts each situation presents.

A feasibility assessment is a road map. Here we outline phases through which workers have travelled before opening their businesses, including decision-making points where votes need to be taken.

Most new businesses, including worker-owned cooperatives, typically go through four phases in their development: (1)

Organizing. A three to six-month period when the decision is made to organize. A feasibility study is carried out, a business plan developed, the legal organization is completed, and the financing is obtained.

Startup. This phase usually lasts for six months and is that period during which the basic business strategy is tested.

Growth. During this phase the markets are expanded, management techniques are refined, production techniques altered as dictated by experience, personnel practices refined, and the workforce expanded. The end of this phase is signaled by the firm reaching its initial growth projections. This phase may last for several years.

Consolidation. The period during which the membership assesses the experience in reaching the targeted growth and uses that assessment to develop its goals and strategies for the next three to five years.

During the organizing phase several important tasks must be carried out by prospective worker-owners as they decide whether they really want to establish a worker-owned and democratically managed business. The group must come to understand the basic principles of worker-ownership, and once those are grasped, decide whether to go forward or not. The group needs to learn how a cooperative works and what the potential their proposed business has for success. This is an appropriate time for the first vote. Do you want the responsibilities and risks of ownership? That is the question. If the vote is favorable, the group should establish a steering committee to put together the business plan (or carry out a formal feasibility study if the plan calls for a worker buyout of an existing business), and begin writing the governance plan and by-laws. Technical experts and consultants usually help with these tasks. Once the business and governance plans have been completed, the documents should be thoroughly reviewed by the group and another vote held to adopt, modify, or reject them. If they are accepted, it is time to formally organize the cooperative. Then a board of directors must be elected, managers hired, and operations can start if the necessary financing, facilities, permits, etc., are in order.

Important Questions in Starting a Worker-Owned Business

The feasibility assessment process in starting a new worker-owned business revolves around five questions:

1) What are the reasons for starting a worker-owned business? Are they good reasons?

2) What are the options? What are the possibilities? What are the probables?

3) Will it sell? Is there a demonstrated need for the product or service being considered?

4) What will it take in terms of people, money, time, buildings, equipment and other factors, to start the business? Will the sale of products or services generate enough revenue to cover costs and return a profit on the investment?

5) Can it be done? Does the group have the skills, resources, time, and perseverence to do the job right? Is there a plan of organization in mind?

Explore the Reasons for Starting a Worker-Owned Business

What are the real reasons for starting a worker-owned business? Do you fully understand and embrace the concepts of worker-ownership and want to practice them in a real live setting? Are you bored with your current career or job conditions and do you want to experience new challenges and seize new opportunities? Or is it because your firm is about to be shut down and this is the only alternative you can think of to save your jobs? Establishing a good reason for starting a worker-owned business is an important part of the groundwork.

If a plant closure is the main reason for considering starting a worker-owned business, advance notice and early preparation increase the likelihood of developing an appropriate response to threatened job loss. Early warning systems permit employees and the community to plan for potential closures, and to be prepared to act quickly to save jobs. Appendix A provides a checklist of early warning signs of plant closings.

Identify the Options

Those wanting to start a business have three basic options: (1) starting a totally new business from scratch; (2) establishing a link with or obtaining a franchise from an existing business to produce or sell the other firm's product(s); or (3) the purchase of an existing business—including a worker-buyout of the business from their employer.

List the Possibilities

Usually there are many more potential businesses to start than one thinks possible. Make lists of possibilities. Seek out ideas from fellow workers and respected sources. Observe existing businesses for ideas that may be used to help design the new business. Once the reasons for starting the worker-owned business are identified and agreed upon, the group has a basis from which to look for possible marketable ideas.

Narrow the Possibilities to Several Probables

After identifying and learning about the many possibilities, the list must be narrowed. Ask "what if" questions. "What if" we started this business? "What if" we spent all our time for a month conducting a feasibility study? "What if" we decide to buy the plant? "What if" we build the proposed product? Narrowing the possibilities to probables will provide answers to those questions.

Consider Marketing Issues

Will it sell? This question focuses on marketing the product(s). Who are the customers? What do they want? How much? At what price? Who is the competition? Is there enough demand for the product or service to justify another supplier in the market? Can sufficient market share be obtained by providing better quality, faster delivery, a differentiated product or service, or lower prices? These questions should be answered on the local, regional, and national level, if possible. How much business can a worker-owned firm generate before opening up, within a year or five years? Will potential customers make a definite commitment to buy? Can the market be tested on a small scale before more ambitious plans are carried out? Will a market survey help?

Obtaining Human Resources

What skills do we as a group, have? What skills are missing? Sometimes it is more difficult to find the right people to do the job than it is to find the money to get started. Not only must workers be able to manufacture the product or provide the service, but they must also be willing to work cooperatively and to actively participate in self-governance. As one observer noted,

> "Reasons assigned for the general failure of worker cooperatives in the United States in recent years have been the unwillingness of the workers to hold firmly to cooperative principles; inability to function as cooperatives, that is, to get along together, and to avoid serious dissenting, lack of managerial and executive capacity among the workers, and lack of marketing ability."(2)

Many potential worker-owners know how to do their jobs, but lack experience when it comes to "knowing the business." Doing the same job at a stamping machine for seventeen years means they know how to do that task or series of tasks on that machine. A new job on a lathe or shaper could prove difficult. On the other end of the spectrum, people who have been out of work for long periods can find their skills outdated or rusty. Managers are seldom used to workers having a say in running the company. There are many factors to weigh when considering the available human resources.

Operating a business successfully requires many different skills: financial, managerial, operational, and technical. Cooperative organizers must possess the necessary range of business and technical skills among themselves or arrange to acquire them by learning, hiring, or some other way.

Calculating the Costs

Gathering the facts to make a preliminary estimate of what

49

it will cost to get a new undertaking off the ground can be difficult, even when at this point only close approximations are needed. Calculating what the expenses will be for rent, payroll, insurance, equipment (if it is needed), telephones, raw materials, advertising, and a host of other business costs which are unique to each firm must be done if estimates are to be accurate. Figuring expenses is not complicated, but the omission of one item can make a major difference in the final price, especially if that item proves costly. Once a price for the product or service is established, workers must ask two tough questions: Is the price at or below the competition? Will the product or service sell at this price?

Making Comparisons

With those answers in mind, it is possible to make some comparisons. In effect, the data gathered so far sketches out a model business. But what would a typical business in the same manufacturing or service industry look like? How much would sales revenues total each year? How many people would the firm employ as managers, in production, and sales? How do its prices compare to the competition? To get this information, workers can go to banks, trade associations or, if they are union members, to their union to learn what a typical business in the industry looks like, or if that industry is adding or losing customers annually. Some business schools and universities have such data too.

Assessing the Risks

What are the risks? Going into business involves risks for every worker-member. Assessing the risks early on is one way to avoid costly mistakes. It is a useful way to chart group and individual attitudes. The authors of one book for persons interested in starting a business advised, "In business, as in life, there is clearly no way to avoid risk-taking. When you take risks you discover your own abilities; and you become better able to control your own future." (3)

Two Types of Preliminary Feasibility Assessment

A preliminary business feasibility assessment and a preliminary risk assessment should be done before your group proceeds to either start a cooperative from scratch or purchase an existing business. The preliminary feasibility study can screen out likely failures. The preliminary risk assessment focuses on how serious the group is about putting up both their labor and their capital.

The Preliminary Business Feasibility Assessment (4)

How to Get Started. The preliminary feasibility study is relatively quick and inexpensive. It should take several weeks to complete and be of moderate cost. Members of your group can do it alone or with the aid of public interest or nonprofit technical assistance groups, qualified volunteers from community or government offices such as the state office of economic or business development, or professional staff from university small business development centers. The preliminary feasibility study should use readily available sources of data that answer the specific questions in Chart 3-1.

Chart 3-1

A PRELIMINARY BUSINESS FEASIBILITY ASSESSMENT

Question	Yes	No
1) Do industry sources anticipate stable or growing demand for your industry products or services?	☐	☐
2) If there is a recession or slump in your industry, is it projected to end within 6 months to a year?	☐	☐
3) If there are new or existing products taking market share away from or replacing your product:	☐	☐
a) Can your plant produce the competing product?	☐	☐
b) Are there new markets or niches for your product?	☐	☐
4) Are other producers of your product maintaining or increasing capacity or production levels?	☐	☐
5) Are foreign firms or plants expected to maintain constant or declining shares of U.S. sales over the next few years?	☐	☐

6) If your product will be sold to other industries (rather than consumers), do industry sources indicate strong demand for these industries' products? ☐ ☐

7) Will the sale of products or services generate enough revenue to cover costs? ☐ ☐

8) Does your group have the skills needed to organize and manage the proposed business and produce and market the products or services? ☐ ☐

9) Can you obtain sufficient funds to finance the startup of the business? ☐ ☐

Additional Questions in a Worker Buyout. If the business being considered involves the buyout of an existing firm or one that is being closed, additional information is needed. The absence of even one of these critical factors can abort employee efforts to purchase their company. (Appendix B outlines in more detail the specific questions which need to be answered, and what data collected as part of a preliminary feasibility assessment for a worker buyout of an existing business.)

1) Is sufficient time available to organize an employee purchase, i.e., time to organize a cooperative, ESOP, or other form of legal structure, conduct a feasibility assessment, create a business plan, obtain funding, and negotiate with the present owner(s)?

2) Will the firm to be purchased be viable? What is its competitive potential?

☐ Does a market exist for the product(s) currently being produced? Is the plant operating in a stable or declining market?

☐ Will the sales revenue cover the firm's costs? Will the plant be able to provide products and services of equal or better price and quality as its competitors and keep up with technical and product changes in the industry?

3) Have all of the appropriate groups been mobilized: the employees and community, including union, elected officials, labor, local business, media and other support groups? It is especially important to have the support of the local and international union (if a union is present). The support of community and elected officials is also important if public funds are to be used to help purchase the plant.

4) Can the plant make a smooth transition from the existing ownership to a worker-owned business?

   ☐ Does the plant have all of the necessary business functions (marketing, sales distribution, finance, etc.) to operate successfully? Was it previously operated as a separate entity?

   ☐ Did it previously receive any critical inputs from other plants or transfer outputs to other plants?

   ☐ Is competent management available to run the business under the new ownership arrangements?

5) Is the current owner willing to sell to the workers? Success is more likely if current owners are willing to cooperate in terms of early notification, a fair selling price, access to financial, technical and marketing information, providing adequate time to complete the transfer, and developing reasonable financial arrangements.

6) Is adequate financial backing available? The availability of sufficient capital is crucial to a successful worker-buyout and conversion to a cooperative. Funding is necessary to buy the plant, inventory and equipment, for operating expenses, and for the feasibility study which may be necessary prior to assembling the business plan. Are lending institutions familiar with employee-owned and controlled companies, and are they willing to loan money to support them? Will they be willing to accept the assets as collateral?

7) How will the new business be organized?

8) Is qualified technical assistance available including accountants, attorneys, cooperative or ESOP specialists,

53

valuation specialists? And can we afford their help?

9) Are there other products the plant could make? Can you answer the above questions for those alternatives in the affirmative?

10) How does your proposed product compare to that of other domestic and foreign producers? Industry analysts and plant managers can provide answers to this question.

   □ Is average quality equal or better?

   □ Are average prices equal or lower?

   □ Are customers' perceptions that your product is equal or better?

54

11) Is it possible for your plant to be an efficient producer in your industry?

   □ How does the profitability of your plant or firm compare with other firms in your industry?

   □ Has your plant been maintained and can major capital expenditures be avoided?

   □ Is the technology current or will it be outdated soon? Technology can be up-to-date but in poor repair. It can also be well maintained but obsolete.

Sources of Data. The preliminary feasibility analysis should use sources of data that are available at any local college, bank, or state business library and include:

□ **Standard & Poor's** industry surveys

□ **Value Line Investment Survey**

□ **Department of Commerce's U.S. Industrial Outlook** (Annual)

□ **Moody's Industrial Manual** for firms in your industry

□ Dun & Bradstreet, Inc., **Key Business Ratios**

☐ Trade journal articles on your industry located through the **Business Periodicals Guide** and **F & S Guide**

Industry experts whose opinions you should seek include:

☐ The analyst for the appropriate industry from the Bureau of Industrial Economics, Department of Commerce, Washington, D.C. Often, your congressional representative, or senator, can put you in touch with these persons.

☐ The trade association staff for your industry's trade association.

☐ Market analysts from market research firms or security analysts for your industry (ask the reference librarian at a business library or get names from articles in trade journals).

55

☐ If possible, sales and production personnel from firms in the same industry.

Using data sources and industry experts, it should be possible to find good answers to most of the basic questions of feasibility.

Interpreting the Results. In an ideal situation the answers to all of the questions in Chart 3-1 will be yes. The most important questions are numbers 1, 2, 7, 8, and 9. While there may be special circumstances, responses about the market and the product or service efficiency should be positive.

A Time to Vote

If the results of the preliminary feasibility study indicate that prospects for founding a successful worker-owned firm are good, a group must decide whether to proceed on their own to develop a comprehensive business plan. Should you hire outside experts to assist? It is time to take another vote. The question is: Do we go on or stop now?

When employees want to buy or convert an existing firm to a worker-owned cooperative (or other form of employee-owned enterprise, such as an ESOP), a formal, costly procedure is usually necessary. If the preliminary feasibility study indicates that a buyout is potentially feasible, a second "full-scale" feasibility study is needed. The second study provides a complete assessment of risks and opportunities, and financial data. Formal feasibility studies are usually conducted by financial consultants, co-op or ESOP experts who help organize the buyout, and lawyers who negotiate the purchase. In some cases, a real estate appraiser will be needed. The formal feasibility study and follow-up for an employee buyout will cost at least $20,000 and may cost over $100,000. Appendix C outlines questions which need to be asked, and data needed.

Preliminary Risk Assessment

Becoming a worker-owner is risky. Everyone considering such a step should evaluate his or her own needs and motivation before deciding to take the risk. Some of the questions you should ask before making any decision involving risk include: Is the goal worth the risk? How can the risk be reduced? What do we need to know before taking the risk? What people and other resources can help to minimize the risk and achieve the goal. Is it important to take this risk? What will be achieved? What preparation do we need to make before we take the risk? This questioning procedure is essential. Taking a risk before answering these questions may lead to failure.

If the group has experience in manufacturing a product or providing a service, most of the answers to these questions are based on experience and common sense. For groups with less experience, answering these questions can provide the data needed to make a realistic decision *before* undertaking more costly, time-consuming market analysis, business planning, and legal incorporation. A few profitable worker-owned firms have opened before answering these questions; they have started on little more than intuition. On the other hand, the Basques in Spain, who have founded over eighty successful worker-owned cooperatives in thirty years, insist that steering groups spend at least two years planning every aspect of a proposed new business. Only three of the worker-owned firms organized by them have failed.

The preliminary risk assessment in Chart 3-2 is a simple, unscientific way to measure individual and group attitudes about the risks involved. It is one means of determining whether to take the next step. Each person in the steering committee or working group undertaking the preliminary

Chart 3-2

STARTING A WORKER-OWNED BUSINESS:
A PRELIMINARY RISK ASSESSMENT

		Agree		Neither		Disagree
		1	2	3	4	5
1)	The goal (becoming worker-owners) is worth the risk.	☐	☐	☐	☐	☐
2)	The risks can be minimized to acceptable levels.	☐	☐	☐	☐	☐
3)	Information needed before taking the risk has been obtained.	☐	☐	☐	☐	☐
4)	Taking the risk is important.	☐	☐	☐	☐	☐
5)	We are willing to try our best to achieve the goal.	☐	☐	☐	☐	☐
6)	We can achieve our goals by taking the risk.	☐	☐	☐	☐	☐
7)	We are not missing skills or resources which add to the risk.	☐	☐	☐	☐	☐
8)	Everyone will share equally in the risk.	☐	☐	☐	☐	☐
9)	There is no major reason to be fearful of the risks.	☐	☐	☐	☐	☐
10)	The organizing group has sufficient commonality of interests to work effectively together and make the venture succeed.	☐	☐	☐	☐	☐
11)	There is reason to be optimistic about the prospects for success.	☐	☐	☐	☐	☐

TOTALS: *Individual* ☐☐☐☐   *Group* ☐☐☐☐

57

Chart 3-3
_____

DECISION PLANNING AID
_____

Steps in Conducting A Feasibility Analysis	Completed	Not Completed	Action to be taken
I) Reasons for starting a worker-owned business have been fully explored.	☐	☐	☐
2) Options have been identified.	☐	☐	☐
3) List of possibilities identified.	☐	☐	☐
4) List of probables identified.	☐	☐	☐
5) Information on marketing of proposed products has been gathered.	☐	☐	☐
6) Availability of resources determined.	☐	☐	☐
7) Estimated costs of starting the business have been determined.	☐	☐	☐
8) Comparisons between proposed business and other businesses in the industry have been made.	☐	☐	☐
9) The assessment results have been interpreted to determine feasibility.	☐	☐	☐
10 A decision has been made.	☐	☐	☐
11) Pre-startup guidelines and governance procedures have been drawn up and approved.	☐	☐	☐
12) Pre-startup educational programs have been organized.	☐	☐	☐

feasibility study should answer the questions using numbers from one to five, indicating their degree of agreement with the statement. To figure the group's response, total the numbers given by each individual and divide them by the number of persons responding.

58

A Time to Vote

If the totals for the individuals or group filling out the preliminary risk assessment form is 25 or higher, the risks in starting a worker cooperative are perceived to be quite high. Some additional thinking and planning probably needs to be done before further investment of money is made. Now is another good time to have a vote. Should we invest more time or money? That is the question.

Chart 3-3 is a simple planning aid to help the organizing group think through and carry out the steps needed to complete the preliminary feasibility study. It can be used as is, or as the basis for designing more complex planning charts.

Every step of the preliminary planning process can be charted out in this fashion. Taking the time to create a planning and decision-making chart for the organizing group can save days of frustration.

59

Pre-startup Activities

Education and Training
Even at this early stage, workers who have started successful cooperatives have found it important to begin an extensive educational program. Putting democracy to work takes some getting used to as well as learning new patterns of behavior.

In Philadelphia, for instance, in 1982 grocery store clerks were faced with the loss of their jobs when the A&P Company decided to close most of its stores in that city. The Philadelphia Association for Cooperative Enterprises (PACE) was asked to assist them in planning a buyout of two A&P stores slated to be closed. Local 1357 of the United Food and Commercial Workers Union, which represented many of the threatened workers, commissioned a feasibility study by PACE. While it was being done the union asked PACE to undertake an extensive education and training program to help the prospective worker-owners grasp the essentials of workplace democracy, and learn how to run a business most of them had been employed in for years.

The supermarket had hardly shut the doors on its stores when classes started. Over 600 workers attended the first round. Eventually A&P agreed to reopen a number of stores under the Super Fresh name, and many of the former A&P workers decided to return to work in the new division—at lower wages. Fifty persons voted to buy two stores from A&P. PACE designed a program for the prospective worker-owners, consisting of formal presentations, small and large group discussions, and a lot of homework. In addition, they learned about cooperative legal structures, supermarket business and financial planning, and the details of cooperative management. (5)

Learning the Fundamentals of Governance

As part of their preliminary educational work, the grocery store workers and PACE staff developed seven working rules. These played an important part in the successful buyout campaign. They are:

1) Any rule established by the entire group is to be uniformly enforced (by the temporary leaders).

2) Until people get used to each other in new working roles and gain a sense of each other's abilities, leaders will be elected for no longer than 45 days.

3) All meetings are to be organized to insure work gets done while allowing for the greatest possible participation.

4) Anyone accepting a task is to get that job done on schedule.

5) Personnel and personal conflicts are to be resolved, if possible, as they occur (and without assigning blame).

6) Problems are to be worked through in a timely manner.

7) The group is to figure out a way to evaluate the effectiveness of meeting goals, deadlines, and solving problems. (6)

Additionally, workers have learned that sorting out who makes what decisions can avoid conflict. Democratic control of the cooperative does not mean necessarily that every member must take part in every decision. At this stage, the general membership should be voting on broad policy matters. For example, "Do we want to pay for a full-scale business plan?" A steering committee, if one has been established, should be empowered to make the decisions necessary to insure that the preliminary feasibility study is done completely and on time. This group might be empowered to identify or hire a management team that would be responsible for actually doing the formal business plan, or to oversee any consultants who might be hired to help. Alternatively, the general membership group may decide to formally organize as a cooperative, elect a board of directors, who will in turn hire a manager to direct the process. In short, it is the general membership's responsibility to decide where the cooperative is heading. It is the board of director's and manager's responsibility to get the cooperative where the members say they want to go.

Deciding cooperative policy can be another hurdle for prospective workers who would be owners for the first time. Policies are statements which guide or control the company's future actions. Policies should be written down, using the exact words meant by the persons making policy, usually a board of directors, or, in the startup stages, by a steering committee. Usually, boards or steering committees make two kinds of decisions: first, they decide policy; second, they decide on implementation of policy.

For example, the steering committee or board of directors (when organized) may decide that the worker-owned business they are planning will hire people regardless of race, sex, national origin, religious or political persuasion. That would be a statement of policy. To implement that policy, the committee or board could ask managers to prepare a hiring plan which would assist in recruiting prospective worker-owners in accord with that policy, and instruct management to recruit with that policy in mind.

There are four steps in policy-making. Formulation comes first. This begins with a suggestion, usually by the membership, but it could come from the steering committee, or board of directors and management if they have been identified. Assessing the suggestion, debating its pros and cons, drafting a statement, along with a time for review and comment by the general membership are all part of the formulation process. Once the cooperative has been organized a committee created by the board, or the board itself, usually formulates policy.

Policy is decided upon by the board of directors in a cooperative. Members and managers do not determine policy. Policies should be made in the spirit of democracy—during open meetings—where speech is disciplined yet unbridled by board or management restraint.

Policy implementation is management's responsibility, although the board of directors could assign a committee of the board to carry out its will. No matter who is designated to put the policy into practice, it is vital that responsibility for policy implementation be fixed in writing. For example, if management is charged with implementing an open hiring policy, the board should expect management to provide a plan of action, including times, goals, etc.

Finally, policies give the membership a means of evaluating management performance. Evaluation is an important part of governing a cooperative, but is often overlooked. Judging management performance by its own plan of action can eliminate subjective, or personal judgements, thus avoiding potential anger. And when it comes time to vote, the board bears full responsibility for policy oversight.

These are simple tools, developed over the years by worker-owners to make the job of democratic self-governance easier, and to facilitate working together cooperatively. Learning to use them during the early stages of the feasibility study will improve the chances for success.

A Time to Vote

After carefully reviewing and completing the appropriate preliminary business feasibility questions in Chart 3-1 and completing the preliminary risk assessment in Chart 3-2, your group should vote on whether to take the next steps, including: (a) conducting of a formal business feasibility assessment if a worker buyout of an existing business is being considered; or (b) preparing a business plan if you intend to start a new worker-owned cooperative; (c) organizing a pre-startup educational program; and (d) drawing up pre-startup work rules and governance procedures.

If the decision of the group is to proceed, the start-up process mandates that the organizers take the following steps:

☐ Make a conscious, all-out commitment to begin the enterprise.

☐ Elect a steering committee to put together the plan of action, including the governance plan, and by-laws.

☐ Develop a business plan (or carry out a formal feasibility study if a worker-buyout of an existing business is contemplated).

☐ Get the necessary legal and other professional help needed to organize as a worker-owned business.

☐ Gather the finances.

☐ Acquire and prepare the facilities.

☐ Recruit and screen the potential worker-owners. Involve them in the planning and other tasks.

☐ Set a target date for start-up of the business and begin working towards it.

63

Lobbying to Gain Support for Worker Buyouts

If the proposed business involves a worker buyout of an existing business or one which is being closed, some additional actions may be necessary. For example, lobbying of government agencies will probably be necessary to obtain funds for feasibility studies and grants or loans for use in the actual enterprise purchase. Lobbying efforts may also be required to convince a reluctant employer or absentee corporation to sell the plant, make a contribution of money for a feasibility study, or make the plant available at a reasonable (realistic, reduced) price. Effective use of the press and mobilization of community support for the buyout may also be important factors in getting the owner to sell the workers an existing business or one slated for closure.

The importance of mobilizing community support and lobbying is illustrated by the experience of 227 worker-owners at Seymour Specialty Wire Company in Connecticut. While at first somewhat skeptical of the idea of a worker buyout of their brass mill, National Distillers and Chemical Corporation soon became more open to the possibility. Corporate officials later indicated that "the community support effort, which included letters from two Bishops and many political organizations, gave the employees some credibility." Not only did National Distillers agree to postpone their sale deadline, but they reduced the asking price, and as well, contributed over $25,000 toward the feasibility study. The state of Connecticut added $7500 and the town of Seymour $2500. The successful lobbying effort was organized by Ken Galdston and the Naugatuck Valley Project, an alliance of church, labor and community leaders formed in 1982 to "assert workers and community interests in response to threats of plant closings." (7)

4 PREPARING A BUSINESS PLAN

If the preliminary prospects appear good for founding a successful worker-owned firm, prospective worker-owners now confront a crucial question: Where do we go from here?

The answer, and the next step, is to develop a comprehensive business plan. This will be followed by efforts to obtain financing, and legally organize the business. Few worker-owned businesses have succeeded without careful planning, regardless of how marketable their product or service, or how high the enthusiasm and qualifications of the worker-owners. Planning a worker-owned business on paper before the doors open for business offers three important advantages.

First, many members from the workforce can participate in developing parts of the plan by serving on committees and task forces. The entire workforce can easily review and assess the plans when they are on paper. New ideas may suggest themselves, gaps in data can be quickly identified, and unexpected problems can surface. The extensive research and thinking necessary to prepare the business plan also demonstrates just how much knowledge is required to start and operate a business, and serves as an important learning experience for the prospective worker-owners.

Second, most new businesses require some outside finance, especially worker-owned firms being started by persons who may be short on cash. A thorough business plan offers evidence to potential lenders that the worker-owners know what they are talking about. Without a business plan most lending agencies, even ones anxious to see the idea of workplace democracy flourish, are reluctant to contribute financing.

Third, a lot of money can be saved and pitfalls avoided.

What Should a Business Plan Contain and How Is It Prepared?

Putting a business plan together takes time, money, and expertise. The organizing group must decide whether they want to develop a thorough, carefully documented business plan by themselves, or whether they should ask a technical assistance organization for help. Some of the sections will be used in the formal business plan submitted to potential lenders. Other sections will help the prospective worker-owners develop the basic ideas and policies to be used in setting up and operating the business. Regardless of how the work will be done, the following are parts of a business plan which should be completed.

☐ Product Plan

☐ Marketing Plan

☐ Raw Material Plan

☐ Financial Plan

☐ Taxation Plan

☐ Personnel Policy and Staffing Plan

☐ Governance Plan

☐ Social Audit Plan

☐ Education Plan

The list boggles the mind, but better to be momentarily upset than to empty your wallets for want of forethought. Dividing the job into parts can make gathering the information easier. Workers themselves need to be familiar with the tools professionals use, and should do as much of the business plan as possible. After all, the aim is to found a *worker-owned and worker-managed* enterprise. If the organizing group is a small one, completing one section at a time eases the chore. If the group is a large one, separate committees can complete sections, then report to the entire group, both in writing and verbally. If technical assistance is secured from outside organizations, workers should learn how to do the plan with the help of professionals.

Worker-owners of the Philadelphia O&O Supermarkets participated in planning the re-opening of the closed A&P Supermarkets with technical advice from consultants. They met three times a week for seven months. Nine planning committees were formed, including one on governance, the union role, management selection, and worker education. A steering committee with one representative from each of the nine committees, plus three union officials, was at the center of planning activity until a board of directors was elected. Other worker-owned companies have organized similar pre-startup planning groups. (1)

Putting a business plan together costs money. A budget should be prepared which contains two sections:

Pre-start costs: money to carry out the planning process, including administration, market research, property surveys, travel, legal costs, and, if technical advisors have been hired, their costs.

Pre-start capital costs: costs of facilities, equipment, books, office furniture, computer, telephones, and other equipment to complete the prospectus.

Planning a business takes time, especially when being done by three or four individuals alone or, at the other end of the scale, when a large number of prospective worker-owners are involved. Good planning of time is required. Planning how to plan can shorten the time. Establish a time schedule before starting. When assigning tasks, make sure each job has a deadline. Usually, several drafts will be required of each section of the plan before it is finally approved.

A sample time schedule might look like this:

Chart 4-1
TIMELINE FOR DEVELOPING A BUSINESS PLAN

Project Work Tasks — Week or Month

Project Work Tasks	1	2	3	4	5	6	7	8	9	10	11	12
Product Plan	▓	▓	▓	▓	▓	▓						
Market Plan		▓	▓	▓	▓	▓	▓					
Raw Material Plan			▓	▓	▓	▓	▓					
Financial Plan	▓	▓	▓	▓	▓	▓	▓	▓	▓			
Taxation Plan								▓	▓	▓	▓	▓
Personnel Policy Plan		▓	▓	▓	▓	▓	▓	▓				
Governance Plan		▓	▓	▓	▓	▓	▓	▓				
Social Audit Plan								▓	▓	▓	▓	▓
Education//Training Plan								▓	▓	▓	▓	
Verify Data								▓	▓	▓		
Type/Copy each Element										▓	▓	
Present to Members											▓	
Decision Making Process												▓

The length of time noted here is for illustrative purposes only and does not suggest that a business can be planned, its supporting data verified, and the social processes involved be accomplished in only twelve weeks, or even twelve months.

Two other charts complement the Time Chart. One is an Accountability Chart (Chart 4-2). The other is a Skills Allocation Chart (Chart 4-3). The Accountability Chart designates the person or group responsible for preparing a particular part of the business plan, when and where preliminary and final reports will be presented to the entire workforce, and what technical assistance is required—if any. The Skills Allocation Chart can be used to insure that shop floor workers or clerks serve with supervisors and managers on all committees.

The Skills Allocation Chart 4-3, which would be especially useful in the formation of a medium to large size firm, might look something like this:

Chart 4-2

ACCOUNTABILITY CHART

Task	Person/Group Responsible	Report Dates: Preliminary	Final	Technical Assistance
Product	————	————	————	————
Market	————	————	————	————
Raw Materials	————	————	————	————
Finances	————	————	————	————
Taxes	————	————	————	————
Personnel Policy	————	————	————	————
Governance	————	————	————	————
Social Audit	————	————	————	————
Education & Training	————	————	————	————

Chart 4-3

SKILLS ALLOCATION CHART

Task / Committee	From: Shop	Supervisor	Management
Product	☐	☐	☐
Market	☐	☐	☐
Raw Materials	☐	☐	☐
Finances	☐	☐	☐
Taxes	☐	☐	☐
Personnel Policy	☐	☐	☐
Governance	☐	☐	☐
Social Audit	☐	☐	☐
Education & Training	☐	☐	☐

Once assignments have been made and a timetable set for reporting to the entire workforce during periodic meetings, and then later in writing, committee members must know what is expected of them as a group. With a large group a coordinating committee should be elected. Each subgroup could report to this coordinating committee—which presents the entire business plan to the members in accord with the timetable. Additionally, the coordinating committee would be responsible for preparing a general overview or opening statement for the business plan. Each subgroup or participating member should:

☐ Gather answers to all of the questions in their assigned section of the business plan, and any others which might surface.

☐ Prepare and give a preliminary oral report to the entire workforce.

☐ Write and submit for verification the information or description required in their section.

☐ Coordinate their work with the other subgroups, or with the coordinating committee, as needed.

☐ Carry out all work in a timely manner.

Components of the Business Plan

A business plan answers questions, and, therefore, should be well organized, easy to read, and free of spelling or numerical errors. It should be free of jargon, especially cliches which are known only to persons in a particular industry. It should include the information that each worker-owner will want to know; after all, each member is being asked to invest both labor and money. And potential outside lenders will want a comprehensive business plan for analysis. It should make a clear and persuasive case for why the business will succeed.

Summary of the Plan

Usually a business plan opens with a short summary, not over one page long, which presents the project idea, key objectives and goals, an outline of the financial requirements, and why it will work. Because the plan is for a worker-owned enterprise, a brief statement about cooperative aims is useful.

Product Plan

Why a product plan? This section offers a precise description of what the worker-owned firm intends to manufacture or the service it intends to provide. Any person—butcher, bartender or banker—will want to know what the product does, how, and its general description; the same for a service. The description should include costs and selling prices. Special features should be identified. Outline any future plans to improve the product or to develop new ones. Describe how the firm's proposed prices compare with competitors' prices and how the proposed product or service differs from the competition. The firm's pricing policies with regard to distributors should be set forth if such firms are going to be used. Discuss how quality will be maintained, indicate if a guarantee or after-sales service will be offered, and whether there will be a faulty goods return policy. Include details on color, design, finish, and packaging. Keep in mind, however, that whatever is said here must be something the firm can back up, both in terms of overhead costs and contractual requirements.

Marketing Plan

A marketing plan serves one purpose: to help worker-owners estimate the size of the market today, next year, and a few years down the road. Prospective customers and the competition are identified. A market analysis helps determine the amount, costs, and timing of the firm's capital requirements, equipment needs, and human resources. If this information is incorrect, the costs can destroy your company.

Markets are usually quite large, but can be described in distinct parts or segments. Carefully identify the market segment at which your product or service is aimed. Worker-owned businesses, at least very early in their history, usually are small firms. Their size, plus the limited capital available to any small business, obviously limits their choice of a market segment. Geography is another factor which can limit a market.

The marketing plan should describe what is unique about the proposed product or service. Every competitor should be listed, along with the characteristics of their products, their wholesale and retail prices, which prices apply, and the strategies the worker-owned firm plans to use to secure a share of the market. Being a worker-owned firm is a claim for

71

distinction, but some particular price, quality, value as substitutes, service or other advantage must be spelled out. Potential customers want bargains plus a product best suited to their needs, quality, and service, not necessarily a new way to organize work.

All firms require marketing plans which include a sales analysis in quantitative terms, both in units sold and monetary value, and all available market research data. However, if sales are dependent upon a few customers, background information on their buying records, credit records, and peak demand periods becomes important. In some cases it may require a market survey of the top 15 or 20 customers if the cooperative is a new business or entails reopening a closed operation. The survey should include the product mix and margins on products as well as volume.

Raw Material Plan

Why account for raw materials? For service cooperatives, describing sources of raw materials is an easy task when preparing a business plan. For manufacturing firms which depend upon only two or three items to make a new product, the task is simple too. But in many worker-owned enterprises insuring a steady flow of raw materials is a must. This means establishing ties with a reliable supplier or suppliers and then identifying possible backup sources. Frequently, binding contracts must be negotiated to insure supplies.

The firm must plan for raw material supplies because their purchase generates accounts payable and inventories for both the raw materials and the finished products. Keeping accounts receivable balanced with accounts payable is one major management task. Purchasing large amounts of raw materials at one time, or too few materials, can throw a small firm's cash flow management into a tailspin.

Financial Plan

Financial documents are the heart of any business plan. Potential investors review this section very closely. Be sure to provide complete and accurate data about the financial condition and needs, whether it has been operating for some time or is just getting started. If the firm has been in operation for some time and new capital is required, hiring an accounting firm to provide an unbiased, thorough financial analysis might be useful.

Include any audited financial statements, comparative profit and loss statements from previous years, and projections for at least three years. Make certain that sales charts, labor cost tables, administrative overhead, and tax statements or projections are included. Industry business ratios should be highlighted if they put the firm in a good light, and explained if they don't.

If the worker-owned firm is seeking funds for the first time, the amount sought for the proposed project must be justified through the business plan. Specify exactly how the money will be used and the precise nature of financial arrangements with every individual lender or agency. Any money which will be used for construction of new buildings or to buy capital equipment must be explained along with cost estimates. If additional funds will be needed during the next five years, indicate the amount, the dates needed, and proposed method of repayment, plus all finance charges. It is important to know the lending policies, collateral requirements, and grant requirements of each of the financial institutions and government agencies from whom funds will be sought, and to address their specific concerns.

In keeping with two basic principles of worker-ownership, the business plan should declare that while loans can be received from any source, only worker-members have a policy-making say in the firm. Labor hires capital. Investors should be advised beforehand that their loan provides them rights to indirectly constrain or restrict decisions, but that only worker-members directly control the firm. Arrangements may be made for outsiders to make equity investments, but only in non-voting stock. However, debt financing in the form of loans which must be repaid at a specific rate of interest over a set time is increasingly available for worker-owned firms.

Taxation Plan

Tax law and tax regulations are best left in seasoned hands. But taxes are inevitable. They must be paid or, if not, data must be prepared to demonstrate why not. The federal government and some states give cooperatives special tax breaks. Worker-owners should ask both local or national tax officials for details when the business plan is being prepared.

Ordinarily, corporate earnings are subject to double taxation. The corporation pays corporate income tax on its taxable income and the individual shareholders pay personal income tax on their share of corporate earnings distributed as dividends. Subchapter T of the Federal Internal Revenue Code enables a cooperative to avoid this double taxation by legally avoiding the corporate level tax—by deducting from corporate taxable income any earnings allocated to members on the basis of work performed (called "patronage," often measured by hours worked). The procedures of Subchapter T can provide a dual benefit: the cooperative can avoid double taxation and, at the same time, retain and reinvest a portion of the earnings allocated to members (in addition to ordinary cash wages).

The benefits of Subchapter T are available, in the words of the Tax Code, to "any corporation operating on a cooperative basis." This has been interpreted as meaning (1) a worker cooperative must allocate earnings on the basis of patronage, as opposed to relative capital investment; and (2) the cooperative must be democratically controlled by the members.

It is also important to note that the particular state-level incorporation statute is not controlling for federal tax purposes. For example, if the cooperative is incorporated as a business corporation but operates on a cooperative basis, it can still qualify under Subchapter T.

The mechanics of using Subchapter T are simple. No prior election or approval is necessary. A corporation that is operating on a cooperative basis simply files the appropriate IRS forms (1099-PATR and 1096) when paying taxes. A note of caution: consult with your lawyer before relying on Subchapter T.

Among the federal tax forms which have to be filed on a regular basis by corporations and employers are the Corporate Income Tax/Return (Form 1120), which is due by the 15th day of the 4th month following the end of the year. The payment of taxes per the return are due in equal installments by the 15th day of the 3rd and 6th months following the end of the year. The Corporate Estimated Tax/Form 503 is used for the deposit of estimated taxes. Deposits are due the IRS in equal quarterly installments on the 15th day of the 4th, 6th, 9th, and 12th months of the taxable year. Payroll taxes/quarterly return (Form 941) of combined withheld income, and employer's and employee's social security taxes (FICA), are due on April 30, July 31, October 31, and January 31. Taxes are paid with the return unless business is required to make deposits to the authorized depository. The individual witholding (Form W-2) and reconciliation statements (Form W-3) are due the last day of February. Employers must furnish employees with Form W-2 by January 31st.

For purposes of the business plan, it should only be

necessary to state whether you plan to qualify as a cooperative for federal tax purposes, and that you intend to obtain the benefits of Subchapter T.

If the proposed business is to be organized as an Employee Stock Ownership Plan (ESOP), there are substantial tax breaks available to these businesses. An ESOP permits the firm to repay both the loan principal and interest in pre-tax dollars, and thus save the company taxes. This information should be included as part of the business plan.

Personnel Policy and Staffing Plan

"How do people get fired if they are owners?" The question, or something like it, has come up during hundreds of meetings called to explain the idea of worker-ownership. So is the question's other side: "How do you get hired?" Or, a third question asked with equal frequency, "How do you handle grievances?" A personnel policy is to worker-members what the business plan is to bankers. From the shop floor, or job station, the cooperative's worth is measured by the ways people are treated, and, as well, by its return on their investment of labor and money.

Only a short summary of personnel policy and staffing plan need be included in a comprehensive plan submitted to lenders or investors. It should spell out the salaries and wages of the key managerial employees, and in a worker buyout where there is a union it should indicate the financial provisions of the existing collective bargaining agreement or any modifications which will be made as part of the buyout. But a fully developed personnel policy—how personnel decisions will be made and by whom—needs to be spelled out in full by worker-members, along with a timetable for formulation, review, decision-making, and evaluation.

Setting out individual responsibilities and rights is one way to start a personnel policy. Defining each job and its qualifications is another. Advancement policies, criteria and procedures for job rotation, disciplinary procedures, a system to handle grievances, and leave time are among the many issues which must be addressed.

Additionally, some procedures should be developed by which personnel policies are proposed, reviewed, adopted, evaluated and revised as need dictates.

Potential lenders will want information on how the firm will be managed on a day-to-day basis, including reassurance that decisions will be reached in the most orderly, efficient manner. Many lenders wrongly think worker-owned firms

75

cannot make decisions quickly and efficiently. The personnel policy section should spell out the distinction between authority vested in management and that residing with the workforce or its elected boards and committees. Finally, the section should briefly note the internal means established to resolve disputes between individual members, worker-owners and management, board members and management and, if a union is involved in the firm, between it, the management, and worker-owners. In sum, the personnel policy section of the plan should demonstrate consistency with democratic values yet contain efficient administrative procedures for handling human resources.

Governance Plan

Another key element needed to assure workplace democracy is the means of self-governance. The cooperative's by-laws are the framework for governance. These are supplemented by written operating rules agreed to by the members or board of directors. By-laws set forth the democratic rights and responsibilities of member-owners. They provide the means by which workers can exercise their guaranteed rights. Finding words for a democratic governance system is easy; putting those words into operation can be difficult. Three criteria should be used to establish governing by-laws: the responsibilities of the membership as a whole, the responsibilities of the board of directors, and the responsibilities of any special grievance council or internal social committee. Each should be absolutely clear, giving each group real decision-making authority. The governance system established should be simple and accessible to members. The ICA model by-laws are provided in Appendix F.

Only a summary of the governance plan is necessary in the formal, public business plan. However, the governance statement should affirm the enterprise's intent to adhere to democratic principles, especially with regard to one-person/one-vote governance.

Social Audit Plan

If a balance sheet is the means by which a firm's performance as a business is measured, then the social audit is a way to measure its human worth. A worker-owned enterprise which operates only on the material criteria of profitability ignores the humanitarian principles of cooperation. Conversely, a worker-owned enterprise which operates only on humanitarian criteria without regard to the realities of the business world will soon go bankrupt. A social audit can measure the firm's social achievements. There are three principal elements in a social audit: democratization of work, humanization of work, and product/service contribution.

☐ **The Democratization of Work** element includes equality, decision-making, communications, governance structure, control, ownership, and, if applicable, union relations.

☐ **The Humanization of Work** element includes job design and job satisfaction, pay, job site conditions, degree of responsibility, opportunities for training or skill upgrading, and individual recognition.

☐ **The Product/Service Contribution** element includes customer satisfaction, adherence to environmental regulation, truthfulness in advertising, and availability of the firm's practices and policies in the community.

77

When such an audit is constructed according to the vision of the worker-owners and when each element is a numerical value, the social audit measures the impact the cooperative is having on the lives of worker-owners, the immediate community, and serves as a tool by which worker-owners can gauge financial constraints. If done regularly, a social audit can document how the firm balances what is financially practical at a given moment with what is democratically or socially desirable.

While the consideration and preparation of a social audit plan are an important part of the preparation for starting a worker-owned business, the inclusion of this material or section in the formal document to be submitted to financial lenders is not necessary or appropriate.

Education and Training Plan

Learning the vocational, managerial, interpersonal, and democratic skills necessary to run the cooperative may well determine the ultimate financial success. The abilities of worker-owners to handle production, manage their own business, and make democracy function inside a worksite are the skills upon which the firm's future depends.

The role of education and training in a worker-owned enterprise is to assist workers to obtain the skills and capabilities which increase their control over and responsibility for corporate decisions, resources, and outcomes. If individual members fail to grow in these areas, the venture may fail. One problem facing many potential worker-owners, fully engaged in the process of organizing the business or arranging for a worker buyout, is that they find themselves struggling with the problems of finance, organization, marketing, production, and other issues, and feel that they do not have the time or money to plan for education. The feeling is that educational activities can wait "until we are on our feet and have solved the more pressing problems." The experience of the Basques and others suggest that this is a dangerous course to follow. From the outset education and training for worker-member-owners should be treated as a vitally important concern and should be pursued accordingly.

Like the sections on governance and the social audit, this part of the business plan need not be given to financial sources. But the document should set forth the principles upon which any program of education and training rests, as well as goals and methods. How will education and training needs be identified? Who is responsible for education, and how and when will the education or skill training be provided? If appropriate, both on-the-job and off-site learning options should be noted.

Verifying the Business Plan

After completing the drafting process, but before having the entire business plan typed for presentation to members or delivering the shorter version to potential lenders, worker-owners or the coordinating committee may wish to verify the data. Verifying the business plan requires an analysis of each section to insure financial targets set to provide sufficient margins to accomplish other stated responsibilities. Verifying is a way to look for any weaknesses which may cause difficulties down the road. Ask yourselves: Will the business generate an acceptable level of financial efficiency? The answer to this question is arrived at by comparing the net margin, gross margin, and expense margin of the worker-owned company's plans with a traditionally organized company of about the same size and industry. The verification of the business plan may require the assistance of an accountant or other financial advisor.

The Break-Even Point

What will be the break-even point of this business? The

Chart 4-4
BREAK EVEN ANALYSIS

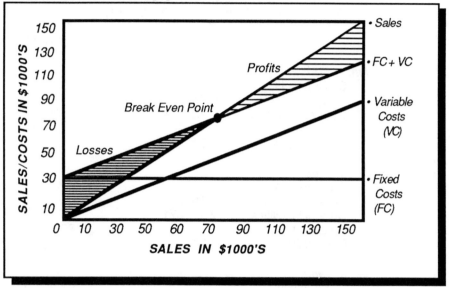

break-even point is where sales cover basic operating expenses, but generate no surplus. It is a key target and can be figured on weekly, monthly or annual sales. Another ratio called the margin of safety can be figured by calculating the percentage sales can fall below your estimates before the break-even point is reached. Chart 4-4 illustrates graphically the concept of a break-even point.

Risk Cover: Current and Quick Liquidity Ratios

Have the risks been reduced? There are at least three ways to figure the degree of risk before starting up the business. One is to divide all cash or cash equivalent assets by all cash or cash equivalent liabilities. The number yielded by this formula is called the "risk cover." The more available dollars in cash or its equivalent, the better. To gauge the impact of loans, including those of worker-owners in the Internal Membership Accounts, a two-step calculation is required. Chart 4-5 is an illustration of this formula for a risk cover as applied to The Worker-Owned Cooperative Pro Forma Balance Sheets shown in Appendix H, Exhibit 10.

Of course, there are other ways to verify the financial data in a business plan. Worker-owners may want to take this process further, but these are the essentials. Other issues should be discussed as part of the planning process. For example,

Chart 4-5

CURRENT AND QUICK LIQUIDITY RATIOS
FOR THE WORKER-OWNED COOPERATIVE

	Current Ratio	*Quick Ratio*
Jan. 1, 1987		
Quick Assets		$228,601
Current Assets	$370,391	
Current Liabilities	$285,972	$285,972
Quick Ratio		.80
Current Ratio	1.30	
Jan. 1, 1988		
Quick Assets		$242,037
Current Assets	$418,663	
Current Liabilities	$301,071	$301,071
Quick Ratio		.80
Current Ratio	1.39	
Jan. 1, 1989		
Quick Assets		$354,206
Current Assets	$566,060	
Current Liabilities	$422,285	$422,285
Quick Ratio		.84
Current Ratio	1.34	

does the group have adequate management skills? If not, how are they to be obtained? Will the proposed product or service have acceptance in the marketplace? Will the financing provide an adequate cushion during the start-up phase, etc.?

Presentation of the Business Plan to Members

A Time to Vote

Before making an appointment with potential lenders, the business plan should be presented to the workforce for study, modification, ratification, or rejection. The particulars of this process are up to the group. Once approved, however, the formal business plan should be typed or printed with one last thought in mind: its purpose is to get financial backing. It will be the first impression prospective lenders receive. If the business plan looks sloppy or hastily done, the many hours devoted to putting it together can come to nothing because lenders are likely to not take you seriously even if you rework it. The longer and more detailed version of the business plan should be used by the prospective worker-owners as a basic document to help them during the organizational and start-up phases of their new business.

A Final Note

Putting a business plan together may take a few weeks or as long as a year, even with outside help. The business plan is the blueprint for any business, but for worker-owners who must compete in a marketplace dominated by traditionally organized firms, the document is both blueprint and keystone.

The business plan, revised on the basis of knowledge gained through interaction with lenders and by experience, becomes the framework for operating the business in its critical early stages. Thus, a poorly thought out plan or one based on inaccurate data—or the disregarding of a carefully prepared plan—may quickly lead the business into serious financial, marketing, or operating problems. The knowledge and experience gained by the prospective worker-owners while researching and writing the plan can prepare them to more effectively operate their business when it is started, and substantially increase the probability of making it a success. Failure to take the planning process seriously, or to depart from it without good reason may lead to failure.

The Rainbow Workers Cooperative, after only 13 months of existence, failed in May 1986, due to financial inexperience, overly fast expansion, and unrealistic expectations. The group added bathing suits to its original product line of tents and parkas, without carefully assessing the market situation or its financial plan. Entry into the low price swimsuit field placed them in direct competition with low wage producers. The co-op more than doubled its work force in five weeks, characterized by Rainbow president Betty Chisolm as "too much, too fast," leaving them unable to pay salaries and unwilling to reduce wages. The group also suffered from a lack of business experience and inadequate education in worker-ownership. According to Chisolm, too many worker-owners saw their company as "a regular job," and not requiring ex-

81

tra effort to make it a success. (2)

Appendix H contains a sample business plan for the worker-owned cooperative to illustrate how an actual plan might be constructed.

Each element in any business plan can be divided into a set of questions which, if answered fully, will give a systematic look at the business being considered. Basic questions are set forth in Chart 4-6 below; obviously, each situation will present other, perhaps more suitable questions in each category. Once the business is started, it is important to develop good information systems to compare the operating results to the plan.

Chart 4-6

CHECKLIST OF BASIC QUESTIONS TO BE ANSWERED IN A BUSINESS PLAN

1) The Product Plan

A) Describe the product or service offered.

B) Define the market segment, all potential customers, and all competitors.

C) Define the costs of the product or service, comparing those costs with competitors' substitutes.

D) Is the product patented, or should it be?

E) Are there any restrictions on its manufacture or distribution?

F) Are there any by-products which might be sold, now or in the future?

G) Is the product or by-products of its manufacture harmful in any way to anyone young or old, worker or customer?

H) If the product or by-products of its manufacture could be harmful, what steps will be taken to insure safety in its manufacture or use?

2) The Marketing Plan

A) Who might buy the product or service, and how does the firm plan to let them know the product or service is available? This is called market identification.

B) How many businesses or persons buy the product, or use

the service being planned? Why do they use it? Will a change in prices change sales? How much of a product can be sold, or a service be used?

C) Will the product be distributed directly to buyers, or sold only through wholesale distributors? And how: by mail, truck, ship, air, or person to person? And what will it cost?

D) Will the product or service sell in some seasons but not others? If so, why? How will this affect how work is organized, cash flow, sales, etc.?

E) The seasons aside, are there other outside factors which will influence when sales are made.

F) What are the product's unique features , or what makes the service important?

G) Will the product have a particular problem with getting spoiled, broken or damaged between the time of production and final sale? What can be done to prevent those or similar problems?

H) Can the sale of the product or service be sheltered? That is to say, can the prospective worker-owned firm be assured in writing that the product or service will be purchased by another firm or person for a specific period of time, and at a set price or price schedule.

I) Will sales persons be worker-owners? Will they be paid a commission as well as a salary or wage?

J) How will the product or service be identified to potential customers on the firm's stationary, packages (if needed), advertising, business cards, and telephone directory?

3) The Raw Materials Plan

A) Who will supply the worker-owned firm with raw materials? Is there one or more suppliers? What are their policies on delivery, prices, credit?

B) How much (or how many) will the worker-owned firm have to buy from a supplier at a time? What is their discount policy, if any?

C) What will shipping and storage cost? Are there any special taxes on inventory, and when must they be paid?

D) Will stock levels be maintained by total cost, or by volume?

E) How will the firm control the inventory, keep records on the inventory, and keep it secure after delivery, either from theft, fire damage, deterioration, or spoilage?

F) How much will insurance cost for stock? And how many worker-owners or how much time will be required to handle the inventory?

4) The Financial Plan

A) List every available source of financial help, including the name, title, address and telephone number of the contact person in each financial institution, and loan size, decision-making schedule and criteria.

B) Develop a complete list of all the equipment needed, the cost of each item, and potential suppliers, including an assessment of their ability to service the equipment, and any related service costs.

C) Prepare balance sheets.

D) Prepare a break-even analysis.

E) Prepare a projected income statement for the first year of operation.

F) Based on the projected income statement, prepare a cash flow analysis for three years.

G) If possible, prepare a spread sheet, or deviation analysis showing what could happen to the firm if prices dropped, increased, or any other variables.

5) The Taxation Plan

A) How will the Internal (or Individual) Membership Account be treated by tax law in the state the firm is to be located?

B) Exactly how does that state tax worker-owned cooperatives?

C) How does the national government tax worker-owned firms?

D) If an ESOP is planned, how will it be treated by tax law?

E) Are there any particular laws in that state which apply only to the kind of business being planned? If so, list them and estimate their cost.

F) Using the projected income statement, prepare an estimate of all taxes the company will face, and a schedule of payment dates, if possible.

G) List all necessary licenses, tax and regulatory permits which must be in possession of an operational business of the sort being planned?

6) *The Personnel and Staffing Plan*

A) How many people will be needed to do exactly what work? Spell out each job, set forth a description, and indicate the number of hours daily that work is required. Identify any special skills or training (and licenses) that may be needed by workers.

B) How are wages, benefits, and the Internal (or Individual) Membership accounts to be calculated, and by whom?

85

C) Are potential members with the necessary skills available? If more member-workers will be needed to start the enterprise, how will they be recruited?

D) If some potential members lack some skills needed by the firm, can training be provided, or obtained nearby? At what cost to the company?

E) What are the health, safety, sex equity, and wages and hours laws which apply to the firm? Are there special state or federal laws which apply?

F) How long must a person be employed before becoming eligible for full membership, including purchasing the membership share? What are the procedures for work performance before membership?

G) What are the procedures for reviewing work performance after a worker becomes an owner?

H) How will a member be fired? What procedures for due process will be used for disciplinary purposes including firing?

I) Will the firm adopt a policy of job security? What will be the basic elements of this policy? If layoffs for seasonal reasons are necessary, what procedures will govern that process?

J) Is there a policy, and a plan, for job rotation? Will it operate without regard to sex? Is there a policy, and a plan, for skill upgrading and providing workers with higher level skills?

K) How will conflicts between worker-owners at the job site, or between worker-owners and elected managers be resolved? By a specially elected body, or on an ad hoc basis?

7) *The Education and Training Plan*

A) How will internal educational programs be calculated as a factor in the cost of production or service delivery?

B) Will every fully-vested member have the right to learn any job in the firm? Will on-the-job training or off-the-job training be paid for by the company or individual? If by both, then in what proportion and amount? If by the company only, what limits will apply?

C) What criteria will be used to judge applications for education, either vocational or managerial?

D) How will the effectiveness of educational programs be judged?

E) Who will manage the educational programs, a person outside the firm, a worker-owner, or a committee?

F) Will there be regular educational efforts to improve the collective skills and understanding of self-management?

G) Will the firm inventory on a regular basis the educational interests of worker-owners?

8) *Governance Plan*

A) Will the firm's by-laws spell out the democratic rights and responsibilities of each member?

B) Will the by-laws establish a plan for electing board members and other officers on a regular basis?

C) Will the by-laws provide for the rotation of leadership by limiting the terms any officer may hold office?

D) Will the firm's manager have the right to vote on policy matters before the board of directors? Or will the manager's role be limited specifically to proposing and carrying out board policy?

E) What are to be the exact responsibilities of: (1) the membership as a whole; (2) the board of directors; (3) the various committees; and (4) the management.

F) How will changes be made in: (1) policy; (2) the by-laws; or (3) management practices?

G) Will the by-laws or any other governance documents or policy statements be written as clearly and simply as possible, and be available to every member?

H) Will restraints be included in these documents to prevent any single group from wielding unchecked power within the firm?

I) Will the firm have a separately elected Grievance Committee to assure independent protection of the rights of individual worker-owners, and to settle disagreements, perceived inequities, or allegations of mistreatment?

J) Will the firm develop a clear statement outlining decision-making powers for worker-owners, committees, the board of directors and management at the shop floor, administrative, governance and policy-making levels?

K) Will the firm have any of these committees, or all of them, and will their duties be specifically stated: governance, finance, grievance, education, management oversight, personnel, executive, long-range planning, and elections?

L) Will all policy-making committees hold open meetings? Will there be an annual meeting at which officers are elected, policy reviewed and decided upon?

9) Social Audit Plan

A) Will the firm establish specific norms by which social performance can be measured with regard to democratic control, worker-owner participation in elections and decision-making, job re-design, product production and creation?

B) Will these annual social audits be used to influence cooperative action and policy? If so, how?

C) Will results of a social audit be available to all members, the outside public, and to other worker-owned firms?

5 PUTTING CAPITAL TO WORK

SOURCES OF CAPITAL TO FINANCE
WORKERS' COOPERATIVES

INTERNAL FINANCING

EXTERNAL FINANCING

Money primes the pump of any business. Worker-owners, despite their own capital contributions—which are frequently substantial and when combined often total as much as 40 percent of the fixed capital required—need to know the principles of business finance, the distinctive finances of labor-managed cooperatives, and potential sources of capital.

Money is needed to organize the firm, to provide equipment and a place to work, to meet the expenses of daily operation including salaries and taxes, and to use when the going gets tough. There are two kinds of capital in the labor-managed enterprise—equity capital and debt capital.

Equity capital is provided by worker-members. It is the sum of their membership contributions, and it is what makes workers owners. On a balance sheet, equity is called net worth, and the sum of money left when all the liabilities (money owed to any other firm or person) are subtracted from the total assets. The formula can be stated this way: "Total assets minus total liabilities equals net worth or owner equity."

Debt capital is the short and long-term credit extended by banks, other businesses, individuals, or governmental agencies. There are two principle kinds of debt capital: mortgages which are most often used to finance fixed assets like buildings or equipment; and lines of credit, credit certificates, or straight loans, all of which are used chiefly for current financial needs like payroll, inventory, and purchasing raw materials. The firm's working capital can be measured by subtracting total current liabilities from total current assets. The formula is: "Current assets minus total current liabilities equals working capital."

Current liabilities include accounts payable to suppliers, to members (including the individual membership accounts), accrued expenses such as taxes, interest payments on loans which are unpaid, notes payable to lenders within one year, and payroll. Current assets include cash on hand or in banks, all accounts receivable, inventory, notes that are collectible within one year, prepaid rent or insurance, and any other expense paid for but not used until some time in the future.

The balance sheet of a worker-owned enterprise differs in several ways from a traditional firm where capital controls labor, and from an employee-owned corporation such as an ESOP. In a traditional firm, profits are distributed to shareholders. In most firms a portion of the profits are retained to provide a reserve or to expand the business by purchasing new buildings or equipment; the remainder is distributed to shareholders who may or may not be workers but who have voting rights. The retained earnings increase the value of each share of stock. Therefore, the bulk of the capital value gained goes to those holding the largest number of shares. A contribution of capital, not of labor, gives the right to vote. The more capital contributed, the more votes furnished to control the firm.

In a pure labor-managed cooperative only workers are shareholders, and each may own only one share of stock. When profits are distributed, either as retained earnings or as actual cash or "patronage dividends" to each shareholder, every worker benefits in proportion to rate of pay, skill level, experience, and responsibility. This idea is one of the Basques' most important contributions to the historical development of cooperatives. The Basques' way of putting capital to work has been adopted around the world.

They divide a member's share into two parts, giving each differing but related functions. First, a member's share insures a right to vote, certain other membership rights, and the right to a share of any profit or loss. These constitute the political rights of worker-ownership. Second, a share assigns the net worth of the company's assets to a system of internal member savings accounts. One account must be established for each worker. The initial balance in these accounts is the membership contribution. These are the economic rights of the worker-owners. They derive from the contribution of labor, not the purchase of shares.

When the worker-owned cooperative divides net income at the end of a fiscal year, every member's account is credited with a sum equal to that of all other workers making the same wages at the same skill level, experience, responsibility, and number of hours worked. If the firm loses money or, in balance sheet language, the net income is negative, each member's share of the loss is subtracted from the balance. Interest is paid on funds in each account at a rate determined by the board of directors.

On the Basques' balance sheets these devices are called internal accounts. David Ellerman, staff economist for the Industrial Cooperative Association who first applied this idea to American worker-owned cooperatives, called them internal membership accounts. Regardless of what they are called, the Basques' ingenious way of adding value to each member's share while adding value to the cooperative has solved two vexing problems which prevented labor-managed enterprises from flourishing. First, they were able to keep the cost of a membership share low enough to allow new worker-owners to buy in when older members wanted to leave the cooperative or retire. And second, they provided a way to prevent shares from being sold to outsiders, resulting in the loss of worker control. These problems were major impediments to maintaining worker control in the Pacific Northwest plywood cooperatives; their origins can be traced to Rochdale. The system of internal accounts also solved the problem faced by marketing co-ops which distributed all of their net income to their member-patrons on an annual basis, a practice that left them with no working capital each new year.

A look at the differences between a conventional balance sheet and one appropriate for the distinctive needs of a labor-managed enterprise is useful. Charts 5-1 and 5-2 illustrate how members in a worker-owned cooperative can put their money to work.

Sources of Capital to Finance Workers' Cooperatives

Historically, banks or similar lending agencies have been loathe to put a nickel at risk in worker-owned firms. They have offered nearly as many excuses for this reluctance as there have been efforts to get loans. Governments have been familiar with cooperatives for many years and have promoted them actively among farmers, fishing or craft industries, and for marketing farm products. But they, too, have kept away from and even refused to assist worker-owned industrial

Chart 5-1

CONVENTIONAL BUSINESS BALANCE SHEET

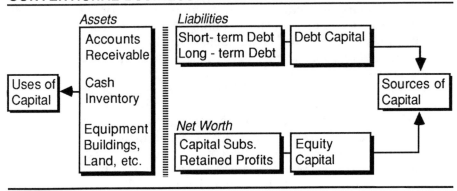

Chart 5-2

LABOR-MANAGED COOPERATIVE
ENTERPRISE BALANCE SHEET

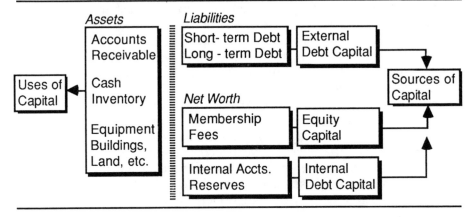

cooperatives until recently. Capital has been hard to come by for workplace democracy.

Internal Financing

There was no lending agency to finance the Basques who founded the first worker-owned factory during the height of the Franco regime. Money came from their own pockets or from friends and relatives. From the start, Mondragon workers used internal accounts to finance their own growth. Ellerman has said that the internal accounts "helped insure the stability and dynamic growth of the whole complex." (1)

At first, Basques reinvested 70 percent of the net income (profits) in the cooperative by crediting each member's internal account. The remaining 30 percent was divided into two parts with about 10 percent going to provide education aimed at fostering new vocational skills or cooperative abilities within the company or community, and about 20 percent going into the collective retained earnings account for the proverbial rainy day and to finance capital expenditures. Today, those figures have been revised. Usually 50 percent of net income is contributed to the internal accounts, 40 percent to retained earnings, and 10 percent to education.

Over the years the value of a share of stock in a successful business increases, this is called capital gains. As workers retire they want to pocket the accumulated result of their labor. In conventional employee-owned corporations, like the plywood cooperatives in the Northwest, the tendency has been to sell shares to outsiders. Younger potential worker-owners cannot afford to buy a share (at a price of $50,000 or more) and enter the firm. Gradually, as more and more shares are sold to outsiders, workers are no longer owners controlling corporate affairs.

When a worker-owner retires from or quits one of the Basque cooperatives, the membership certificate or ownership share is automatically forfeited back to the cooperative. The balance in the member's internal account—the original membership fee plus accumulated earnings and interest—is paid to the former worker-owners over a specified period of time. The internal accounts keep the price of a share at a level which job-seekers or potential members can afford. A person hoping to join the cooperative pays a membership fee to purchase one share, which is a capital contribution equal to the contribution of every other member, thus putting that person "at equal risk" with fellow workers. This contribution can be paid in installments, or all at once.

The internal account for a new worker-member, which starts with only the value of the one share, grows with the addition of the member's share of net income each year, plus interest paid for the use of the money. In effect, the Basques established a generational revolving loan fund which provides capital for expansion and modernization, and prevents shares from escaping worker control. At the same time, the system allows each worker-owner to receive a share of the profits earned over the years of membership, which can be withdrawn at the time of departure or retirement.

The balance sheet of a worker-owned cooperative at the

93

Chart 5-3

THE WORKER-OWNED COOPERATIVE
BEGINNING BALANCE SHEET

Assets		*Liabilities*	
Current Assets			
Cash	$43,000.00	Short term debt	$0.00
Accounts Receivable	0.00	Notes Payable	100,000.00
Inventory	75,000.00	Accounts Payable	0.00
Prepaid Supplies	12,000.00		
Prepaid Expenses	13,500.00	*Long term debt*	
		Term Loans	
Fixed Assets		Payable	25,000.00
Land & Buildings	250,000.00	Mortgage	
Equipment	100,000.00	Payable	200,000.00
		Total Liabilities	$325,000.00
		Net Worth	
		Membership	
		Fees (equity)	175,000.00
		Individual Accounts	0.00
		Reserves	0.00
Total Assets	$500,000.00	*Liabilities & Equity*	$500,00.00

time of start-up would appear something like the illustration in Chart 5-3. The figures used are those in the business plan for The Worker-Owned Cooperative in Appendix H.

Charts 5-4 and 5-5 show how the individual member's internal account would reflect the net profits, or growth, of The Worker-Owned Cooperative over periods of five and twenty years. (The approximate working life of an average member-owner is twenty years.) For the sake of illustration, we assume sales growth of 42 percent in 1987, 23 percent between 1988 and 1990, 17 percent from 1991 and 1995, 13 percent between 1996 and 2000, and 8 percent from 2001 and 2005. The charts also assume that all 35 original workers are paid the same wage rate and work for the full 20 years; 50 percent of the annual net income is allocated to the members' internal accounts, 40 percent to reserves (retained earnings), and 10 percent to education. The charts assume a constant net profit margin of 7.7 percent per year during each of the

Chart 5-4

THE WORKER-OWNED COOPERATIVE
CUMULATIVE VALUE OF MEMBER INTERNAL ACCOUNTS 1986-1990

	1986 $	1987 $	1988 $	1989 $	1990 $
Sales	1,250,000	1,779,250	2,182,235	2,679,236	3,293,000
Sales Growth	---	42%	23%	23%	---
Profit Percentage	0.03	0.05	0.08	0.08	0.08
Net Profit	39,625	71,704	102,566	200,943	246,978

Allocation of Profits in Total for 35 workers

Internal Accounts @ 50%	19,813	35,809	51,163	100,242	123,044
Reserves @ 40%	15,850	28,682	41,026	80,377	98,790
Education @ 10%	3,962	7,170	10,257	20,094	24,697

Allocation of Profits by Worker/owner

Internal Accounts per worker per year	566	1,023	1,462	2,864	3,516
Cummulative Internal Accounts (Distribution for current year + previous balance + interest)	566	1,589	3,051	5,915	9,431

NOTE: Interest of 7.5% on the previous year's internal accounts balance is subtracted from the total (50 percent) allocation to worker-owners before distribution.

17 years following the first three-year start-up phase when profits were 3.17 percent, 4.03 percent and 4.7 percent respectively, and that the board of directors have voted to pay an annual interest of 7.5 percent on the member internal account balances.

Chart 5-5

THE WORKER-OWNED COOPERATIVE
CUMULATIVE VALUE OF INTERNAL ACCOUNTS 1986 - 2005:

	1986 -1990 $	1991 -1995 $	1986 -2000 $	2001 -2005 $
Allocation of Profits				
Net Profit	661,812	2,026,888	3,965,100	6,320,989
50% (less 7.5% interest on member allocations for prior years) to internal accounts	330,072	1,006,261	1,960,844	3,112,839
Allocation of Internal Accounts per Worker -Owner				
5- year allocation	9,431	28,750	56,024	88,938
Cumulative balance	9,431	38,181	94,205	183,143

The use of internal financing mechanisms poses dilemmas for North Americans. In order to maintain incentives and encourage reinvestment of surplus, a significant portion of the capital must be owned by individual worker-members. America and Canada have dynamic economies with constantly changing conditions and technology. This makes labor mobility desirable. And that is a dilemma. How do you minimize the conflict between the three objectives of high mobility, equity accumulation, and appropriately structured incentives for reinvestment of surplus?

If the time horizons of cooperative worker-owners are short, as they seem to be in capitalist corporations and their shareholders, then capital accumulation to finance investment may be inhibited and plans for long-term growth distorted.

The historically low mobility of the Basque workforce has diminished the conflict between these objectives, permitting rapid growth and capital accumulation. Their experience suggests that in America these obstacles may be less severe when internally financed, or when worker-owned businesses are established in rural areas or as part of a regional development strategy. It also suggests that the successful worker-owned businesses must adopt effective human resource development policies encompassing quality of worklife programs to minimize turnover, and including implementing job rotation, retraining, and skill upgrading to facilitate workforce flexibility, adaptability, and internal mobility. Worker-owners must be able to acquire new work skills and take on new job assignments as business conditions change.

External Sources of Capital

Self-financing aside, there are additional sources of financing to help purchase or start a worker-owned business. Listed below are general categories of these lending sources. (2)

Special Credit Sources for Cooperatives. At this writing there are three special credit sources available to worker-owners in the United States. Each has its own set of objectives and requirements. For additional information contact them directly.

97

☐ **The Industrial Cooperative Association Revolving Loan Fund,** 58 Day Street, Somerville, MA, 02144. Tel: (617) 629-2700. The ICA Revolving Loan Fund provides a source of conventional loans and "membership equity" financing to worker cooperatives in their initial stage, making it easier for low-income, blue-collar or women workers to put together a successful financing package.

☐ **The Self-Help Credit Union,** P.O. Box 3259, Durham, NC, 27705. Tel: (919) 683-3016. The Self-Help Credit Union supports worker-owned businesses and fosters local community development in North Carolina. In addition, the Self-Help Ventures Fund, a non-profit subsidiary, arranges financing for worker-owned firms in low-income, and minority communities.

☐ **The National Cooperative Bank,** 1630 Connecticut Ave., N.W., Washington, D.C., 20009. Tel: (202) 745-4600. The National Cooperative Bank (NCB) was created in 1980 to provide loans and technical assistance to consumer, housing, and worker cooperatives. The bank was originally established by the federal government, but became self-sufficient through the sale of stock to customers. The bank is now a private institution, but it has established a companion private foundation to give technical assistance and lower interest loans to eligible borrowers. Under its charter, the NCB can extend up to 10 percent of its assets to worker cooperatives.

NCB loans are made at market rates for up to 10 years. The bank provides both senior financing and subordinated financing, has fairly conventional underwriting standards, requires cooperative members to have an equity investment, and prefers co-participation by local private lenders. Borrowers are required to purchase NCB stock and must pay the loan closing costs out of their own resources.

☐ **Church and Foundation Sources.** Several churches have established loan programs for cooperative, community-based or minority business ventures. Some foundations make program-related investments to worker-cooperatives or help capitalize other investment sources which act as intermediaries. Because these philanthropic sources provide high-risk capital at favorable rates of interest, they should be explored by worker cooperatives who have low-income members, by minority or blue-collar workers facing job loss, and by women.

☐ **New State and Provincial Programs.** During the past few years several states and provinces have responded to the problems of plant closings by passing legislation to save threatened firms and revitalize their economies. In New York, Massachusetts, Pennsylvania, Connecticut, Michigan and Oregon, this legislation has included loan funds to provide money for modernization, employee buyouts, and other capital needs of threatened firms.

In Canada, in October 1985, the provincial government of Manitoba launched an Employment Cooperative Program (ECP) to foster the creation of new worker co-ops, conversions, and rescues of threatened firms. The ECP assists prospective co-ops with "bridged" financing until a satisfactory financial package including worker equity and private sources can be put together. The bridging financing can include loans, forgivable loans, grants, loan guarantees, or various combinations as needed.

The Oregon Economic Stabilization and Conversion Fund was created in 1986 to underwrite feasibility studies and provide partial financing (matched with other private investments) to workers and other groups in the state desirous of saving their jobs and creating new jobs to further process the raw materials produced in Oregon. The intent of the legislation is to foster worker and community-owned enterprises. Money to finance the program is coming from a state lottery.

In 1985, the Michigan legislature extended and expanded a program started in 1979 to encourage employee purchases of firms threatened with closure or transfer of operations.

Typically, a variety of sources, both internal and external, are tapped to obtain financing for a worker-cooperative. Be sure and find out whether your community or state has any special financial programs available to help start worker-owned businesses, either new start-ups or conversions of existing businesses.

Private Financing Sources

There are several major private financing sources for small businesses, including labor-managed cooperatives—commercial banks, asset-based lenders, commercial mortgages, leasing, and venture capitalists.

Commercial Banks. Commercial banks will lend money only when they can reasonably predict if and when a company can repay. As a result, they offer short-term, medium-term, or long-term debt financing to businesses which can demonstrate in a business plan the ability to repay loans.

Commercial banks usually require some form of collateral to secure loans and, in the case of closely held companies, personal guarantees. They do, of course, lend primarily against the strength of the business. If a customer is financially strong, a bank may lend on an unsecured basis. A worker-owned cooperative should establish a good relationship with a local bank to obtain credit on reasonable terms, and for other banking services.

Insurance Companies. While insurance companies have not been lenders to cooperatives, the investment division of Consumers United Insurance Company is now considering loans to worker-owned enterprises.

Asset-based Lenders. Another financial institution is the asset-based lender, including commercial finance companies and secured lending departments of banks, e.g., C.I.T. Financial Co. or Chase Commercial Co. They lend to high-risk companies that more conservative lenders shy away from, securing loans with accounts receivable, inventory, or machinery and equipment, while generally charging several interest points above the prime lending rate. Asset-based lenders do not lend on an unsecured basis. They depend upon the self-liquidation of collateral to repay loans and to cover losses on their higher risk.

Because these lenders look for quality receivables and readily marketable assets, service businesses and construction companies are considered poor lending prospects.

Commercial Mortgages. Purchasing land and buildings as well as refinancing them are the main purposes of commercial mortgages. Commercial mortgages are available from commercial banks, thrift institutions, insurance companies, and commercial finance companies. They make loans of up to 80 percent of the value of property on the credit strength of the business. Loans are typically made at interest rates several points above residential mortgage rates and for 10 to 25 years.

Leasing. Leasing is an alternative to purchasing buildings, machinery, or equipment. Banks, equipment-leasing companies, private-leasing arrangements and limited partnerships are among the sources of lease financing for small businesses. Lease payments represent a business expense when figured for tax purposes. This provides a tax advantage compared with the purchase of a comparable asset on credit; the loan enters the books as a liability on the business' balance sheet. A leased building or piece of machinery is considered to be an "off-balance sheet" form of financing which does not worsen a business' debt/equity ratio. Also, IRS regulations require different types of leasing arrangements to meet certain criteria in order to receive favorable tax treatment.

Venture Capitalists. Venture capitalists make high-risk investments in new businesses, usually on an equity basis (common or preferred stock, convertible debentures or debt with warrants). They invest expecting significant capital gains—which requires the firm being financed to experience a combination of growth and liquidity. Normally, this means the business eventually will be sold or will "go public" with a stock offering.

Venture capitalists usually want repayment terms which are tailored to support growth. For example, the principal payments on debentures are waived until the business is on solid financial ground. Venture capitalists also often want to be represented on the board of directors. Because they want an equity stake and representation on the board of directors, obtaining money from venture capitalists is generally not compatible with the ideal of worker-ownership and control.

Public Financing

Three federal agencies offer funds to help small businesses, including the Small Business Administration (SBA), Economic Development Administration (EDA), and Department of Housing and Urban Development (HUD). Additionally, some states have agencies which provide funds for economic development.

Small Business Administration. The SBA has several programs intended to help small businesses acquire capital. However, two cautionary notes about the SBA: First, SBA procedures are slow and cumbersome, making it time consuming and difficult to obtain loans. Second, Congress recently debated abolishing the SBA or its major loan guarantee programs, voting to reduce the loan funds available to the SBA. For more information about SBA loan programs contact an SBA office. (See Appendix E)

☐ **Regular Small Business Loan Guarantee Program (7a)**. This program offers loan guarantees to small businesses unable to obtain financing in the private market. Funds are available for construction, expansion or conversion, and the purchase of fixed assets and working capital. SBA loan guarantees are available to worker-owned cooperatives. Guarantees are for up to 90 percent of the loan amount with a maximum of $500,000. The borrower must find a local bank willing to lend with the loan guarantee and demonstrate that the firm is unable to obtain funds without the guarantee. Interest rates are 2.75 points above prime for a loan of seven years or more, and 2.25 points above prime for a loan of less than seven years. SBA also asks for personal guarantees when collateral pledged is not considered sufficiently strong.

Under the Small Business Administration Employee Ownership Act of 1980, ESOPs became eligible for SBA loan guarantees with terms similar to the 7a loan guarantee program.

☐ **Local Development Companies (Section 503)**. The SBA Local Development Company Program offers financing to individual firms through intermediary Local Development Companies (LDCs). LDCs are local corporations established specifically to leverage SBA funds. The SBA guarantees the debentures floated by the LDC to raise money for small business financing. LDCs lend for 'bricks and mortar" or to buy land and buildings, for plant construction, expansion or modernization, and to purchase machinery and equipment. Businesses receiving assistance must have a net worth of under $6 million and net profits of under $2 million. The SBA can guarantee up to $500,000 in debentures issued by the LDC; however, 50 percent of the cost of any project financed must come from outside sources. Interest rates for the money made available by the LDC vary depending upon when the debentures are sold.

☐ **Small Business Investment Companies (SBICs) and Minority Enterprise Small Business Investment Companies (MESBICs).** SBICs are privately owned venture capitalist firms which provide financing assistance to small businesses through equity-type lending: common and preferred stock, long-term loans of five to twenty years, and convertible debt or loans with warrants. The SBICs are licensed and regulated by the SBA. To qualify for assistance a business must have assets of less than $9 million and a net worth of less than $4 million.

Economic Development Administration (EDA). Under EDA Title IX, special assistance grants can be made to community economic development organizations to aid communities faced with "severe and sudden economic dislocation." The dislocation, usually a major plant closing or bankruptcy, must have occurred within the previous twelve months or be expected to occur within two years. EDA Adjustment Planning Grants are available to develop long-range plans for economic stability and to implement approved adjustment plans. These grants range from $200,000 to $5 million. The federal government usually funds 75 percent of the plan. Funds can be used for many purposes, including starting revolving loan funds.

Community economic development organizations can use Title IX financed revolving loan funds to make loans which retain or attract new businesses in distressed areas. They also provide money for technical assistance, and loan guarantees on amounts over $500,000. However, they do not provide assistance to enterprises in industries faced with overcapacity, and all applicants must pass this test. An EDA Title IX grant was used as part of the financing for the South Bend Lathe ESOP buyout.

Department of Housing and Urban Development (HUD). Local governments can use Urban Development Action Grants (UDAG) to revitalize economically distressed urban areas. UDAG grants have been used for low-interest loans to finance employee buyouts. As the loans are repaid, the money can be used for additional business lending within the community. Funds are designed to complete industrial, commercial or residential projects, create jobs, strengthen tax bases and contribute to economic revitalization. UDAG money has dollar and financial leverage standards. To be considered, a project must have a written commitment of private matching money and have the local political jurisdiction's support. UDAG grants range from $100,000 to $14 million. UDAG funds were part of the financial package used in the Hyatt-Clark Roller Bearing employee buyout in New Jersey, and in the Rath Packing worker buyout in Iowa. However, in 1985 Congress reduced UDAG grant funds by 20 percent.

For more information about UDAG grants, contact local community officials.

Farmers Home Administration (FmHA). FmHA has a Business and Industrial Loan Program which makes loan guarantees for businesses in rural areas. FmHA is a quality lender, not a lender of last resort. Loan guarantees can be made for normal business purposes and range from $11,000 to $50 million. Collateral is required to secure the loan guarantees and normally amounts to 10 percent equity for existing businesses and 20 percent for new businesses. Loans cannot exceed 30 years duration for land, buildings and permanent fixtures, 15 years for machinery and equipment, and 7 years for working capital.

For more information about FmHA programs, contact your state FmHA office or the national office in Washington, D.C.

The Department of Health and Human Services, Office of Community Services has made some money available for worker buyouts, as has the National Rural Development Office in the Department of Agriculture.

State and Local Sources. At the state and local levels there

103

are several potential sources of funding for worker-owned cooperatives.

☐ **Industrial Revenue Bonds (IRBs).** IRBs are interest-bearing debentures issued by state or local governments through Industrial Revenue Authorities to make direct loans to businesses. The interest rates are usually somewhat lower than commercial loans because the interest on the loans is exempt from federal income tax and from state income tax in some states.

A business applying for IRB financing must find a lender who will accept the bonds. Funds then flow from the lender to the state or local government Industrial Development Authority which passes them through to the business borrower. Loans are repaid with revenues generated.

IRBs have generated some opposition in Congress which has tightened their rules. They are supposed to be used for construction, acquisition, or improvement of commercial or industrial plants or to buy equipment. Working capital cannot be financed. While IRBs vary in size from $200,000 to $10 million, typically businesses receiving funds of less than $1 million have no restrictions on capital spending.

☐ **Other State and Local Programs.** Many states have funded high-tech capital funds to attract Silicon Valley style growth. Massachusetts and Wisconsin have created public or quasi-public community development finance corporations. Information about these agencies can be obtained from local or state offices of economic development or commerce.

Several communities have used UDAG money to set up venture- capital funds to attract new businesses to their communities. North Greenbush, New York, used a $750,000 HUD economic development grant to invest in eight start-up companies, including a biotechnology concern and a computer-networking-system business. Some observers say the town is limiting its return on investment by restricting money to companies that settle within its boundaries. Community leaders nevertheless expect that in five years they will double their money while generating 1,500 new jobs. The town plans to cash in its investments if the eight companies start making money. Profits, if any, can be used to pay for future development. HUD approved a second grant of $400,000 in 1985 to keep the program going, and the town expects to apply for at least one more grant. The success of the North Greenbush program is attracting considerable attention. (3)

A Time to Vote

Having reached the point where finances are seriously discussed, and plans have been drawn up, your group may want to take another vote *before* signing any loan agreements. The question to decide is: Do we agree to take the risks associated with this loan?

105

6 USING CONSULTANTS

FREE OR LOW COST SOURCES OF TECHNICAL ASSISTANCE
FEE FOR SERVICE RESOURCES
INFORMATION FROM GOVERNMENT AGENCIES

Many persons resist doing a business plan. Some, after looking at a typically comprehensive plan, such as outlined in Chapter 4, will throw up their hands, figuring, incorrectly, they are incapable of putting such a document together. Others might figure it would be a waste of time. In the face of their objections, experience has provided two irrefutable arguments for spending the time, energy and thought required.

First, it is the single best way to avoid looking back after a business fails and saying regretfully, "If only we had planned...." And second, for potential worker-owners, doing a business plan together may be the single best means of getting to know the business and to know each other—even though you have worked together for years, but in a conventional company where democratic rights were left at the front door. A third reason for preparing a plan is that workers starting a new business or buying their firm may have strong personal and emotional commitments or dependence upon one idea, and the desire to open the enterprise can make them want to be blind to or gloss over issues examined in a business plan.

Some workers may feel they lack the skills to put together a business plan, but are nevertheless convinced such an objective analysis is in their best interests. For them, and others, help is available.

Some technical assistance sources are free, or nearly so. However, obtaining consulting assistance from firms or individuals set up specifically to help workers become owners will cost something. Deciding whom to get help from can be difficult. Word of mouth recommendations may not be the best way to hire someone. Before outlining the resources available, some simple forms have been provided which can make a hard job easier. It is useful to try to identify and list what kind of help is needed before seeking assistance which may be very costly. Chart 6-1 is a technical assistance assessment sheet for identifying the tasks needing attention. Chart 6-2 is a monthly calendar providing a timeframe for scheduling technical assistance interviews.

The resources included here open doors. No one agency or group will have all the answers. Some may be totally inappropriate. Hiring and using technical providers demands diligence to insure that your particular needs are served. The sources listed here are for information purposes only.

Free or Low Cost Sources of Technical Assistance

Free or easily accessible sources of technical assistance available to worker-owned cooperatives are the first, sometimes best, resources.

Fellow Workers

If the workers in an existing business are considering buying their firm and converting it to worker-ownership, they are a good source of information, especially about daily operations. During the business planning phase or when operations start up, some organizational procedures and routine should be established to insure that every member is invited to share his or her experience about how to make the conversion a success. Usually, workers, be they accountants or janitors, know important and useful facts about the business and its operations.

Suppliers

Suppliers prosper when the businesses they service succeed. They may object to the idea of worker-ownership, but they have few qualms about wanting the money your firm will spend. They can explain how other firms they service operate. They can suggest new, less costly machines, products, or operational procedures. Usually the best of them will collect data about the industry or service, and might share that knowledge.

Chart 6-1

TECHNICAL ASSISTANCE ASSESSMENT

Responsibility/ Task	*Technical Assistance Needed*	*Agency/Person to be Contacted for Assistance*	*Help to be Requested*
————	————	————	————
————	————	————	————
————	————	————	————
————	————	————	————

109

Chart 6-2

MONTHLY CALENDAR FOR TECHNICAL ASSISTANCE INTERVIEWS : THE WORKER-OWNED COOPERATIVE

Year_____

January	*February*	*March*	*April*
May	*June*	*July*	*August*
September	*October*	*November*	*December*

Customers

If the firm has not yet opened its doors and has no customers, its competitors will. Potential customers can be invaluable sources of information about the products or services they buy or would like to see on the market. Customers can often suggest ways to improve a product or ways of doing business. However, a note of caution is in order. Information received in this manner should be analyzed by someone who has sufficient experience and expertise in sales and manufacturing as well as some knowledge of costs to insure that overzealous customers do not push ideas or products that may be unfeasible or more costly to produce.

Other Businesses

Most businesses have common problems, and those in a particular industry or service likely share difficulties. If the businesses are not competing directly for the same customers, some managers or owners may be willing to exchange ideas, solutions or data.

Libraries

Libraries, especially in large cities, governmental centers or universities, have books, periodicals, reports, newspapers, and trade journals which contain useful data for the business plan or for operating the business intelligently. Using these resources increases the likelihood that worker-owners' decisions are based on fact, not speculation.

Trade Associations

Trade associations keep extensive data for lobbying, training, education, services to members, and to keep up with new technologies. Information is usually available for the price of a membership. Trade groups typically publish newsletters or have some other means to communicate with members. Many exist to provide information about new developments or trends in their industries, and some publish extensive data series.

Business Extension, Productivity, and Innovation Centers

Frequently, the finance, accounting, engineering, or management departments of universities maintain special libraries or have professors who can work with worker-owners. But some may not be willing to because of ideological issues or because they command high fees and only work for such. Nearly twenty universities and colleges have state or regional productivity centers designed to aid businesses and solve productivity-related problems. Several state land-grant universities have small business development programs in their agricultural or business extension services. Finally, a handful of colleges and non-profit organizations serve as incubators for business development and to foster innovation. For further information and addresses see Appendix E.

Education and Training Programs

Literally hundreds of education and training programs are offered by colleges, universities, proprietary schools, non-profit organizations, and private entrepreneurs to improve management, technical, and business skills. Some are free, others are very expensive. They vary widely in quality and usefulness.

At this writing, only a few educational programs have been designed specifically for prospective worker-owners. Among them are the Boston College Program in Social Economy, the Cooperative College of Canada, Cornell University Program on Employment and Workplace Systems, Guilford College Democratic Management Program, New Hampshire College Program in Community Economic Development, and the Utah State University Cooperative Management Program. Each year, the North American Students of Cooperation holds workshops in Ann Arbor, Michigan, on cooperative operation.

111

Fee for Service Resources

Getting Value for Your Money

Sometimes the help worker-owners need can only be obtained with cash. There are at least two useful ways to determine the potential value of consultants before spending scarce dollars for their service. The first is to ask businesses who have used them about their performance. The second is to ask potential consultants in person the questions in Chart 6-3, A Guide for Evaluating Consultants. You should request a resume with details on specific jobs they have carried out. It also helps to get a fixed price for the whole job or parts broken down in various ways, such as so much per day/hour. Otherwise you may wind up with a very expensive bill.

Chart 6-3

A GUIDE FOR EVALUATING CONSULTANTS

Question   *Notes on Answers*

How long have you been
practicing?

_____

What is your relevant experience?

_____

What approach(s) do you use?

_____

What are your areas of speciali-
zation?

_____

What different types of expertise
does your group possess?

_____

Have you worked with worker-
owned firms before?

_____

Have you worked with firms in our
industry or service before?

_____

Will you give us the names and
addresses of five businesses
you have assisted?

_____

Can we terminate our contract if
your work does not meet our
expectations?

_____

How do you calculate your fees?
How do they compare with other
professionals in this field?

_____

What are the terms of payment
for your services?

_____

Will you furnish us with a record
of what you will do for us and the
way you will do it?

_____

Will you teach one or several of us
to do all or part of this work in the
future (if professional codes or
the law permit)?

_____

What help do you expect from us?
Will our work be figured as part of
your fees?

_____

When can you start and how long
will it take before we have a
report from you?

_____

Business Consultants

Consultants are hired to analyze or solve problems in personnel, plant layout, engineering, production, office systems, financial control, training, safety, marketing, waste disposal, exporting, data processing, policy development and implementation, or any of the myriad matters which face worker-owners. Each consultant should have verifiable credentials, based upon attendance at a bona fide college and from actual work experience. For most aspects of worker-owned business, including the theory and practice of labor-managed enterprises, there is a reputable, potentially useful consultant available. Generally the work of consultants falls into three broad areas:

113

- ☐ Reviews of policies and practices; annual audits of a firms' books.

- ☐ Solutions to one-time or emergency problems in production, governance, marketing, personnel, or education and training.

- ☐ Preparation of feasibility studies, or the business plan.

- ☐ Money/investment finding.

A note of caution: In many cases, especially buyouts of existing businesses, great difficulty is experienced with finding enough capital. This can also be true with a new firm start-up or the opening of a firm that has been closed for a long time. Workers become desperate and are frequently approached by consultants who claim they have links with wealthy investors; that they have a great reputation and contacts with banks and other financial lending institutions; and can get the capital for you in return for a substantial fee. In most cases these persons are phonies, but they invariably seem to appear, and sometimes in large numbers.

Once you have decided why a consultant is needed, and the

consultant has been selected, worker-owners will want to have a written agreement with the hired experts concerning:

☐ Specific tasks to be accomplished.

☐ Length of time to complete the work.

☐ How and where the work will be accomplished.

☐ Written report(s) the worker-owners will receive.

☐ Estimated costs and any controls on costs.

☐ (If a large business consulting firm is selected) exactly which person(s) will be doing the work.

A Time to Vote

Once such an agreement has been presented to your group, and reviewed by the membership, it would be wise to vote on final approval.

There is a small number of non-profit organizations and business consultants who are knowledgeable about setting up worker-owned enterprises. An even smaller number of organizations and consultants possess specialized knowledge about workers' cooperatives. Among them are:

Center for Community Self-Help
P.O. Box 3259
Durham, N. C. 27705
(919) 683-1584

Center for Economic Organizing
Suite 406, 1522 K Street, NW
Washington, D.C. 20005
(202) 755-9042

Industrial Cooperative Association
58 Day Street
Somerville, Mass. 02144
(617) 629-2700

Ball, Hayden, Kiernan, Livingston
& Smith
108 Washington Street
Newark, N.J. 04102
(201) 622-4545

Business and Economic Development Services
Utah State University
Logan, Utah 84322-3505
(801) 750-2283

Michigan Employee Ownership Center
1975 Penobscot Bldg.
Detroit, Michigan 48226
(313) 964-5040

Philadelphia Assn. for Cooperative Enterprise
133 S. 18th Street, 3rd Floor
Philadelphia, Penn. 19103

Worker-Owned Network
50 S. Court Street
Athens, Ohio
(614) 592-3854

Midwest Center for Labor Research
3411 W. Diversey, #14
Chicago, Illinois 60647
(312) 278-5418

Locker/Abrecht Associates
198 Broadway, 7th Floor
New York, N.Y. 10038
(212) 962-2983

National Center for Employee
Ownership
426 17th Street
Oakland, CA. 94612
(415) 272-9461

Co-Operative Work (Toronto) LTD.
357 College Street
Toronto, Ontario M5T 1S5
(416) 928-9568

Center for Community Econ. Dev.
Community Service Society
105 East 22nd Street
New York, N.Y. 10010
(212) 254-8900

Bankers

Large banks and investment firms often have officers or entire departments which keep track of certain businesses or industries. Bank loan officers are usually seasoned in one or more community business trends. Most banks have no familiarity with worker-ownership. Finding a banker or lending officer who is not biased against the idea of worker-ownership can be important but difficult. Some questions to guide selection of a banker include:

☐ Does the bank have a bias against worker-ownership?

☐ Will the worker-owned firm work with one bank officer or anyone who happens to be at work that day?

☐ Will the bank help up-date business plans and, if so, at what cost?

☐ What service fees does the bank charge for checking accounts, and other services? Do they provide any special services?

☐ What are their lending policies and interest rates?

☐ Do they know the industry?

☐ Who makes the decision on the type of loan we need?

Lawyers

Attorneys are another group worker-owners will need. Attorneys should spell out alternatives, offering legal or administrative justification for each alternative and, if asked, make a recommendation. But the final decisions must be made

115

by the cooperative management, the elected board, or membership. Two questions should be asked of any potential lawyer: What is their area of legal expertise? Are their fees on a per case basis, or on retainer, and how much are the fees?

You should have legal advice before signing a long-term contract, when dispute negotiations with another firm, or a worker-member, cannot be settled, or if the worker-owned firm is sued. Legal assistance should be sought if government regulations or laws need interpretation, and to maintain the integrity of the Individual Membership Accounts.

Accountants

Certified public accountants (CPAs), like lawyers, must pass professional exams and be licensed to practice. CPAs are employed to gather business data and assemble so it can be easily understood. Their work must meet professional accounting and legal criteria. Bookkeepers are not accountants. They enter records on a day-to-day basis, but are restricted from preparing certified audits which are vital to secure loans or credit and, frequently, for tax purposes.

An accountant can suggest alternative strategies for financing, credit, taxes, and improved financial planning. If the elected board does not know how to read and interpret the firm's balance sheets, then teaching those skills should be a part of the accountant's responsibilities.

Accountants should be used when setting up the business, helping worker-owners make certain the firm's financial framework is sound. An accountant should help design an appropriate record-keeping system, and teach worker-owners how to maintain it. The accountant may also advise on cash-flow management, credit systems, cost control and pricing, and taxes.

Insurance Agents

Every business must have adequate insurance for worker's compensation and health, directors' and officers' liability, vehicle or product liability, fire and theft, and essential machines or equipment. There are as many kinds of insurance as there are agents. Finding the agent and coverage which is most suitable to the firm's needs and which fit the budget is not a task which should be taken lightly. Three or four steps are advisable:

☐ List the most desirable insurance coverage and the minimum needs.

☐ Ask at least five reputable firms or agents to prepare bids.

☐ Have the bids reviewed by an attorney, an accountant, and the board of directors.

☐ After selecting the most promising bid, negotiate a final contract with assistance from an attorney and accountant.

Information from Government Agencies

Federal, state, and local government agencies collect large quantities of business information, partly to keep up on their potential to pay taxes, but also to promote economic development. Government agencies publish technical reports, tables, newsletters, and other documents with invaluable insights about taxation, production, competition, markets, business development, and trade opportunities. They must give you any legal or administrative regulations which you, as worker-owners, will be required to follow.

Most governmental agencies have had little or no experience with worker-owned businesses, but increasingly are aware such firms are flourishing and that state legislation is being enacted.

Federal Government Agencies.

The U.S. Department of Commerce and Small Business Administration (SBA) unfortunately, have virtually no materials on or experience with worker-owned businesses per se. The U.S. Department of Agriculture has an extensive body of literature relating to the cooperative movement and marketing, chiefly related to agricultural producer and marketing cooperatives. Each agency might be helpful in other ways. The U.S. Department of Labor provides assistance to develop labor-management cooperation and worker participation, and to prevent plant closings.

U.S. Department of Labor, Bureau of Labor-Management Relations and Cooperative Programs. The Bureau Labor-Management Relations and Cooperative Programs encourages cooperative labor-management and employee participation programs to improve productivity and enhance the quality

117

of work life. The unit also provides assistance in plant closings. A variety of services and information is available without
cost, including technical assistance, conferences, and resource
materials. For additional information contact: Bureau of
Labor-Management Relations and Cooperative Programs,
U.S. Department of Labor, Frances Perkins Building, 200
Constitution Ave., Washington, D.C., 20216. Telephone:
202-357-0473.

**U.S. Department of Commerce, Minority Business
Development Agency.** The Minority Business Development
Agency (MBDA) was created to assist minority entrepreneurs.
MBDA awards grants to and signs cooperative agreements
with state and local government agencies, profit and nonprofit
business development organizations, or trade associations to
provide management, marketing, financial, and technical
assistance to minority entrepreneurs. MDBA has the following programs:

☐ **Minority Business Development Centers (MBDC)** are
   located in areas with large minority populations. They
   provide management, marketing, and technical assistance
   to increase business opportunities for minority
   entrepreneurs.

☐ **The Acquisition Assistance Program** provides technical
   support services to minority buyers of medium- and large-
   sized manufacturing firms or high-technology industry
   such as energy, telecommunications, and medical in-
   strumentation. Assistance is available for business acquisition analysis and negotiation.

☐ **The American Indian Program** provides American In-
   dians, Eskimos, Aleuts, or their tribal governments, with
   business management and technical assistance. Consultants are provided through grants or cooperative
   agreements. The goal is economic self-determination for
   individual and tribal business.

☐ **The Minority Business and Trade Association Program**
   offers information and technical services to members of
   the minority business community. Services include
   negotiation of trade discounts and liaison with federal,
   state, and local activities.

☐ **Minority Export Development Consultants** expose minority businesses to international marketing networks, market information, and/or product and service delivery. Services include identification of potential markets, specific trade leads, technical assistance to complete international transactions, plus coordination with public agencies to increase minority business participation.

For further information about these programs contact the Minority Business Development Agency, U.S. Department of Commerce, Washington, D.C., Tel: 202-377-2648.

U. S. Department of Commerce, National Minority Supplier Development Council. This agency conducts a national marketing program to attract private sector business opportunities for minority businesses and to increase procurement from minorities. For further information contact the Washington office of the Minority Business Development Agency listed above.

Small Business Administration (SBA), Office of Minority Small Business and Capital Ownership Development: This office formulates and coordinates policies benefitting eligible minority small businesses. It provides direct assistance to minority businesses and works with other agencies, banks, or industry to increase the number of minority-owned businesses. For further information contact an SBA Regional Office. (See Appendix E).

SBA Office of Procurement and Technology Assistance. This office provides small or struggling businesses with opportunities to secure federal contracts. For further information contact an SBA Regional Office. (See Appendix E).

Service Corps of Retired Executives (SCORE). Retired men and women who voluntarily provide free management counseling. They often have experience which is useful to small retail, wholesale, service, or manufacturing businesses. For further information contact an SBA Regional Office. (See Appendix E).

Active Corps of Executives (ACE). Executives from private business and industry give free advice on managerial, professional, and technical topics to small business owners and managers. For further information contact an SBA Regional Office (See Appendix E).

119

Small Business Institute (SBI) Program. This program uses college business majors as counselors to small business. Students work in teams guided by a professor, to meet with and counsel small business owners and managers. There is no charge. For further information contact an SBA Regional Office (See Appendix E).

Small Business Development Centers (SBDC). Located at several colleges and universities around the nation, these centers work with local trade and business groups, Chambers of Commerce, and SCORE and ACE volunteers to support small business. Specifically, the centers provide management and technical assistance to small business owners. For further information contact an SBA Regional Office or see Appendix E for a listing of existing SBDC's.

National Science Foundation (NSF). Through a handful of Innovation Centers located in regions throughout the country and through the Small Business Assistance Program, the NSF provides information and guidance to small research and technology-based businesses, or firms owned by women or minorities. For further information contact the Office of Small Business Research & Development NSF, 1800 G Street, N.W. Room 511-A, Washington, D.C. 20006. Telephone (202) 357-7464.

State and Local Agencies

Most states and many local governments have offices of business and economic development. Although their primary function is to attract new businesses, some aid existing businesses. The California Department of Economic and Business Development assists workers who want to buy their firms if threatened with closure. The Michigan Department of Labor has been providing modest technical assistance to foster employee ownership through worker buyouts since 1979. The legislation authorizing these services was renewed and expanded in 1985. Massachusetts and Oregon are developing similar advisory services. Many states and communities use the federal Job Training Partnership Act, or other state legislation, to help train or retrain workers for new business skills as a way to save jobs.

In Canada, the province of Manitoba has introduced legislation to set up a tripartite Workplace Innovation Centre to help employers and employees deal with the impact of technological change. In addition, the government has set up an Employment Cooperative Program to provide technical assistance to workers wanting to organize "employment cooperatives" (defined as a cooperative whose main objective is to provide employment to its members).

A Time to Vote

Having gotten technical assistance and weighed their advice, do you as a group, continue to believe starting a worker-owned firm is wise? It is time for another vote. A yes vote means go ahead; no means let's stop here and think before acting.

121

7 THE LEGAL STRUCTURE

CHOOSING A LEGAL STRUCTURE
NEW DEVELOPMENTS IN COOPERATIVE LAW
INCORPORATING A LABOR-MANAGED COOPERATIVE
CREATING A DEMOCRATIC ESOP
MEMBERS' AND DIRECTORS' CHECKLIST

Choosing a Legal Structure

Workers have organized and structured their businesses with great diversity. There is no single "accepted" legal or organizational structure for worker-owned cooperatives. Many resemble each other but there is frequent debate as to what principal elements should be included, what organizational structure should be adopted.

Although worker-owners can manage their internal affairs cooperatively regardless of how a business is legally set up, the legal form establishing the firm makes a difference in its long-term survival, its operation as a cooperative, and as a democratically-managed business. The legal structure also makes a difference in how earnings will be taxed, the legal liability of members, the way profits are distributed, and in the types of activities which may be conducted. Making a decision on organizational form is the next step. A worker-owned cooperative can be created in many ways: sole proprietorships, partnerships, associations, joint ventures, corporations, not-for-profit corporations, and cooperative corporations. It is also possible, to set up an Employee Stock Ownership Plan (ESOP). A few co-ops, particularly small food co-ops, have begun operations with no legal structure at all. Until recently, most co-ops have been organized as partnerships or some type of a corporation.

While it might be useful to describe all of the various types of legal structures which can be used to organize a cooperative, we believe that the cooperative corporation or the corporation outlined below best meets the criteria for a democratically-run, worker-owned business. Additional information comparing workers' cooperatives and conventional corporations is included in Appendix D.

Corporation

A corporation is a legal entity, or "legal person," and can make contracts, accumulate assets, borrow money, and pay taxes all in its own name. Corporations are licensed by state governments according to rules established in each state.

Unlike other forms of business ownership such as the sole proprietorship or partnership, corporations do not automatically dissolve when a shareholder dies or sells the stock, and they have limited liability. A corporation continues to exist "in perpetuity" or until the shareholders vote to liquidate it, or a court liquidates it in bankruptcy. Stockholders are not subject to loss of personal assets or property to pay debts or legal judgments made against the business. In a corporation, you normally lose only your investment. However, officers in the corporation can be held personally liable if they mismanage the business or misappropriate its assets for their own private gain. And stockholders can be held legally liable for unpaid back taxes.

Corporations issue and sell shares of stock to raise capital. People who buy the stock become stockholders and owners. The more stock a person owns the more say he or she has in the business operation. Stockholders receive one vote for each share of stock they own. In some instances, a corporation may issue two classes of stock, 'common stock" and "preferred stock." The voting rights normally go with the common stock, and the preferred stock has no voting rights but receives a higher dividend or a fixed dividend. If the company prospers, preferred stockholders receive dividends before the holders of common stock. Shares of stock in corporations are usually freely transferable, meaning the owner can sell them to anyone willing to buy.

Overall guidance of a corporation is in the hands of a board of directors elected by stockholders. The board sets policy and hires management to direct day-to-day affairs. In smaller corporations, directors may also be managers and shareholders.

Corporations pay income taxes on profits, and stockholders pay taxes on the dividends they receive. However, this double taxation can be avoided in small closely held corporations by paying out most or all the income as salaries or bonuses to the employees and leaving no profits to pay out as dividends. Employees then pay taxes on the income they receive. Another option is to retain some of the profits, using them to expand.

There are two kinds of corporations, for-profit and non-profit corporations. Both enjoy the same benefits. However, a non-profit corporation does not distribute "gains, profits or dividends" to stockholders during the corporation's life. A non-profit corporation may retain profits for its own use, donate them to other non-profit corporations, or pay out profits as wages to member-employees if the wages are reasonable when compared with wages paid for work in similar fields.

Non-profit corporations are chartered by the states. They may not issue corporate stock or certificates of ownership, although issuing memberships is normally permitted. Some states have specific definitions, responsibilities and privileges for members of non-profit corporations.

Non-profit corporate status provides some tax benefits, including exemption from paying state income taxes, state employment taxes, and state franchise taxes—which is the minimum state income tax on corporations. Federal non-profit tax exempt status is available only to non-profit corporations which meet the requirements of Section 501(c) of the Internal Revenue Code. These tax exempt categories are well defined and strictly limited to particular types of organizations. If the organization carries on a business with the general public similar to that engaged in by for-profit corporations, tax exempt status is routinely denied.

125

Cooperative Corporation

When a cooperative is incorporated under a state's cooperative statutes, it is called a cooperative corporation. Cooperative corporations are a hybrid form of organization entitled to benefits common to all corporations: limited liability, perpetual existence, and tax-deductible fringe benefits for employees. In addition, cooperative corporations may obtain advantages available to cooperatives such as: being able to use the word "cooperative" in their name, being able to issue memberships instead of shares of stock—with restrictions on transfer to non-members, obtaining exemptions from or having simpler procedures for registering memberships with the federal Securities and Exchange Commission and state counterpart agencies, payment of patronage refunds based on participation, and receiving possible exemption from stock permit fees required of most for-profit corporations. (1)

Cooperative corporations may also take advantage of Subchapter T of the Internal Revenue Code, which allows cooperatives to avoid the double taxation imposed on corporate profits. Subchapter T is expressly available to worker cooperatives, although it originated as a tax break for agricultural cooperatives. However, it is important to know that the particular state-level incorporation statute is not controlling for federal tax purposes. This means that if the enterprise is incorporated as a business corporation but operates in substance on a cooperative basis, it can still qualify for the tax advantages under Subchapter T.

Although organizing a cooperative corporation appears to be an appropriate form of legal structure for a worker-owned business, prior to the 1980s few were organized this way. Many states made it difficult for co-ops to incorporate as cooperative corporations. Today, each state has its own cooperative laws, and no two states' laws are alike. Most states have no worker-cooperative statutes, and in others only large agricultural co-ops qualify. Unfortunately, prior to 1982, only a few states had co-op statutes which allowed any type of cooperative to incorporate under the cooperative corporation rules. Beginning in 1982, the legal climate for worker-owned cooperatives began to change. (2)

If your state has not yet passed a law providing for cooperative corporations or your state's existing co-op laws are too limiting, it is possible to incorporate in another state such as Delaware or Massachusetts as a "foreign incorporation." Whatever the case, we suggest that you and your fellow workers review co-op statutes in your state with a qualified attorney before proceeding.

New Developments in Cooperative Law

In the United States, and in varying degrees in other nations, the statutory laws pertaining to cooperatives have failed to establish a corporate structure which encourages growth, permits workers to receive the fruits of their labor while exercising democratic management control. The pioneering Basque cooperatives created an organizational framework for the cooperative labor-enterprises which "promoted the principles of stability and the rational, growth oriented, behavior of labor-entrepreneurship (and) promoted innovation and change." (3) Their success prompted the Massachusetts legislature in 1982 to enact the first statute in the United States which incorporates the principles of democratic self-governance with labors rights in property. Similar legislation has since been adopted by Connecticut, Maine, New York, and Vermont, and is being considered by other states.

Massachusetts Worker Cooperative Law

The Massachusetts worker cooperative law is a model statute which specifically includes the key principles of the successful Basque cooperative labor-enterprise system. Chapter 157A, Massachusetts General Laws or the "Industrial Cooperative Association Law," as it is commonly referred to, has four principle parts:

1) It expressly converts a corporation, as is customarily defined in law, into a membership organization which is democratically controlled by the workers.

2) It permits equitable allocation of earnings and losses to members based on their relative contribution of labor, not their relative capital investment.

3) It authorizes a capital structure along with a system for internal or individual accounts.

4) It sets forth a capital allocation procedure consistent with the federal (United States) Internal Revenue Code, Subchapter T.

Membership. The Massachusetts statute codifies the principle of democratic worker control. Membership is based on the contribution of labor. The worker cooperative must issue a class of voting stock to members who work full or part-time and who vote their membership share on the basis of one person, one vote. Other classes of stock may be issued if specifically authorized in the articles of incorporation; but, with two exceptions, no other class of stock enjoys voting rights.

These exceptions add flexibility but do not inherently jeopardize labor's control over capital: persons holding non-voting stock have the right to vote as a class on any article or by-law amendment which could adversely affect their rights; and members may amend the by-laws or articles to authorize voting stock for stockholders other than working members.

127

Cash Distribution. A second principle derived by the Basques—the apportionment of earnings or losses to members on the basis of labor contributed—is also codified. The allocation of net earnings or patronage dividends may take the form of cash distributions or credits to an individual member's account, or in the form of a written obligation. Because the Internal Revenue Service Code recognizes labor-managed enterprises as businesses which operate on a cooperative basis, the firm itself does not pay taxes on the earnings which it distributes to members. Under Subchapter T of the United States Tax Code, the worker-owned cooperative deducts any earnings allocated to patronage dividends from taxable corporate income.

As a result, members of a worker-owned cooperative enjoy two benefits: their firm avoids being taxed on the corporate net earnings and on stock dividends; and they can retain some portion of the earnings allocated to members and reinvest them in the firm. Basques use this principle to generate within their own firms the capital needed for reinvestment or growth.

Internal Membership Accounts. A third feature of the Massachusetts legislation enables worker-owned cooperatives to maintain a fixed entry fee for members by allocating any increases in the cooperative's net worth to the workers rather than shares of stock. This prevents the membership shares which worker-owners must purchase from becoming prohibitively costly. The internal or individual membership accounts reflect any increase in the value of the cooperative. Prior to the enactment of the Massachusetts law, the membership shares of most, if not all, statutory worker-cooperatives carried net book value. They could not be used as membership certificates. This presented a dilemma: giving each new worker-owner the mandatory membership certificate amounted to making an unwarranted gift; but the price of membership shares could be prohibitively expensive, making membership open only to persons able to raise the cash.

Under the Massachusetts statute, when members quit or retire from the workforce, the fixed cash value of the membership certificate plus a share of accrued profits and interest over time is their due. As the cooperative's value or worth increases, worker-members benefit financially, while letting others who join enjoy similar financial reward without prohibitively costly membership fees.

The internal membership accounts separate membership rights from personal property rights. Membership rights become personal rights. Personal property rights are assigned to each worker's role and are measured by total wages or hours worked and are evidenced by the balance in each worker's account.

The Massachusetts law stipulates that each worker's internal account is strictly accounted for, and that interest is paid on the mandatory membership fee and on the member's allocated share of retained earnings.

Incorporating a Labor-Managed Cooperative

The Massachusetts Worker Cooperative Law opened the way to organize democratically run worker-owned businesses in the United States on a solid legal foundation. We believe this form of organization provides the best framework for organizing a worker-owned and managed cooperative. When your planning group completes the feasibility assessment and decides to incorporate you will probably need an attorney. Corporation law is complex and confusing, with differences abounding among state laws. While the following discussion briefly explains articles of incorporation and the by-laws, and the appendix provides examples of each, your group will need to carefully study the laws in your state to determine specific legal and tax requirements.

129

Articles of Incorporation

Every corporation must prepare and file a copy of their articles of incorporation with the appropriate government agency. These are the constitution or business charter. The articles are written in general terms and remain a permanent part of the firm's legal framework. The articles can be changed or amended, but the process is rather difficult. The articles usually contain:

☐ The cooperative's official name and address.

☐ The cooperative's purpose stated in very general terms; for example, the articles might say the purpose is "to engage in any lawful activity primarily for the benefit of the members who shall be the primary producers of the goods and services of the cooperative." All possibilities should be covered because the cooperative's direction may change over time.

☐ The number and names of the original directors.

☐ How the stock or memberships will be issued and the total number of authorized shares or memberships which will be made available for sale. Depending on which state the cooperative is incorporated in and whether or not it is a cooperative corporation will determine whether there are any restrictions which limit the co-op from commencing operations until a certain percentage of the authorized shares or memberships are sold. We recommend that the articles of incorporation structure the memberships along the lines outlined in the Massachusetts laws.

☐ Some states specify that certain operations or procedures are governed by the articles of incorporation. We suggest that you carefully research your state's laws to find out what must be included in the articles in addition to the basics above.

130

By-laws

By-laws add the meat to the bones provided by the articles of incorporation. They can be general or specific. General by-laws give room to maneuver and fewer limitations; specific by-laws make it easier for member-workers and others to understand the cooperative's purpose and how it operates. Depending on your state's laws, there may be certain things that must be covered in the by-laws. By-laws typically include:

☐ The name and location of the worker-owned firm.

☐ How it will carry out its purpose.

☐ The principal business office.

☐ Who can be a member or shareholder, including any restrictions on owning and transferring memberships.

☐ Privileges and responsibilities of members. For example: How many hours a week a worker must work in order to qualify for membership. How and under what circumstances can a member-worker be fired or expelled from membership?

☐ When and where membership meetings will be held. Provisions for special meetings are set out, including the percentage of members who must request one. Notice of meetings must be given.

☐ The number of directors, the length of their term in office, how they are elected, when they should meet, how they can be removed, how many constitute a quorum to conduct business (usually 50 percent of the directors must be present at a meeting in order to vote and make decisions).

☐ The voting rights of members, which is one vote per member.

☐ The names of officers.

☐ The method for amending by-laws.

☐ The distribution of net earnings or losses to member-workers is set forth on the basis of labor contributed. This may take the form of cash distributions, credits in an individual member's account, or a written obligation.

☐ How the firm will distribute its assets if it dissolves (usually it is in proportion to the participation of each member).

☐ Any other items wanted or specified or which may be required by the state in which the cooperative is incorporated.

Directors

As in most corporations, directors of worker-owned firms determine the basic policy. They approve annual budgets, major contracts, and a plan of work. They are responsible for the records of member meetings, elections, and for annual financial statements. The board also selects professional help such as accountants and attorneys, and hires or fires top management.

Responsibilities usually come with rights. Regardless of which legal statutes control the internal structure of the worker-owned firm, every elected board member assumes legal responsibilities. As an owner, every member bears certain responsibilities, but these have not yet been as clearly defined as the case law surrounding corporate board members. This body of law derives principally from the experience of agricultural cooperatives, but no doubt applies to labor-managed cooperative enterprises.

Worker-owners who are elected to the board, serve in essentially the same capacity as directors of any corporation. Historically, courts have applied the principles of corporate law when questions have arisen about cooperatives. Virtually no case law has been established by United States courts on worker-owned production cooperatives, chiefly because they are a relatively new phenomenon.

The U.S. Department of Agriculture has advised cooperative board members that the "simplest way. . .(to). . .reduce the risk of an adverse legal action is to resist the temptation to do something wrong or achieve personal gain at the expense of the cooperative. . ." while exercising the greatest care and honesty in official action. (4)

While board members are subject to civil and criminal suits for some disputed behavior, they can be sued for:

- ☐ Failing to give annual reports to members.

- ☐ Paying patronage dividends in cash exceeding current savings.

- ☐ Authorizing preferential treatment for directors.

- ☐ Violating by-laws or articles of incorporation.

- ☐ Failing to require financial statements with the result that some harm comes to the cooperative.

- ☐ Misappropriating or misusing property or assets.

- ☐ Negligence, fraud, commission of crimes, antitrust violations, securities law violation, or theft.

- ☐ Failing to attend board meetings to the extent that harm comes to the cooperative.

- ☐ Operating a business which competes with the cooperative.

- ☐ Failing to adequately insure the cooperative's assets.

In sum, when a director violates duly established cooperative rules, common law, or statute law, he or she can be held liable. Directors can be sued by federal or state officials, third parties, other directors, and by worker-owners. Lest you be overwhelmed by the personal legal liability risks when serving on a co-op board of directors, you should know that most corporations and cooperatives purchase directors' and officers' liability insurance.

Some states specify a minimum and maximum number of directors, usually between 5 and 25. Selecting an odd number helps prevent tie votes. Too many directors can make the board unwieldy. Too few directors leaves the power in too few hands.

The terms of the directors should be staggered. For example, if the board has 9 directors, one third should be elected each year, each serving three-year terms. That way there is a sufficient number of experienced directors to insure operational continuity.

Directors usually meet once a month. Notice of meetings is given in advance. The by-laws (or state law) requires that a quorum be present for the decisions made to be binding.

133

Managers or Officers

The managers are responsible for the day-to-day business operations. They are appointed by the directors or, in some cases of small co-ops, the entire membership may participate. Officers have the "legal authority" to enter into obligations and contracts on behalf of the corporation. A person may be both a director and an officer. In a few states the president may be required to sit on the board.

Shareholder-Worker-Members

In the traditional corporation, shareholders elect directors but otherwise have little say in the business. They also have the right to vote on changes or amendments to the articles of incorporation and by-laws. In a democratically-run cooperative, worker-members have substantive representational involvement in business operations.

Voting

In traditional for-profit corporations, each share of stock is worth one vote. The shareholders with the most stock exercise the greatest control; those with few shares in a large corporation have little effective say.

In a labor-managed cooperative enterprise each member-worker has only one vote regardless of how much money is in the individual's internal account. If state law does not specify one member/one vote, worker-owners need to make this voting arrangement clear in the by-laws. Because many state laws specify that voting in for-profit corporations goes with shares—one vote per share—be sure to specify that each worker-member receives only one share of stock, and that no one may hold more than one voting share.

Sharing the Net Profits (or Losses)

In addition to providing jobs, a second purpose of the labor-managed cooperative business is to make money for member-owners. Net profits or net margins (or losses if they occur) belong to the members. In for-profit corporations profits are distributed in proportion to the number of shares owned. In a worker-owned cooperative profits are paid into each member's internal account in proportion to the amount of labor contributed, usually based on earnings. Some profits may also be retained as capital to buy new equipment or expand the business. Some profits should be used for education, too.

Transferring Shares or Memberships

Stock is bought and sold in a for-profit corporation by owners who want control of the firm, or who hope to make dividends, or appreciate the stock's value. In a small corporation, major stockholders may want to sell out or retire. Anyone able to put up the money can buy control of the business if they can purchase a majority of the stock.

Cooperatives organized as for-profit corporations which issue stock need to protect themselves from purchase by non-worker outsiders. In this situation, workers must include a provision in the articles of incorporation or by-laws indicating the cooperative has first right to buy back stock when a member leaves or dies. The price paid should be what the member originally paid plus any inflationary adjustment and accrued interest. In addition, the articles of incorporation and by-laws should specify how a departing member is paid the net worth and interest which has accrued in his or her internal membership account.

Sample articles of incorporation and by-laws for a democratically run worker-owned and managed cooperatives are included in Appendix F.

Creating a Democratic ESOP

Employee Stock Option Plans (ESOPs) are legal devices for providing workers with stock ownership in a traditional corporate business enterprise. This approach has been used frequently during the past decade as a means of preventing plant closings or allowing managers and/or workers to buy a business from its previous owners. ESOPs enjoy generous tax advantages, both to the company and investors, a principal reason for their popularity.

One problem is that the ESOP provides a legal framework for some form of workers' capitalism, but does not automatically provide a mechanism to insure workers' control, or create a labor-managed cooperative. In a typical employee-leveraged buyout through an ESOP, the employees can only vote their shares of stock as the loans obtained to buy the company are paid off. In the meantime, trustees appointed by management and the bank control the firm.

Advocates of worker-ownership and workplace democracy, including the authors of this book, are reluctant to recommend the ESOP as a legal form for a worker-owned business, even to facilitate an employee buyout of an existing business. Is there any way out of this dilemma? Can an ESOP be restructured to make it more democratic and to put more control in the hands of the employee-owners? The answer is "Yes-but!"

Economist David Ellerman has suggested that there are two ways to structure an ESOP to make it more democratic: (1) the two-tiered scheme and, (2) the two-share classes scheme.

> In the two-tiered scheme, the votes are not passed through even on allocated shares, so that all votes are exercised by the trust committee. But then the ESOP agreement also specifies that the trust committee will follow the voting instructions of the employee-owners. The employee-owners vote, on a one person/one vote basis, about how to instruct the trust committee to vote the shares. In the two-share classes scheme, there would be voting and non-voting stock. Each employee-owner would get one share of voting stock and the vote would be passed through. The remaining shares would be non-voting. This scheme seems preferable because the votes are directly exercised by the workers. (5)

Variations of the two-tiered scheme to satisfy the one person/one vote rule have been used in several democratic ESOPs such as the Solar Center in San Francisco, Atlas Chain in Pennsylvania, and Seymour Specialty Wire in Connecticut. Although there have been no legal or government challenges to the two-tiered idea at this writing, some concern has been expressed by Ellerman: "It is not clear how to reconcile the fiduciary duties of the trustees with the agreement to obey the instructions of the beneficiaries (workers) should a case arise where there is a perceived divergence between the two obligations." (6)

Similar reservations exist about the two-share classes scheme. The status of this scheme is unclear under present federal legislation. Current law requires ESOP shares to have the highest combination of voting and dividend rights, commonly interpreted to exclude non-voting shares. Ellerman argues that "pending a definitive interpretation of the law or new legislation, a one person/one vote ESOP, using the two share classes, is potentially in conflict with ESOP law." (7)

If legal, the two ideas make the ESOP more acceptable as a form of worker democracy by overcoming the barrier the ESOP trust puts between workers and their voting rights. But there is another major shortcoming to ESOPs. How can ownership of the enterprise be kept in the workers' hands over time? Under an ESOP, as workers leave or retire, their vested shares are issued to them, and those shares can be sold to outsiders. While recent legislation allows a company to insure maintenance of the shares in the ESOP trust through a buy-back arrangement, shares normally can leak to outsiders. This problem caused the worker-owned corn mill established by the Rochdale Manufacturing Society to fail. Outsiders bought a majority of the stock and it ceased to be a worker-owned enterprise. Similar outcomes were experienced by the Vermont Asbestos Group and the Herkimer Library Bureau.

Recent legislative developments have significantly changed the legal situation regarding the use of ESOPs. The new 1986 Tax Reform Act replaced the cumbersome arrangements preventing the use of the ESOP as a financial structure and the cooperative as a form of democratic governance. The new law contains an explicit provision for ESOP/co-op combinations, allowing a company to allocate one vote to each member instead of a vote to each share. Corey Rosen, an ESOP expert, has stated that "Co-ops can now participate in all tax benefits of ESOPs without changing their governance systems." (8)

Greater experience with ESOPs has demonstrated some additional advantages to this form of financial structure, particularly in conversions of existing businesses to worker ownership. As noted by Ellerman;

> Co-ops tend to be all or nothing affairs, while many situations call for a gradual ramp-building up to a majority or full, worker ownership. The ESOP affords a tax-favoured hybrid structure which allows the workers to block-vote their share of ownership as determined by a worker majority on a one-person/one vote basis.
>
> It can also be an advantage to have a separate ESOP trust holding workers' shares. An ESOP trust contains share-capital accounts which, for the most part, simulate Mondragon-type internal capital accounts. . .The trust also avoids the "petty capitalist" problems resulting from individually-marketable shares in partially worker-owned firms.
>
> An ESOP provides a much-needed "third-party" in a gradual worker buyout from a retiring owner. For many reasons, it is not appropriate for workers to be buying shares individually from a retiring owner. Tax laws mitigate against having the company buy back or redeem the shares and then issue the shares to the workers. A worker-controlled ESOP is a useful third party which can take out a loan to buy shares from the owner and then secure a tax break in paying off the loan. (9)

137

With some of the legal uncertainties previously clouding the acceptance of the one person/one vote now removed, the ESOP is becoming more acceptable as a mechanism for converting existing businesses to worker-ownership. However, we suggest that serious thought and study be undertaken and good legal advice be obtained before using the ESOP as the financial framework for creating a democratic worker-owned business.

Members' and Directors' Checklist

Chart 7-1 is a checklist which may be used to determine how the articles of incorporation, by-laws and other internal governance devices created for your firm match up with an optimum standard devised over the years. It can also help you assess the duties and responsibilities of directors.

Chart 7-1

MEMBERS' AND DIRECTORS' CHECKLIST

Members Do The Following	Yes	No	Other
1) Adopt and amend by-laws.	☐	☐	☐
2) Adopt resolutions at annual meetings.	☐	☐	☐
3) Elect or remove directors.	☐	☐	☐
4) Approve and formulate policy.	☐	☐	☐
5) Approve major changes in capitalization or additions to the firm.	☐	☐	☐
6) Receive an annual accounting of the firms performance			
a) in writing	☐	☐	☐
b) by oral reports from managers.	☐	☐	☐
7) Assist in financing the firm.	☐	☐	☐
8) Require that directors and managers carry out policy set by worker-owners.	☐	☐	☐
9) Take an active part in governance of firm by serving on committees, attending meetings, etc.	☐	☐	☐
10) Cease being a member when leaving the firm for retirement or other reasons.	☐	☐	☐
11) Set forth policies which are approved by membership.	☐	☐	☐

12) Hire management and delegate only those powers designated by the membership. ☐ ☐ ☐

13) Elect officers of the board and firm. ☐ ☐ ☐

14) Raise capital, borrow money, individual membership accounts, oversee financial matters by approving budget, etc. ☐ ☐ ☐

15) Select lawyers and accountants. ☐ ☐ ☐

16) Can remove managers for cause. ☐ ☐ ☐

17) Can fill vacancies on board. ☐ ☐ ☐

18) Keep records of all board meetings and insure that those records are open to members for inspection. ☐ ☐ ☐

19) Make contracts, leases, and loan arrangements. ☐ ☐ ☐

20) With the Social Council, establish personnel policies for approval by membership. ☐ ☐ ☐

21) Evaluate the firm's performance, formulate plans for growth or future operations. ☐ ☐ ☐

22) Seek to perpetuate the firm in the interests of its members. ☐ ☐ ☐

23) During an annual meeting present to the membership policies, records, budgets, and any proposed resolutions or by-law amendments for vote. ☐ ☐ ☐

139

If fourteen or more of these questions are answered yes, then workers have significant voices in self-governance. Fewer than fourteen affirmative answers could spell marginal control. If "other" answers dominate your response, be cautioned to have expert clear-headed advisors help restructure by-laws and articles of incorporation.

A Time to Vote

When your group has completed drafting the by-laws, and the membership has read them thoroughly, it is time to adopt or reject them by vote.

140

8 MANAGING WORKER DEMOCRACY

PRINCIPLES OF DEMOCRATIC DECISION-MAKING
LEVELS OF DECISION-MAKING POWER
AREAS OF POTENTIAL CONFLICT

Workers govern through elected representatives. They administer and control through management. Governance is a political function; management is an economic function. The way decisions are made is what counts in any democracy; the quality of the decisions is what counts in business. The two functions, which have been separated in traditional capitalism or when the state runs businesses, should be united when workers own and run the firm. Practicing the concept can be difficult. Relatively speaking, only a few workers have ever had management experience. Even fewer managers have been trained to plan and allocate democratically.

Principles of Democratic Decision-Making

While worker-owners will want to draw on their experiences to fashion the political and economic tools governing their own unique situation, organizational principles from other labor-managed enterprises suggest guidelines. The pioneering Basques fashioned some. Others derive from Yugoslav workers who have managed state-sponsored enterprises since World War II. After years of study a Yugoslav worker-manager, Branko Horvat, outlined six principles which assure democratic, efficient decision making. (1) In small firms, the principles come into play almost as a matter of course. In large firms, however, organizational communication demands more attention to detail and perhaps additional decision-making tiers. While described in terms suited for mid-sized firms, Horvat's principles derive from both extremes.

The first decision-making level should be what Horvat calls the work unit. Each basic work unit has social and management characteristics which correspond to the firm's larger political and economic functions. As the primary part in the production or service delivery process, each work unit is a small, homogeneous group. Informal communication is the norm. Participation in decisions is direct and face-to-face. Everyone understands how decisions are reached. Willful, unjustified opinions seldom prevail. Opinions are infrequently manipulated.

These basic work units join or "federate," with similar economic units as a work community. These, in turn, federate as the enterprise community. Communication needs more attention at each new level. Decisions have to be delegated. An electoral process—formal or informal—is necessary.

His second principle acts to guarantee democracy: whenever a work unit's decision will substantially affect the interests of other work units, those decisions are pushed up to the work community level or, if necessary, to the enterprise level which might be management or the board of directors.

His third and fourth principles seek to insure that the best possible decisions are made and implemented efficiently. While work units have the right to make certain clearly stated decisions, they also bear the responsibility for any outcome. Rights are balanced with sanctions which are specified in advance and well-known. The administration and implementation of decisions demand competence, not democracy. Thus, the basis for managerial authority is established.

The fifth principle makes additional distinctions between the firm's political and economic functions. Policies are formulated politically, deriving from the work unit to the work community and finally the board. Administration of those policies is a professional or qualitative matter. Authority for creating policies derives from the principle of one person/one vote; authority for administration derives from technical competency.

So far the ideas make sense, and seem neatly suited to the principles governing a labor-managed enterprise's internal dynamics as we have outlined them. But life isn't neat, nor is the struggle to manage work. Recognizing this reality, Horvat suggests in his sixth organizational principle that worker-owners devise and institutionalize controls which are beyond democratic or bureaucratic tinkering and which provide a means of resolving conflict. The Basques created such devices through their Social Councils. Their Social Council is the elected voice of the cooperative members and is vested with wide prescriptive and advisory powers in all aspects of personnel management. Its decisions are binding in such matters as safety and hygiene at work, accident prevention, wage levels, administration of social funds, and health and retirement programs. The members vote by department to elect the Social Council. The council normally meets once a month. In addition to its function as an advisory body the Social Council serves as a means of communication, transmitting information from the board of directors to the workers and the workers' opinions to the board of directors. (2)

This suggests a role for unions in worker-owned firms. With extensive skills and experience with matters the Basque Social Councils oversee, unions in conversions to worker-owned cooperatives or ESOPs could evolve a role as collaborative representatives of labor rather than adversaries or business representatives of labor. Here, as elsewhere, Ellerman has plowed new ground, suggesting unions in large worker-owned firms serve as "the loyal opposition," a metaphor he derives from British parliamentary experience. (3)

143

Organizational Chart 8-1 below is based on the collective experience described so far in this book. The social audit committee could serve as a means of resolving conflicts and facilitating communication. This committee, elected by the membership, voting by department, would function in much the same way as the Basques' Social Council, and also perform a social audit of the business on a periodic basis.

Sorting out who will make what decision, when, how, and why is a difficult task for worker-owners. Keep in mind that political decisions are most often clearly and efficiently arrived at through a well-conceived electoral process. Economic decisions are essentially strategic. They must be made in response to particular situations, with due speed, and within a politically authorized policy framework.

The starting point for both is the individual worker within each work unit and the work unit. Having a direct say in, or the right to be heard on issues arising out of job assignment, safety and health, hiring and firing, wages, hours and other aspects of the daily routine are of greatest importance. Power here will evoke willingness to participate in self-governance on other levels. Political and economic issues at the job site provide a starting point for deciding which deci-

Chart 8-1
ORGANIZATION AND STRUCTURE OF THE WORKER-OWNED COOPERATIVE

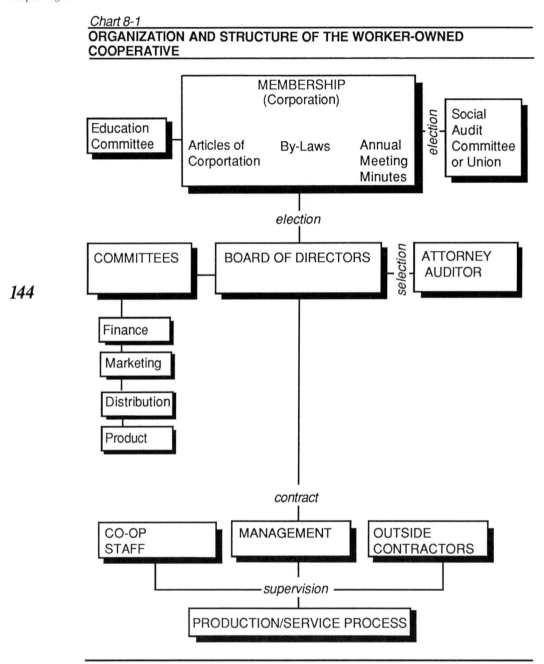

sions fall under the authority of workers, manager, board, social audit committee or union.

Grievances will surface. Some can be resolved swiftly; others may end up in arbitration hearings or other forums outside the firm. Here again, the extensive experience of unions in setting up and operating grievance procedures and their understanding of law from a labor point of view could provide worker-owners with important resources. Adequate machinery for handling grievances and other complaints of workers, fairly and expeditiously, must be established in accord with case or administrative law, and it is in this area where union members' experience can be especially helpful.

For many workers, if not most, it is who says how and when they do their jobs that matters most. Designing jobs as if people counted is critical if the worker-owned firm is to prosper. Even worker-owners with a financial stake at risk need to feel their work is meaningful, has variety and significance, and to be certain of a measure of autonomy. The Basques learned this lesson the hard way. The only strike in the Mondragon group's history occurred when, in part, worker-members felt they were being treated as cogs in a factory system. The strike was short-lived, but today, job design and job rotation are integral parts of the Mondragon planning and management processes. Workers are insured a voice in those decisions. In America, workers at South Bend Lathe and Hyatt-Clark—firms purchased by the employees through ESOPs—struck their firms for similar reasons. Behavioral scientists are finding that principles of job enlargement seem to transcend ideologies. What makes a job important in a traditional firm is the same in a labor-managed enterprise. By combining tasks, forming natural work units, making sure each worker-member knows the results of his or her labor on a regular basis enriches jobs. Essentially, however, assuring worker-owners the responsibility for deciding on work methods, for the time work is done, on the priority given each task, and for advising or training new workers in the workplace makes work meaningful. (4)

Over the years, the Basques have used job rotation plans not only to insure high worker-member morale, but, as well, to curb seasonal slumps, or economic downturns faced by particular cooperatives. Most Basque worker-members learn several jobs either to perform in their own or in another firm within the group. Thus, when employment demands rise due to seasonal sales growth, or economic upturns, work needs can be filled without resort to boom or bust hiring policies.

145

During the long European recession which occurred in the late-1970s, no single worker-member of the Mondragon group was terminated despite the fact that unemployment in the Basque provinces reached 24 percent at times.

Levels of Decision-making Power

An appropriate process of decision-making can be outlined at each level to insure some degree of uniformity and dispatch. Most decisions are made to solve or prevent problems. Solving problems usually involves six steps:

☐ Recognizing or defining the problem.

☐ Having the work unit or an individual bring the problem to the attention of others.

☐ Gathering data and sorting out options for a solution.

☐ Discussing the options and making the decision.

☐ Implementing or taking action on the decision.

☐ Monitoring the outcome(s) and making any corrections.

Space Builders, an eleven-person worker-owned construction cooperative organized in 1978, learned the importance of developing effective decision-making procedures the hard way. Several times in their early years people without the skills and motivation to match the business' needs were hired impulsively. They found that failure to establish adequate performance standards and appropriate procedures for making and implementing decisions, including delegating authority, could threaten the productivity, peace, and possibly survival of the group as a whole. Over time, Space Builders learned to develop accurate job descriptions, write down their operating policies to insure that each new member would understand the group's norms and expectations, and make and implement decisions in a timely manner through appropriate organizational levels.

Space Builders' success has been earned through hard work, dedication, and strong commitment to the democratic decision-making process. Regular, productive, well-attended meetings have been the key to effective democratic management. We meet for two hours every week (after regular working hours) to discuss major policy and planning decisions such as budgeting, wage evaluations and raises, marketing strategy, and changes in operating policies. We also talk about short term concerns such as current construction projects, scheduling, and cash flow...

We have learned which decisions should be brought to a meeting and which are appropriately made on the job. We lost a couple of good construction managers before we realized that we must allow them some authority to go along with their burden of responsibility. (5)

Establishing a suitable framework for decision-making is complicated by the legal relationships created by a worker-owned cooperative between worker-members, appointed management, and elected board. Establishing reciprocal relationships between these groups requires time, education, and, above all, trusting patience. But the process need not be left to chance. Having earlier outlined the duties and responsibilities usually accompanying membership in worker-owned firms, and of directors, it is appropriate to describe the powers often delegated to managers and their responsibilities. While not inclusive, the list below is representative and can be used as a guideline:

147

Responsibilities of Managers

☐ To coordinate and administer the firm's affairs in keeping with policies agreed upon by the board of directors.

☐ To develop reports and budgets, financial projections, and lending summaries to the board of directors and membership.

☐ To maintain an appropriate bookkeeping and accounting system, and to have those records examined by auditors outside the firm on a regular basis.

☐ To attend all meetings of the board of directors, make available to them appropriate business and financial reports, and offer options for decision, but not vote on those decisions.

☐ To devote full time to the firm's affairs and not engage in business concerns outside the cooperative, or in competition with it.

Rights of Managers

☐ To hire and fire in accord with the firm's policies.

☐ To make recommendations to the board of directors, the social audit committee, union, or any other properly established working group.

☐ To organize, administer, plan and control the financial and administrative operation.

☐ To oversee the production, sales, distribution, etc., of the firm's services or products.

☐ To evaluate and appraise the performance of worker-owners.

☐ To identify and make available suitable training and educational programs to improve political and economic efficiency.

In sum, it is the obligation of management to effectively direct and control the interplay of labor (member-workers), capital (member equity, loans, or assets) and material (raw or unfinished products or undelivered services). The obstacles facing worker-owners and managers are formidable, and difficult to surmount. But for many, including the thousands of workers who manage their own businesses, these hurdles are looked upon as opportunities. The workplace becomes "a laboratory for industrial democracy and participation." *The key is for managers to derive authority from the political and economic wellsprings of those who work in the firm, rather than from capital.* (6)

Chart 8-2, developed by the Industrial Cooperative Association, summarizes the division of powers that normally exists among the worker-owner-members, board of directors, and chief operating officer of the cooperative.

Chart 8-2

DIVISIONS OF POWER IN A WORKER-OWNED COOPERATIVE

Worker-Owner Members	*Board of Directors*	*Chief Executive Officer (CEO)*
1) Adopt and amend by-laws.	1) Defines yearly goals as well as policies necessary to implement goals.	1) Prepares budgets, production plans, marketing plans, and all other plans necessary for the implementation of the goals and policies approved by the board.
2) Elect Board of Directors.	2) Selects CEO, defines duties, and sets salaries.	2) Defines duties of division and department heads.
3) Yearly ratify and semi-annually review the goals of the Business plan.	3) Controls finances a. ratifies financing plans/budgets. b. approves changes in above. c. approve loans.	3) Hires / fires within framework of personnel policies. This power may be delegated.
4) Ratify any drastic alteration of the of the business plan or philosophy.	4) Ratifies personnel policies with the exception of hiring/firing. In the latter case, recommends policies to the membership who then make the final decision.	4) Coordinates the implementation/ administration of all organizational policies.
5) Review any sale or purchase of any major asset such as a building, etc.	5) Evaluates performance of the CEO.	5) Evaluates employees. This power may be delegated.

149

6) Review any job
   which exceeds
   25% of the
   business plan's
   projected
   yearly sales.

7) Ratify hiring,
   firing, and lay-
   off policies.

8) Participate in
   work unit
   decision-making.

As firms grow, or circumstances change, it may be necessary to modify the division of powers among the levels. Informal decision-making procedures involving everyone may work effectively for a small firm with 10 members, but it may not be suitable for a business with 25 or 100 worker-members. Also, major changes in the business climate which threaten the firm may necessitate new approaches to decision-making.

For example, changes in tax laws reduced the market for solar heating by 75 percent, forcing the worker-owned Solar Center of San Francisco to make some major adjustments. The 25 worker-owners decided to reduce their salaries by 10 percent, cut back expenditures, and lay off several workers. The austerity measures were designed to help finance training and equipment for a venture into a different type of heating system.

The firm also moved to a more hierarchical structure, to streamline decision-making. "The former method of having everyone participate in virtually every decision led to exhausting meetings, unclear responsibility for implementation, and postponed decisions," they said. Committees were established so that all employees were not required to be involved in every decision. Overall authority, however, still rested with the entire membership. A board consisting of four workers, the president, and three outsiders now sets policy. Other changes included hiring a general manager and changing the maximum-minimum salary ratio from 2:1 to 5:1 to attract "topflight salespeople." (7)

Peter Barnes, one of the founders of the Solar Center, offered five lessons he 'learned by experience" for others interested in starting a worker-owned business. They are:

Growth is inevitable, so accept it, plan for it, and enjoy it. Remaining small is a romantic notion which does have advantages. Growth also has advantages—excitement is generated, more areas of responsibility are provided, and a livable income is generated.

Democratic organizations need leaders, and leaders need to be supported and rewarded. Entrepreneurs, among other things, envision and create new possibilities, bring together diverse resources, and inspire others. These individuals should be encouraged primarily by intrinsic rewards—the thrill of creating something out of nothing, recognition, and the satisfaction of helping others learn and grow—and secondarily by monetary rewards.

Authority must be matched to responsibility. In order to get things done this concept must be practiced at the individual level. In a democratic structure managers are worker-owners who are ultimately accountable to their peers for carrying out the policies set by all worker-owners.

151

Get sophisticated, not cynical. Hold onto your basic values. But also approach situations with a mind to taking the best and leaving the rest. This can be an exciting challenge to your creativity and even your success.

Never forget to make the organization, and its values, self-renewing. There are three parts to this. First, if power and responsibility are to be shared, risks must also continuously be shared. Requiring new owners to make an investment comparable to the previous owners' is probably the best way to do this. Second, new owners must be welcomed and integrated into positions of responsibility. Third, education is essential. Most individuals have little or no experience in, or even knowledge of a worker-owned and operated business. Instruct them about democratic practices and more especially about your/their company and its history. (8)

Areas of Potential Conflict

According to Louisiana State University Professor Ewell Paul Roy, there are ten chief factors which cause rifts between cooperative board members and management. (9) They are restated in Chart 8-3 as a checklist for worker-owners. Total scores of 30 or higher suggest that there may be some areas of conflict which need to be addressed.

Chart 8-3

MANAGER/ MEMBER/ BOARD RELATIONSHIPS

		Agree 1	2	Neither 3	4	Disagree 5
1)	The firms's objectives have been definitely and specifically understood and agreed to by the manager and board of directors.	☐	☐	☐	☐	☐
2)	The duties, functions and rights of the manager and board of directors have been spelled out and agreed to.	☐	☐	☐	☐	☐
3)	Management's financial and other rewards have been spelled out.	☐	☐	☐	☐	☐
4)	The board of directors do not dabble in administrative matters. They devote their time to long-term policies and planning.	☐	☐	☐	☐	☐
5)	The manager recommends and the board of directors adopt clearly stated policies which guide managment action.	☐	☐	☐	☐	☐
6)	The board of directors establishes policies after consulting management. And vice verse.	☐	☐	☐	☐	☐
7)	The board of directors requires managment to furnish sufficient and appropriate periodic reports so that decisions can be reached on the basis of the fullest possible knowledge.	☐	☐	☐	☐	☐
8)	The manager has not employed relatives or relatives of a director	☐	☐	☐	☐	☐
9)	The individual board members do not assert managerial authority on the work floor.	☐	☐	☐	☐	☐

152

10) Board members have represented the political and economic interests of the entire workforce.

☐ ☐ ☐ ☐ ☐

11) The worker-members actively participate in appropriate decisions made at the level of the work unit.

☐ ☐ ☐ ☐ ☐

TOTAL SCORE [☐]

153

9 DEMOCRACY ON THE WORKFLOOR

EDUCATION FOR OWNERSHIP AND PARTICIPATION

Worker-owners face both ways like Janus, the Roman god whose name perpetually turns the calendar. As workers, self-interest dictates a desire to govern the job. As owners, production demands that jobs be performed predictably, or managed, in accord with cooperative policy. At some point, sooner or later, nearly every worker-owned cooperative comes to terms with two impulses seemingly at odds with management: ownership nurtures the desire in individuals to directly affect workplace decisions and the desire to spread about authority for taking decisions.

For instance, Almarinda Souza, a seamstress at Darwood Manufacturing Company, in Fall River, Massachusetts, told fellow workers during a hectic workforce meeting called at a crucial moment in a buyout effort: "I started sewing at this company nearly thirty years ago. Right after I got here I went to the boss and told him I had an idea I thought would save money. He told me, 'Almarinda, you are paid to sew, not think.' So I have kept my mouth shut since. Now, if we buy this company, if I don't think, I don't get paid." Workplace democracy upends the traditional relationship between capital and labor, but, as well, forces changes in self-concept. Owners want to become owners.

At one level, at least in the early stages of developing worker-owned firms, the democratic election of policy-making boards who, in turn, govern management seems enough to fulfill the reasonable expectation that worker-ownership means self-managed work. Eventually, however, especially in more complex industrial settings where unions have had historically important roles, representational democracy, while necessary, is not sufficient.

To give meaning to the practice of workplace democracy, plans which mediate conflict between managers and workers but which balance power and authority with accountability must be worked out. Would-be worker-owners should also have some tools at hand for this purpose. As much care should be devoted to this vital activity as was given over to writing the business plan, negotiating with lenders, or setting prices.

How twenty-five worker-owners in small enterprises manage their work will differ greatly from the way twenty-five hundred worker-owners must tend to business. Size is only one factor which will shape the way workers govern the workfloor itself. The purpose a business is set up to accomplish influences how it is organized. So do the tools used, or the markets served. Occupational skills and personalities of workers and managers leave their mark. In the end, each worker-owned cooperative—whether just getting started or a conversion—must undertake the sometimes painful process of fashioning the way work itself is governed.

Most, if not all, workers arrive at the democratically managed worksite poorly prepared to participate in enterprise governance, or to usefully involve themselves in decision-making about the job. Some will never want to learn the skills it takes, but for those who do, members, managers and boards must be prepared to address vexingly original issues resulting when the necessities of production mixed with the politics of democracy.

A starting point for any worker-owned cooperative is to look at the assumptions which are taken for granted when work is organized to suit capital. First, workers work for managers, and managers work for the company. Second, managers alone know what is best for the company. Third, managers give orders, workers take them. Fourth, managers and workers share few corporate goals and are separate, adversarial, special interest groups.

Where labor controls capital, and cooperation is the organizing medium for work, the assumptions differ greatly. First, both workers and managers own the company. Second, both workers and managers have information which must be shared for optimal corporate health. Third, because both workers and managers have information which must be shared for optimal corporate health, both must accept the responsibility for a dialogue between equals. Fourth, because they are owners, each with an equal stake and voice, workers and managers share goals which are not mutually exclusive.

Therefore, the first barrier which must fall in the ideally organized worker-owned firm is an educational one. Who gets to learn what must be redefined so that the many cognitive and vocational skills required to make a business prosper are restored to labor, ending the separation between formulation of decisions and their execution. In an unpublished paper written in 1977, Jaroslav Vanek, an early theoretician of worker-ownership in modern-day Europe, wrote:

> The Rochdale Pioneers, forerunners of all cooperative movements today, were well aware of the significance of education for the liberation of the worker. When they wrote down the fundamental principles of their movement some one and a quarter centuries ago, they knew it was the ignorance of the wage earner of how to do things, how to organize production, that enslaved him. Thus, they resolved to allot some portion of their meager resources to education. . . . Education, and more generally, the transformation of the human consciousness, is the precondition and the very lifeblood of any successful and lasting effort to bring about self-management and economic democracy. (1)

157

The place to start learning workplace self-governance is with the job itself. William "Big Bill" Haywood, the legendary organizer for the Industrial Workers of the World, never failed to bring workers to their feet shouting approval when he would declare, "The bosses' brains are under the cap of the working man." Politically and rhetorically, his assertion rang true; in reality, however, workers who have been consigned to repetitious work know principally how to carry out their job, and, generally speaking, they know little related to financing, markets or production. Since the work of putting a labor-managed enterprise commences with a feasibility study, then proceeds to a comprehensive business plan, involving workers in that process at the outset is the single most instructive way to widen the base of knowledge required, both individually and for the collective whole. Learning by doing.

Fashioning a way for dialogue to take place between workers who are owners and managers who are owners, too, is the second critically important step. Marty Zinn, a founder of the Worker Owned Network, based in Athens, Ohio, and Roger Wilkins, former director of the Center for Cooperative

Work Relations, also in Athens, have successfully tested what they call ground rules and cooperative agreements, two tools which foster collaboration. The ground rules are three simple statements which working groups can use to lessen conflict while greasing a decision-making process during "moment-by-moment, face-to-face interactions" on the shop, in meetings, or at the water cooler.

First, avoid intimidation, attempts to control or manipulate a situation, threats, or, as Zinn and Wilkins call such behavior, power plays. "To do this," Zinn and Wilkins say, "we need to learn to recognize power plays, to confront people when we see them pulling power plays, and to set up cooperative ways to resolve problems. You confront a power play by saying how you feel, describe the intimidation, etc., recall how the group agreed to work cooperatively, and suggest a way that can happen."

Second, agree to communicate openly. "This does not mean talking about everything," they say. "It means recognizing those things that relate to the success of our business and the health of our group. This requires us to share our feelings so that anger and resentment don't build up, and to state our needs."

Third, agreeing that every member's opinions are equally valued and deserve equal consideration. "Everyone's needs are not the same. Whenever there seems to be less than enough of something needed, we agree to cooperate to find more, or to compromise, or to find some other solution."

By using those easily understood ground rules, and coupling them with a clearly stated "Cooperative Agreement," or contract drawn up and agreed to before a group of prospective worker-owners starts a feasibility study, Zinn and Wilkins have managed, as consultants, to help potential worker-owners "un-learn" ways of behaving which have sundered many start-ups or conversions. "A start-up group must complete and sign their Cooperative Agreements before they open for business," according to the consultants. The Cooperative Agreements can include policies for hiring and firing governance, working hours, and any work-related topic.

Still another tool available to would-be worker-owners planning to take democracy to the shop floor, is a decision agreement. Decisions may be impossible to reach in a company running three shifts daily, seven days a week, or in a taxicab company where workers are literally all over a city. Decisions are equally difficult to reach if workers are worn out after an eight-hour shift. Coming to an agreement about how decisions are to be made before decisions have to be taken avoids numerous conflicts. The following six points should be considered for inclusion in such an agreement:

1) Exactly who makes which decision—the workers as a group, managers, or the steering committee.

2) Spelling out exactly what decisions each category of persons can make.

3) Using small groups, or task forces, to formulate decision options to a larger group, or to make a decision for the larger group.

4) Separating decisions into categories such as policy, management, shop floor, or between procedural and policy matters.

5) Have a decision appeal, or decision review process in place before a group makes the first decision.

6) Make sure everyone making a decision uses the same information, and that it is accurate and complete.

Still another step which can be used in preparing for shop floor participation and democratic self-management would be to take the time to express the values, or beliefs, which the group hopes will guide policy-making in daily operations. Potential worker-owners who are hard-pressed to find the money to put themselves in business may think a statement of business philosophy is only remotely related to their immediate needs. Others who are already tending their business but who are snagged by internal conflict may think a clear statement of values of little use in cooling emotions. But democratic participation on the shop floor is, in the final analysis, the primary operational relationship between a member and the cooperative. Were such a statement derived from this book, it would read like this:

☐ Workers are responsible and can make corporate decisions.

☐ Workers must have a decisive voice in governing the enterprise, and the democratic principle of one person, one vote serves as the basis for participation.

☐ Corporate values must be balanced with human values.

☐ Income must be distributed equitably and individual membership accounts must be administered prudently.

☐ Groups should be involved in problem-solving to the extent possible within the given situation.

☐ Decision-making authority shifts to the lowest possible level consistent with the principles of sound management.

☐ Opportunities should exist for any person wanting to learn new skills or perform new jobs.

☐ Membership should be open to any person employed by the firm.

160

Obviously, we have expressed other values, but these few illustrate the point. A similar list could be gotten up by any group of workers without much difficulty, and then be used to fashion policies, including one on participation suited to the specific firm.

A way to measure the degree of participation, as a tool for creating participation, appears in Charts 9-1 and 9-2. Here, only two or three categories are listed. Were one to be developed which located the various levels of decision-making within a specific company it would probably contain additional categories.

A specific means to determine what power workers had over their jobs before a buyout or conversion is described in Chart 9-1. By asking fellow workers to fill the form out twice—first to describe the degree of control they had in a traditional company, and again to describe the degree of control they would like to exercise over their work—planners will have data to use for locating decision-making authority in the cooperative. All 5's in each of the three categories probably indicate workers want too much say. All 1's would indicate managers might have too much sway. Here, power is defined as the ability to influence or make decisions dealing with the listed categories. Another list could be worked up to suit your own cooperative.

Chart 9-1

DEGREE OF POWER IN DECISION-MAKING IN A WORKER-OWNED COOPERATIVE

Categories	Degree of Power of Worker-Members				
	None 1	2	*Some* 3	4	*All* 5
Task Related					
Tools used	☐	☐	☐	☐	☐
Schedules	☐	☐	☐	☐	☐
Safety	☐	☐	☐	☐	☐
Training	☐	☐	☐	☐	☐
Quality control	☐	☐	☐	☐	☐
Production	☐	☐	☐	☐	☐
Supervision	☐	☐	☐	☐	☐
Other	☐	☐	☐	☐	☐
Administrative Functions					
Resource allocation	☐	☐	☐	☐	☐
Plantwide work schedules	☐	☐	☐	☐	☐
Cost control	☐	☐	☐	☐	☐
Meeting strategic goals	☐	☐	☐	☐	☐
Budgeting	☐	☐	☐	☐	☐
Marketing	☐	☐	☐	☐	☐
Purchasing	☐	☐	☐	☐	☐
Others	☐	☐	☐	☐	☐
Strategic Planning					
Setting goals	☐	☐	☐	☐	☐
Selecting products	☐	☐	☐	☐	☐
Determining policies	☐	☐	☐	☐	☐
Acquisitions	☐	☐	☐	☐	☐
Selecting management	☐	☐	☐	☐	☐

161

Still another way to look at the same problem is to sort out the degree of power by role—managers, the board, or by workers. Chart 9-2 illustrates this way to describe where power has been vested, or where your group wants it located in the future.

Chart 9-2

DEGREE OF CONTROL EXERCISED BY WORKERS

Types of Decisions	Decisions Are Made By		
	Managers or Board unilaterally	Managers & Workers by consensus	Workers unilaterally
Task Related			
Tools used	☐	☐	☐
Schedules	☐	☐	☐
Safety	☐	☐	☐
Training	☐	☐	☐
Quality control	☐	☐	☐
Production	☐	☐	☐
Supervision	☐	☐	☐
Other	☐	☐	☐
Administrative Functions			
Resource allocation	☐	☐	☐
Plantwide work schedules	☐	☐	☐
Cost control	☐	☐	☐
Meeting strategic goals	☐	☐	☐
Marketing	☐	☐	☐
Purchasing	☐	☐	☐
Others	☐	☐	☐
Strategic Planning			
Setting goals	☐	☐	☐
Selecting products	☐	☐	☐
Determining policies	☐	☐	☐
Acquisitions	☐	☐	☐
Electing management	☐	☐	☐

Another tool workers can use to define the dimensions of their relationships with one another is to look at the roles they must assume. Chart 9-3 is a short questionnaire which elected board members, or supervisors, and managers, might be asked to complete. It evaluates their roles as individually key personnel. Of course, as with previous illustrations, the

Chart 9-3
_____

**ROLE ANALYSIS FOR ELECTED OFFICERS
AND MANAGERS**
_____

A) Expectations

1) What do my fellow workers expect of me?
2) What do my fellow elected members expect of me?
3) What do I expect of myself in this role?
4) Will I have to change or will these expectations be
   modified as I carry out my work?

B) Limitations

1) What are the legal restraints on my job?
2) What are the social limits?
3) What are the financial limits?
4) What are the time constraints?
5) Can or should these be changed?

C) Priorities

1) What are the priorities of the job I have elected to perform?
2) What are my priorities for that job?
3) Are there particular organizational needs at this moment?
4) What skills do I need to learn to do this job?
_____

questions are illustrative only, and would-be worker-owners should formulate their own.

As this is a very subjective questionnaire, there are no hard and fast formulas by which to measure the answers. Answering them may be the single most important outcome.

Worker-owners at Seymour Specialty Wire Company, the largest industrial democratic ESOP in America, extended democratic ideals to the shop floor using techniques similar to these suggestions. They called their program Workers Solving Problems, setting as policy that "any problem which is under the direct control of any working unit can be discussed. Once all the options have been considered, each shop floor working unit can make a decision about those problems."

Management and worker-owners had come to loggerheads at Seymour over issues of work organization, large and small, and the company, while prospering financially, "was its own worst enemy," according to one elected officer. Using consultants, management and worker-owners embarked on a companywide goal-setting process which yielded four goals, one of which surprised no one: to organize democratic ways to make decisions. The WSP program was the plan of action issuing from that goal. Chart 9-4 is an adaptation of the problem and decision-making flow chart used as part of the WSP.

"Every worker has a responsibility to participate in the WSP decision-making process," the company said in educational materials used in the training program set up before implementation. "The elected Shop Floor Representative has special responsibilities. So do the Foremen, Supervisors, the Superintendent and Department leaders. But everyone needs to be clear about who makes decisions."

Workers and managers agreed to initially focus the WSP program on production issues only. The union leadership, giving its full endorsement to the program, insisted correctly that any problem covered in the contract with the company could be discussed in the WSP process, but "subjects that are applicable to the Labor Agreement to be channeled through the appropriate committees for review."

In addition to publishing a guide for the WSP program, each person's responsibilities were spelled out, accountability forms were created to insure that records were kept on who took what decision and when, and a decision-making chart was drawn marking specific decision categories and where they were taken. Chart 9-5 is the WSP decision-making chart.

NOTES ON CHART 9-4

Problem Solving Steps

☐ State problem.
☐ List possible causes.
☐ Choose most likely cause.
☐ List possible solutions.

☐ Choose best solution.
☐ Post for comment.
☐ Implement.
☐ Evaluate.

Additional Requirements

☐ Plant Manager to attend 2 meetings monthly at Shop Floor Level as an observer.

☐ President to attend 2 meetings monthly at the Shop Floor Level as an observer.

☐ Department or higher level meeting to be called by reps. if break in communications arises.

Chart 9-4

SEYMOUR WIRE WSP PROBLEM
AND DECISION-MAKING FLOW CHART/MEETING FREQUENCY

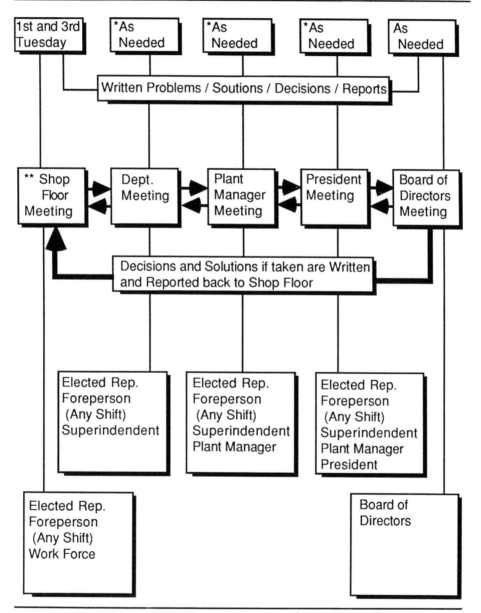

165

* At least one meeting per month required from Level 2 through Level 4 determined by
chairpersons of those levels. If problem involves 2 or more shifts, reps. and forepersons
from those shifts should be present.

** As many problems as possible should be solved here.

Chart 9-5
SEYMOUR WIRE WSP DECISION-MAKING CHART

Type of Decision   *Decisions to be made by

	Shop Floor Level	Fore-person Level	Supt. Level	Plt.Mgr. Level	Pres. Level
1) Tools					
a) Use of	▨	▨	▨		
b) Replacement of	▨	▨	▨		
c) Repair of	▨	▨	▨		
2) Production					
a) Goals	▨	▨	▨	▨	▨
b) Schedules	▨	▨	▨	▨	▨
c) Flow	▨	▨	▨		
d) Requirements	▨	▨	▨	▨	
e) Bottlenecks					
3) Equipment					
a) Use of	▨	▨	▨		
b) Maintenance of	▨	▨	▨		
c) Replacement of	▨	▨	▨	▨	▨
4) Materials and Parts					
a) Ordering of	▨	▨	▨	▨	▨
b) Scheduling of	▨	▨	▨		
c) Handling of	▨	▨	▨		
d) Storage of	▨	▨	▨	▨	
5) Maintenance					
a) Preventative	▨	▨	▨	▨	
b) Equipment repairs	▨	▨	▨		
c) Priorities	▨	▨	▨		
d) Improvements	▨	▨	▨	▨	▨

6) Safety

a) Equipment	☒	☒	☒	☒	☒
b) Elimination of hazards	☒	☒	☒	☒	
c) Education	☒	☒	☒	☒	☒
d) Improvements	☒	☒	☒	☒	☒

7) Quality

a) Product	☒	☒	☒	☒	
b) Level of	☒	☒	☒	☒	
c) Improvements	☒	☒	☒	☒	☒

8) Cost Control

a) Production	☒	☒	☒	☒	☒
b) Energy	☒	☒	☒	☒	☒
c) Material	☒	☒	☒	☒	☒
d) Overhead	☒	☒	☒	☒	☒

*Final decision includes input from all ☒ Levels

Some fifteen working units in every phase of the 250 person firm's operations were vested with decision-making, problem-solving responsibilities. While each shop floor unit was encouraged to take as many decisions as possible, all were cautioned that "two tests should be kept in mind before action is taken":

One is the Extensiveness Test. Each WSP working unit was to ask four questions about the impact a decision would have on fellow workers.

The Extensiveness Test
1) How many persons will be effected, and how?
2) How much time will be involved?
3) How much money will it cost?
4) How much money will be saved?

A second test, the Significance Test, asked what impact will a decision have on Seymour Specialty Wire.

The Significance Test.
1) Will this decision change the basic nature of Seymour?
2) Will the decision effect the survival of Seymour?
3) Will this decision effect the company's profits?

The explanatory materials distributed by the company added yet another cautionary note. "Before taking action, look at all the options, double check the information, and, if there is a strong feeling among fellow workers that the proposed decision makes neither dollars nor sense, respect those feelings. Workers should take the decision to the next level of the program."

Education for Ownership and Participation

The relationship between democratic management and learning is an organic one. Democratic management facilitates adult learning and personal growth because all members have the right to know about the business, but more importantly, they have the *responsibility to know* how their company works and how it can work better. This is the only way that members of a democratically managed firm can make wise decisions about the operations of the firm. (2)

As educators and social critics have noted for years, how work is organized, its purposes, and who controls the way work is done and when dramatically affects any society's stock of knowledge, as well as the ways in which teaching and learning are carried on. In the labor-managed enterprise where the traditional relationships between capital and labor is upended, the ways and means of education are dramatically altered in ways about which, as yet, experts are uncertain. However, at the most rudimentary level, worker-ownership appears to democratize knowledge.

For example, where capital controls labor and the means of production, knowledge is monopolized for the profit of those who own or manage capital. Where the state controls the means of production, knowledge is gained for the benefit of those who govern, both the factory and the state. In contrast, when workers own the factory or their jobs, what they learn adds directly to their ability to control work and their own enterprises. Education becomes one means to achieve economic self-governance. If economic aspirations are to be fulfilled, then learning must be continuous.

The International Co-operative Alliance, a nongovernmental organization established in 1895 and which today represents 355 million members from 170 cooperative organizations in 70 nations, has noted that financially successful cooperatives "make provision for the education of their members, officers and employees and the general public, in the principles and techniques of cooperation, both economic and democratic."

More than a high-sounding principle could be at stake if worker-members omit from their participation plan a suitable educational program. The lack of education has been identified repeatedly as one of the single most frequent causes for cooperative business failure. (3) Conversely, effective workplace education has contributed directly to the success of the Basques. One key to the continued growth of their worker-owned cooperative enterprises is the extensive and integrated educational program they have developed to teach members the essential elements of participation and cooperation as they apply to the modern labor-managed enterprise. The Basque cooperatives allocate ten percent of the net profits to education.

Difficulties in Getting Started

169

Workers have "two barriers to cross if they want to create their own jobs," according to George Burt, chairman of Community Business Scotland: "(1) lack of knowledge, skill and experience; (2) a psychological reluctance—lack of confidence, assertiveness, etc." (4) One of the group of 30 workers who organized the Rainbow Workers Cooperative, the first worker-owned sewing co-op on the West Coast, likened their situation to that of slaves after the Emancipation, who felt both exhilaration and trepidation when there were no longer masters telling them what to do. (5)

The impact of these barriers on new worker-owners is severe, and the consequences can be divisive and destructive. At the Dungannon Sewing Co-op in Virginia, the insecurity accompanying the start-up and operations of a new business "created disruptive gossip and rumors both in the co-op and in the community, which many times lowered morale." The board of directors "lacked the experience and the self-confidence to make the long term decisions on a marketing strategy, and it frequently dissipated its energy with ad hoc issues involving emotionally charged personnel matters." Most of these workers lacked high school diplomas and practical business experience. Their situation indicated a need for education and training, including high school equivalency courses to contribute to self-assurance and prepare them for further business training. (6)

Developing an Educational Plan

How can a suitable educational plan be devised to deal with the problems and issues faced by worker-owners? What kind of education is needed? How should it be organized and delivered, and by whom? Any work experience can be categorized, and most have been over the years. Once categorized it can be taught. Until the idea of worker-ownership came along, however, the assumption had been that owners of capital and their hired managers controlled how work was to be categorized, administered, and consequently, what is taught. When labor owns the workplace, that historic assumption is discarded. To be consistent with the open, voluntary concepts of the labor-managed cooperative, worker-members must insure that any education or training program derives from their collective interests and needs, and that they collaborate with competent teachers in carrying the task of learning forward.

The specific characteristics of such an educational plan will vary from firm to firm, but, in general, will include vocational, performance, political, and cultural elements. Vocational learning will impart or enhance those skills needed to accomplish tasks at hand. Performance learning will improve the way the firm is managed. Political learning will nurture democratic decision-making and participation inside the firm, and outside in the surrounding community. Cultural learning will foster a labor-based vision of social change, again inside the firm and outside.

One conclusion drawn from the two-year experience of the Dungannon Sewing Co-op is that co-ops—especially "limited resource" co-ops in low income areas—need to affirm the development of people, the building of self-confidence and the achievement of personal competence as an integral part of their social goals. "This sort of growth comes not so much from a classroom setting as it does from lived experiences discussed with a group process." (7)

Through the concept of worker-ownership, individuals assume responsibility for their workplaces; through self-defined education, workers gain control over what is to be learned, when, and how. Workers, who recognize what they need to know in order to successfully mind their own business, may need to find teachers with skills in transferring knowledge to help fashion aims, methods, curriculum and a means of evaluation which fit specific needs. Often, however, as peers, they can teach each other.

One important factor influencing the types of educational

programs needed by a cooperative is the size and location of the community in which the business is located. Typically worker-owners living in large cities will feel less well-integrated into their cooperative. The Basque experience indicates that small communities reinforce cooperative solidarity by minimizing the number of reference groups to whose status individual worker-owners can compare themselves. A large city is composed of a greater number of such reference groups with different life-styles and standards of living, which are then reflected in a diverse commercial environment. This suggests a greater need for well-planned and effectively administered educational programs in worker-owned businesses located in urban centers to build and maintain the sense of community among the worker-owners. This is also necessary to minimize mobility and preserve the equity and organizational integrity of the cooperative business over time. (8)

171

Assessing Educational Needs and Interests

A first step toward assessing the educational interests and needs of worker-owners or for selecting appropriate educational suppliers, teachers, and techniques is to conduct a survey of the worker-members. This can be done by using a questionnaire like the one in Appendix G. Devised and field tested by one of the authors in collaboration with the Guilford College Democratic Management Program, the educational needs assessment rests on three assumptions:

1) The opportunity to learn any job in the cooperative is open to any member regardless of race, creed, sex, age, national origin, political beliefs, or educational attainment level.

2) That learning occurs through work itself, from informal dialogue, or formally through organized activities, and that all members have the responsibility to use both informal and formal learning in fashioning the firm's educational program and policies.

3) The aim of education in a labor-managed enterprise is to increase the abilities and skills of all members to control corporate decisions, resources, policies and results.

Once the educational needs survey has been completed by all worker-members, the results can easily be tabulated to reveal how much time could be devoted to what subjects. By using this tool before starting to look for educational providers or teachers, worker-members can gauge who and what might best serve their educational goals.

APPENDICES

Appendix A

PREPARING IN ADVANCE OF A CLOSURE

Checklist of Early Warning Signs of Plant Closings

Even before a plant closure is announced, unions, employees and the community can be prepared for the possible need to act quickly to save jobs. For example, in the case of the O & O buyouts in Philadelphia, the United Food and Commercial Workers Union (UFCW) and Philadelphia Association of Cooperative Enterprise (PACE) prepared several months before the closure announcement by developing a buyout plan for the ailing supermarkets. Developing early warning systems in the community and plant, negotiating collective bargaining protections and monitoring investment can enable the rapid response that is necessary should a plant close. The following checklist suggests issues that can be addressed prior to announcement of a plant closure. Early preparation increases likelihood of developing an appropriate response to threatened job loss.

The following questions often can be answered by employees. Early warning systems permit employees and the community to plan for potential closures.

	Yes	*No*
Is the cost of raw materials, energy, packaging, and trans-portation greater in your region than in other regions where your company has plants?	☐	☐

	Yes	No
Is your plant a considerable distance form sources of raw materials, energy, or from consumer markets?	☐	☐
If your plant is owned by a larger parent company, does your plant or division fall below the company's target profit rate ("hurdle rate")?	☐	☐
Have there been few significant new investments at your plant in recent years?	☐	☐
Has the company stopped doing maintenance tasks? Have maintenance schedules changed?	☐	☐
Has there been a noticeable depletion and non-replacement of parts inventories?	☐	☐
Have there been significant decreases in new or replacement parts inventories?	☐	☐
Has an innovative competitor developed a product that makes the one you make less marketable?	☐	☐
Has your company's share of the market declined?	☐	☐
Has your company lagged behind in developing new products which could be produced at your plant?	☐	☐
Has the range of products produced by your company contracted?	☐	☐
Has your plant or company been bought out by a conglomerate or merged with another corporation?	☐	☐

	Yes	*No*
If it has, has the parent company expanded into new or different activities or product lines where your plant doesn't seem to fit?	☐	☐
Is the new management demanding every possible cost cut?	☐	☐
Have executives in your company recently begun complaining about a "bad business climate," high taxes, or excessive government regulations?	☐	☐
Is the production technology used at your plant being replaced by more up-to-date methods in other companies, regions, or countries?	☐	☐
Alternatively, is new technology going to be introduced in your plant which could lead to significant job losses?	☐	☐
Has your company opened a new plant in a low-wage state or country which makes the same product you do?	☐	☐
Has the company purchased land in a low-wage area suitable for industrial development?	☐	☐
Has your company hired a "union busting" consultant or law firm to represent it in dealing with the union?	☐	☐
Has management been complaining about high wages and benefits or "restrictive" union work rules?	☐	☐
Has management been collecting information which could be used in shifting production to another site?	☐	☐

177

	Yes	No
Has anyone noted any correspondence or visitors from consultant firms which specialize in corporate relocations?	☐	☐
Is there excess capacity in your industry/company/plant? Are plants in your industry/company running at less than 85% of their capacity?	☐	☐
Has employment at your plant decreased over the past year? Five years? Ten years?	☐	☐
Are there less people working at your craft or job description?	☐	☐
Has the workforce gradually become older since you began working at the plant?	☐	☐
Has the company moved any equipment or skilled workers from your plant to other plants?	☐	☐

178

Appendix B

A Preliminary Feasibility Assessment for a Worker Buyout: Screening Out Inappropriate Cases

Adapted from Julia Parzen, Catherine Squire, and Michael Kieschnick, **Buyout: A Guide For Workers Facing Plant Closings,** *Sacramento: Department of Economic and Business Development, State of California, Second Printing, September 1983, pp 27-35.*

Because the preliminary feasibility study's purpose is to be quick and inexpensive, it is only a means of identifying those cases where an employee buyout is very inappropriate (or appropriate). The preliminary feasibility study should take less than a month to complete and cost very little (usually less than $5,000). If funding is not easily available, it can be prepared by qualified volunteers from community or government offices (such as the State Office of Economic Development) on a pro bono basis by university business school faculty and students, consulting firms, or by public interest or non-profit groups with low overhead. Finally, the preliminary feasibility study should employ readily available sources of data that answer the specific questions described in the following sections:

A) *Are the present owners amenable to an employee buyout?*

	Yes	No
1) Is there language in your union agreement giving you first option to buy? (See Union Agreement)	☐	☐
2) Is the standard language in union agreements giving management exclusive rights to manage and ter-		

179

minate employees removed from your
agreement? (See Agreement) ☐ ☐

3) Has management been publicly willing to entertain an offer from
employees or at least been neutral
about such an offer? (Meet with
management, read press clippings) ☐ ☐

4) Is management willing to contribute
a nominal sum toward the feasibility
study or to consider a decision to
dedicate land, structures or equipment to the employees currently or
in the future? (Meet with
management) ☐ ☐

180

If the answer to the first question is yes, then lack of support by management should not be a problem. If it is no, then
the answers to the other three questions are more critical.
If the answers to questions 2 through 4 are also no, then
management will probably be unwilling to negotiate a buyout
with employees. As a result, a successful buyout is unlikely,
and will be possible only if there is both significant media
and public support, and a feasibility assessment indicating
very clear benefits to employees and investors.

B) *Is your firm organized in such a way that a smooth transition to employee-ownership is feasible?*

Yes *No*

1) Do you have an experienced manager,
or group of experienced managers,
who are willing to manage your
employee owned firm? ☐ ☐

2) Do the skills of your workforce meet
the needs of your employee owned
firm? ☐ ☐

3) Does your plant have on-site personnel, marketing, finance, and general
administration functions? ☐ ☐

4) Is your plant operated as a profit center? (Is it required to document both its revenues and costs?) ☐ ☐

5) Does your plant produce its products without receiving inputs from other management-owned plants or transferring outputs to other management owned plants for finishing? ☐ ☐

All of the above questions indicate whether a smooth transition is possible. The commitment of skilled top and middle managers is crucial. Nevertheless, if potential managers exist, expert economic and legal advice by an outside consultant can substitute up to the point that a final decision to proceed is made. If the answer to one or more of questions 2 through 5 is no, then it is important that there be time to reorganize the firm before it closes and that there be committed management. If there are only a few months available (not enough time to reorganize), then an employee buyout is only advisable if plant market factors are both very positive, improving the chances of continued interest once the plant closes.

C) *Are the products produced at your plant facing declining, stable or growing markets?*

To answer this question in the preliminary feasibility analysis, you should rely on published analyses and industry experts. Prime sources of data on your industry available in libraries (such as public business libraries, university libraries, or major bank libraries) or from your company are as follows:

☐ **Standard & Poor's** Industry Surveys

☐ **Value Line Investment Survey**

☐ Department of Commerce's **U.S. Industrial Outlook** (Annual)

☐ **Moody's Industrial Manual** for your corporation or other firms in your industry (Annual)

☐ **Walker's Manual of Western Corporations**

☐ Dun & Bradstreet, Inc., **Key Business Ratios**

☐ 10k report of your corporation (look at statement of President)

☐ Market studies prepared for your corporation

☐ Trade journal articles on your industry located through the **Business Periodical Guide** and **F&S Guide**

Industry experts whose opinions you should seek out include the following:

☐ The analyst for the appropriate industry from the Bureau of Industrial Economics, Department of Commerce, Washington, D.C.

☐ The trade association staff for your industry's trade association.

☐ Market analysts from market research firms or security analysts for your industry (ask reference librarian at a business library or get names from articles in trade journals).

☐ If possible, sales and production managers at your firm.

Using these data sources and others that become available, it should be possible to find sufficiently good answers for screening purposes to the following questions:

	Yes	*No*
1) Do industry sources anticipate stable or growing demand for your industry's products?	☐	☐
2) If there is a recession or slump in your industry, is it projected to end within 6 months to a year?	☐	☐
3) If there are new or existing products taking market share away from (replacing) your product:		

a) Can your plant possibly produce the competing product? ☐ ☐

b) Are there possible new markets or niches for your product? ☐ ☐

4) Are other producers of your product maintaining or increasing capacity or production levels? ☐ ☐

5) Are foreign firms or plants expected to maintain constant or declining share of U.S. sales over the next few years? ☐ ☐

6) If your product is sold to other industries (rather than consumers), do industry sources indicate strong demand for these industries' products? ☐ ☐

183

7) If there are obvious alternative uses for your plant, are the answers to the above questions for the alternative uses or products affirmative? ☐ ☐

8) According to industry analysts and plant managers, how does your product compare to that of other domestic and foreign producers:

a) Average quality equal or better ☐ ☐

b) Average prices equal or lower ☐ ☐

c) Perception by customers equal or better. ☐ ☐

It is important that most of the eight screening questions be answered "yes". It is imperative that at least the answers to 1, 2, 3 and 8 be positive for your product or for alternative products.

D) *Is it possible for your plant to be an efficient producer in your industry?*

To answer the following questions, historical data will be needed on your plant. For part (1) of D in particular, it may be difficult to obtain the necessary data. Thus, if you cannot obtain data on your plant's current profitability, skip part (1) and go directly to part (2).

1) How does the profitability of your plant of firm compare with other firms in your industry?

   a) Data needs include one to three years of historical data for your facility on profits before taxes, sales revenue, net worth, and Robert Morris industry-wide financial data (for the SIC code that most closely corresponds to your firm*) on profit/sales and profit before taxes/tangible net worth.

   b) Procedures for performing the comparison are provided in worksheets 1 and 2.

	Yes	No
c) Criteria for judging the results are as follows: Has your average profit/sales ratio for the last three years been positive? (See line 4 of worksheet 1).	☐	☐
Is the average profits/sales ratio for your firm less than 50 percent of the industry average? (Your firm may not be competitive in your industry.)	☐	☐
Is the average profit before taxes/tangible net worth ratio for your firm less than the industry average for the lower quartile? (Your firm may not be competitive in your industry.)	☐	☐

Exhibit 1

ROBERT MORRIS DATA

	Current Data					Comparative Historical Data		
	0-25M 2 %	150M-1MM 9 %	1-10MM 21 %	10-50MM 6 %	ALL 38 %	6/78-1/77 All 36 %	6/77-1/78 All 38 %	6/78-1/79 All 45 %
INCOME DATA								
Net Sales			100.0		100.0	100.0	100.0	100.0
Cost of Sales			72.1		68.5	63.7	65.1	66.5
Gross Profit			27.9		33.5	36.3	34.9	33.5
Operating Expenses			22.7		28.3	29.3	28.8	28.3
Operating Profit			5.3		5.2	7.0	6.2	5.2
Other Expenses			5.0		6.0	9.0	5.0	5.0
Profit Before Taxes			4.8		4.6	6.1	5.7	4.6
% Profit Before Taxes/			35.2		22.0	38.7	37.2	35.2
Tangible Net Worth			20.9		22.0	24.5	27.5	22.0
Profit Before Taxes			9.0		9.0	10.9	9.9	9.0

*The SIC code for your firm can be determined from descriptions in Standard Industrial Classification Manual, 1972, available at any business-oriented library. Examples of the two rations from Robert Morris that are needed are indicated with arrows in Exhibit 1.

Worksheet 1

PROFIT BEFORE TAXES/SALES RATIO YOUR FIRM

($s in 000's)   *Years*

	19__	19__	19__
1) Total Sales Revenue	$ ☐	☐	☐
2) Profit before Taxes	$ ☐	☐	☐
3) Profit/Sales Ratio: Line (2) / Line (1) multiplied by 100	$ ☐	☐	☐
4) Average of the three years for firm	$ ☐	☐	☐
5) Industry Average Profit/Sales Ratio	$ ☐	☐	☐
6) Average of the three years for the industry	$ ☐	☐	☐
7) 50% of the Industry Average	$ ☐	☐	☐

Explanation for Worksheet One

Line 1) Total sales from top line of the firm's income statement for the last three years years.

Line 2) Profit before taxes located on the firm's income statement for last three years.

Line 3) Line (2) divided by Line (1) multiplied by 100.

Line 4) Sum of Line (3) divided by 3.

Line 5) Industry Average Profit/Sales Ratio from Robert Morris data for same three years.

Line 6) Sum of Line (5) divided by 3.

Line 7) One half of Line (6).

Worksheet 2

PROFIT BEFORE TAXES/TANGIBLE NET WORTH RATIO
YOUR FIRM

($s in 000's)   *Years*

	19__	19__	19__
1) Stockholder's Equity	$		
2) Intangible Assets	$		
3) Tangible Net Worth: Line (1) minus Line (2)	$		
4) Profit before taxes	$		
5) Profit before taxes/ tangible net worth: Line (4) / Line (3) x 100	$		
6) Average of three years for firm	$		
7) Industry Average Ratio (lower quartile)	$		
8) Average of three years for the industry	$		

187

Explanation for Worksheet Two

Line1)   Stockholder's equity from the firm's balance sheet for
          last three years; include common stock plus paid-in
          surplus and retained earnings and subtract the value of
          any treasury stock.
Line 2)   Sum of all intangible assets shown on balance sheet for
          last three years such as "goodwill" and "cost in excess
          of net assets of acquired companies."
Line 3)   Line (1) minus Line (2).
Line 4)   Profit before taxes located on the firm's income
          statement for last three years.
Line 5)   Line (4) divided by Line (3) multiplied by 100.
Line 6)   Sum of Line (5) divided by 3.
Line 7)   Industry Profit before taxes/tangible net worth ratio for
          the lower quartile of firms from Robert Morris data for
          same three years. This figure should be taken from the
          bottom row of figures because this row represents the
          lower quartile.
Line 8)   Sum of Line (7) divided by 3.

2) *Has your plant been maintained and can major capital expenditures be avoided?*

    a) Data needs include plant maintenance records, plant capital spending budget, industry data on technologies employed and new facilities built, and data on profit after tax and depreciation expenses. If these data are not available, use your best judgement.

    b) Criteria for evaluating these data are as follows:

	Yes	*No*
☐ If your plant and equipment are older than the average for the industry, have they been maintained?	☐	☐
☐ Have all major capital expenditures that are necessary to maintain the facility, or meet government regulations (especially pollution) been made?	☐	☐
☐ Does your plant have processes and technologies at least as current as those used by the majority of your industry (based upon your market research)?	☐	☐
☐ *If your plant has not been maintained or has not met government regulations, would the cost be reasonable to make necessary expenditures? A benchmark is whether the cost crudely estimated to get your facility in good condition would be less than six times your plant's average cash flow (profit after tax plus depreciation expenses) for the last three years.	☐	☐
☐ *If your plant's processes and technologies are not current (based upon your market research), would the cost be within reason to make		

necessary expenditures? A benchmark is whether the cost crudely
estimated to make required main-
tainance on your facility and obtain
the new technologies would be less
than six times your plant's average
cash flow (profit after tax plus
depreciation expenses) for the last
three years.   ☐   ☐

* *Skip this question if data on the profitability of your plant
is not available. If these data are available, add together profit
plus depreciation expense for last three years and divide by
three. Then multiply the result by six. The capital cost of new
equipment should be smaller than this result.*

If the answers to the first three questions above are yes, then
your plant is in good condition and up to date. If the answers
are no, then you need to consider how costly it will be to
bring it up to date. A benchmark is provided in the fourth
and fifth questions. If the answers to all five questions are
no, then a successful buyout is unlikely because of poor plant
maintenance combined with high capital costs. A minimal
requirement is that either the plant is adequately maintained
or that costs of achieving adequate maintenance are not
exorbitant.

E) *Summary of the results of the preliminary feasibility
    study*

At the completion of the preliminary feasibility study,
the following questions should have been posed and
answered:

	Yes	*No*
☐ Is there enough time before the closure? (See Factors for Success)	☐	☐
☐ Are the present owners amenable to an employee buyout? (See Section A)	☐	☐
☐ Is your firm organized in such a way that a smooth transition to employee-ownership is feasible? (See Section B)	☐	☐

☐ Are the products produced at your plant facing stable or growing markets? (See Section C) ☐ ☐

☐ Is it possible for your plant to be an efficient producer in your industry? (See Section D) ☐ ☐

In an optimal buyout situation all of the answers will be yes. This will rarely be the case. In most cases, the most important questions are the last three. While there will often be special circumstances beyond the scope of this manual, in general, affirmative responses to the last three questions and, in particular, those about efficiency of production and market for the product, are crucial.

190

Appendix C

THE FORMAL FEASIBILITY STUDY FOR A WORKER BUYOUT: WHO TO DO IT, HOW TO PAY FOR IT, AND WHAT BELONGS IN IT

Adapted from Julia Parzen, Catherine Squire, and Michael Kieschnick, **Buyout: A Guide For Workers Facing Plant Closings,** *Sacramento: Department of Economic and Business Development, State of California, Second Printing, September 1983, pp 27-35.*

If the preliminary feasibility study indicates that an employee buyout is potentially feasible, a full-scale feasibility study is needed. The purpose of the feasibility study is to provide a comprehensive assessment of risks and opportunities for the employee-owned firm.

Several experts are needed to perform the study and guide the necessary follow-up:

☐ Financial consultants to do the study;

☐ ESOP or co-op experts to structure the buyout; and

☐ Lawyers to negotiate the purchase of facilities.

☐ Teachers to help set up educational program.

In addition, in some cases a real estate appraiser will also be needed. The costs of obtaining these experts and the way in which their services will be used is described in the following paragraphs.

Costs That Will be Incurred and How to Finance Them

The cost of the feasibility study will depend upon the specific case, but some estimated costs as of 1985 are provided in Table 1. This table assumes no free services or below market cost services.

The feasibility study and follow-up will cost at least $20,000 and may cost more than $100,000.

Table 1

COST OF FEASIBILITY STUDY

For cost analysis using available data and review of public market research			$ 20,000
If market research is required	+$20,000	=	$ 40,000
If must generate new cost data because of anticipated changes in products and markets	+$20,000	=	$ 60,000
If must appraise assets	+$15,000	=	$ 75,000
If need lawyer and Coop/ESOP expert	+$40,000	=	$115,000

Costs can be minimized by seeking out consultants with low overhead and firms willing to do pro bono work. It can also be done by using consultants who have a good reputation, but do not have a well-known reputation. These consultants can be backed up with an oversight committee. This committee should include local bank officials, co-op/ESOP experts, a law firm, city officials, union representatives and management consultants.

There are a number of sources of financing for the feasibility study. The main ones are described below.

1) Raise money from union members—it is a good idea to request at least a small contribution as a sign of commitment—and from existing owners.

2) Obtain a grant from federal agencies such as the Economic Development Administration—while this approach is time-consuming, it worked for the U.S. Steel Youngstown employees who received a grant to hire a consultant.

3) Obtain technical assistance grants from State agencies—the State of California approved a grant to help General Electric workers in Ontario perform a feasibility study.

4) Local economic development department grants.

5) Local benefactors, perhaps located through the mayor's office.

6) Foundations and churches.

7) Making use of pro bono work by business schools, firms and universities.

How to Find and Choose the Consultants

The most likely sources of consultant support for the feasibility study are management consulting firms, other financial consulting firms, the Industrial Cooperative Association and other non-profit groups specializing in worker-ownership, and university business schools (for both faculty and students).

Finding appropriate people can be difficult, but there are several good starting points. You can ask (1) state economic research offices that have contact with economists and business analysts or state departments that service your industry (Department of Forestry, Energy Commission, etc.), (2) Chambers of Commerce or Industry Trade Associations, whose members may have used business consultants, (3) university MBA programs where you can ask the dean of students whether students undertake business consulting projects and (4) department heads of university marketing, finance, and business policy departments who may know the faculty who do this kind of work. In an attachment there is a list of resources for employee ownership that offers advice on sources of assistance (there is also a list of guidebooks, etc.).

Once you have found one or more likely individuals or groups, there are several questions that you should ask them. These are listed in Table 2.

The Feasibility Study: Content and Interpretation

The purpose of the following discussion is not to describe how to do the feasibility study. The specific steps vary significantly from case to case, and the employees certainly don't need to be able to perform the analyses. Nevertheless, they do need to be concerned about whether the feasibility study deals with the relevant issues, and they need to know how to interpret the results. There are two basic parts to a feasibility study:

1) Market Factors—demand for the product.

2) Plant Factors—viability of the plant with a small investment.

Table 2
_____

WHAT TO LOOK FOR IN POTENTIAL CONSULTANTS

1) Have they done other cost analyses of plants?
2) Have they done any market studies?
3) Have they done financial modeling or prepared business plans?
4) Have they had other business clients?
5) Have they done feasibility studies for plant buyouts or divestitures?
6) Do they have backgrounds with extensive business/finance experience?
7) What are the names of some of their clients, and can you call them to get their opinion of the individuals?
8) Is overhead less than 100% of their hourly cost?
9) Can they get the study done within a few months (depending on your time pressures)?
10) Are they willing to give caveated opinions about issues for which all the data they would like is not available?

While a related area is financing, whether financing is obtainable will depend on the market and plant factors. Thus, financing is discussed separately in a final section.

Relevant Issues to Analyze in Feasibility Study

The following sections describe the relevant points that the consultant should investigate and the results that employees should seek. It may be desirable to have a contract with a consultant that requires the following analyses:

A) *Market Factors*

1) **Future Market for Each Product Produced.**

☐ Short-term and long-term demand outlook.

☐ New uses for your products.

☐ New substitutes for your products.

☐ New potentially profitable product lines.

☐ New competition from abroad.

☐ If your product is an input for another product, short-term and long-term outlook for industry using your product.

☐ Your market share by product line.

☐ Shifts in your market share.

☐ If market changing, niches for your product.

Results sought: Whether you can expect continued demand for your products and, if so, approximately how many units can you expect to sell.

2) Concentration/Competition in the Industry.

☐ Type of market (local, regional or national).

☐ Number or changes in number (new plants, plant closures) of firms in market.

☐ Names of dominant producers and estimates of their market shares.

☐ Changes in imports.

☐ New production technologies; whether your plant has them and their importance.

☐ Integration of your facility relative to competitors.

☐ Distance from markets relative to competitors.

Results sought: Whether your firm has any unique advantages or disadvantages relative to competitors.

3) Feasibility of Competition By a New Entity.

i) Basis of competition for customers in your industry

☐ Importance of brand name.

☐ Number of brands.

☐ Homogeneity of product.

☐ Effectiveness of price cutting.

☐ Whether existing firm is major brand.

☐ How existing firm has competed.

Results sought: Whether the employee-owned firm will be able to compete for customers.

ii) Normal Industry Distribution Channels.

☐ Do most firms in industry use factory direct sales, distributors or manufacturers' representatives?.

☐ Channels existing management has used.

☐ What distribution facilities (ex: warehouses) will the employee owned firm need, and are they available?

☐ Can the firm keep its existing distribution channels and contacts? If not, are there channels it could easily adopt?

☐ Will the firm need to obtain a large new sales force?

☐ Are customers willing to purchase goods from the new employee-owned firm?

☐ Are any large customers willing to provide letters of intent to purchase from the new firm?

Results sought: Whether there is a means of distribution available to the employee-owned firm that will not require a complex, new network.

iii) Sources of Inputs at Competitive Prices.

☐ Current suppliers of inputs (raw materials, etc.).

☐ Potential new sources of inputs.

☐ Do current suppliers serve other facilities owned by your corporation?

☐ Will you be able to keep suppliers?

☐ Will the employee-owned firm purchase a sufficient amount of inputs to command competitive prices?

☐ Are there any very large suppliers of inputs?

☐ Are any large suppliers willing to provide letters of intent to sell to the new facility?

Results sought: Whether the employee-owned facility can expect to have reliable sources of supply at a competitive price.

B) *Plant Factors*

1) **Physical Condition of Plant and Equipment.**

☐ Historic maintenance schedule and changes in maintenance.

☐ Historic reinvestment plan and changes in plan.

☐ Average age of major capital equipment and remaining useful life of equipment.

☐ Age of facility relative to average age for other plants owned by parent firm and by other firms.

☐ Need for major capital expenditures for maintenance, modernization, and/or regulation compliance.

☐ Estimated value of plant and equipment to be purchased.*

197

* A well-qualified appraiser of assets may be needed for this analysis. The appraisal will cover land, buildings, inventory, and equipment that will be useful for the new company. The business is worth the market value of its assets that are necessary to conduct business plus a premium if the business is especially profitable or minus a discount if it is unprofitable.

Results sought: Whether the facility has been maintained enough to allow continued productive use. Whether large capital expenditures can be avoided, at least in the first three to five years. Which of the facilities for sale are needed by the employee-owned firm, and their maximum value to the new firm.

2) **Organizational Structure: Leadership, Functions and Facilities.**

☐ Is facility a profit center or a cost center?

☐ Functions that would be included in purchase of facility, including personnel, marketing, sales, finance and general management.

☐ Personnel needed to fill gaps in functions.

☐ Are the facilities at the plant complete or would additional facilities be required, such as warehouses?

☐ Ability to keep top and middle management on board or attract new experienced management.

☐ Does the existing work force have the necessary skills to operate the employee-owned facility? Is it willing to do so?

☐ Products or services transferred from other plants.

☐ Products transferred to other plants.

Results sought: Whether the employee-owned firm can have a smooth transition. This is determined by whether it can function as an independent facility without needing to be reorganized; whether it can be separated from current ownership without losing key suppliers or markets, and whether it can depend on having a committed management to lead it.

3) **Historical viability of the plant.**

a) Economics of the plant/company

i) Cost structure for last three to five years: for each product line, including costs of materials, labor, energy, maintenance, allocated overhead and number of units of output.

☐ Whether any unit costs are assessed at transfer prices (if so, revalue them to market prices).

☐ Changes over time in the shares of costs and reasons.

☐ Changes over time in the usage of any input and reasons.

☐ Historical capacity utilization and efficient utilization levels.

ii) Operating margins, computed using historical prices and costs.

☐ Trend in prices and reasons.

☐ Product lines with largest margins.

☐ Adjustments to mix that would increase plant margins.

iii) Break-Even Volume.

☐ Minimum volume of output at which revenues equal costs.

☐ Volume of output that maximizes profit margin.

☐ Implications of optimal output for necessary changes in current output and employment for employee-owned firm.

☐ Feasibility of being able to sell optimal output given market projections about size of total market.

iv) Profitability, computed based upon earnings data for facility for last five years or by subtracting from operating margins, unallocated fixed costs, estimated corporate charges, current interest costs and depreciation expenses.

☐ Trends in profitability.

☐ How changes in mix identified above would change profits.

v) Cash flow, for the last five years using the data above on profits (after tax computations), adding back depreciation expenses, and subtracting out changes in working capital, debt repayment and capital expenditures.

☐ Whether cash flow provided by operations has been

199

sufficient to support necessary expenditures (compare profit plus depreciation to capital expenditures and debt repayment).

☐ If there are costs hanging over the plant for deferred maintenance, deferred replacement or regulatory compliance, has plant cash flow been sufficient to finance them? If not, how much outside capital would be needed to finance them?

☐ If the prospective buyout has been an independent business, additions to debt or equity capital in the last five years.

☐ Whether any of the facility's assets are secured by debt.

Results sought: Whether the facility historically has shown economic viability, including whether it has been able to control its costs and maintain profit margins; whether it has operated at optimal levels of output and with an optimal mix of its products; whether the new worker-owned firm could expect a market for the volume of output at which it breaks even and for the volume of output at which it maximizes profits, whether it has been able to finance through internal cash flow its own working capital and at least some of its other capital needs; and whether it has been able to raise any outside capital in the past. For all of the above, what were the reasons why the firm did or did not achieve these profit, output, and financing aims?

b) Plant strengths and weaknesses (based upon the previous market and cost analyses).

☐ Reputation of the facility, including whether it has long-term suppliers and customers and their statisfaction with the facility.

☐ Willingness of suppliers and customers to deal with the new firm.

☐ Quality or efficiency as a producer relative to other producers.

☐ Low or high cost producer in its industry for each product.

☐ Unique product offerings.

☐ Other strengths and weaknesses.

Results sought: Whether the facility has the good will of its suppliers and customers; whether these suppliers and customers will deal with the new firm; and whether its competitiveness with other facilities is enhanced or reduced due to specific strengths or weaknesses.

c) Feasibility of Improving Operating Margins, Profitability, and Cash Flow.

i) Ability to Control Costs.

☐ Cost reductions that could be made and their effect on profit margins; in particular, feasibility of reducing overhead, improving inventory control, reducing spoilage and waste, reducing absenteeism, finding cheaper suppliers, and willingness of employees to trade off ownership for wage reductions (level of deferrals they are willing to consider); generally it is not advisable to trade the pension plan for ownership of the company.

201

ii) Ability to Change Mix and Level of Output.

☐ Change in mix that would raise overall profits.

☐ Changes in output that are within the limits of the market that would raise overall profits.

iii) Ability to Raise Prices.

Based upon market study, is it possible to raise prices and roughly by how much?.

iv) Ability to Introduce New Products.

☐ What are compatible new products (see market study)?.

☐ Operating margins on these products versus existing products.

Results sought: Whether profits can be increased by moderate cost reductions, changes in mix, changes in level of output, the introduction of new products, or price increases.

d) How Economics Would Change for the Employee-Owned Facility.

i) Analyze the effect on profitability and cash flow of:

☐ The feasible changes in costs, prices, product mix and products investigated above.

☐ Different levels of capacity utilization.

☐ Required replacement of management staff and/or corporate functions.

☐ Training costs for new employees.

☐ Lower wages.

☐ Initiating new sources of supply and/or customers.

☐ Making deferred replacement, maintenance, and modernization expenditures.

ii) Compute estimate of *future* operating margins, profits and streams of cash flows for three years, taking into account the effects of the changes in (i) immediately above.

iii) Compute working capital needs. If there is no good basis to estimate working capital needs, an approximation would be total operating expenses for four months (including rent, inventory, wages, leasehold improvements and known interest costs) plus reserve to carry accounts receivable plus petty cash.

iv) Estimate costs of purchasing necessary facilities from existing owners or others (see Plant Factors). Also estimate financing costs based upon your expectations as to sources of financing and potential cost (see Financing Section).

v) Compare the estimated cash flows to the sum of the costs estimated in (iii) and (iv) using net present value analysis.* This step will need to be repeated once financing costs are more exactly estimated.

* Net present value analysis is a technique that allows you to compare income you receive in the future to cash you pay out now to buy the plant. It takes into account the fact that both inflation and the ability to invest money now and earn a return, rather than spending it, reduce the value of income received in the future.

Results sought: Whether the employee-owned firm can achieve a rate of return high enough to maintain an efficient facility, pay back its lenders, and repay the employees for their investment.

Evaluating the Results of the Feasibility Study

Once the results of the feasibility study are obtained, the employees must decide whether to proceed with the proposed employee buyout. In those cases where the results concerning market factors, plant factors, and potential improvements in these factors are overwhelmingly negative or positive, the decision may be easy. Because this will generally not be the case, it will be necessary to weigh the results carefully, considering the difficulties posed by each problem. The following rules will be of some help in this task. Other sources of advice include the consultant that prepared the feasibility study and potential investors in the firm.

The questions in Table 3 below should be answered in the course of the feasibility study. For an employee buyout to be advisable, either:

1) The answers to all of the "market" and "plant" questions in Table 3 should be affirmative; or

2) The answers to all of the "market" questions in Table 3 should be affirmative and any answers to "plant" questions that are negative should be cancelled by positive options under "potential improvements."

Of course, there will be situations in which a decision is made to proceed when these preconditions are not met. The employees in these cases must present to investors and themselves convincing reasons why the new firm will succeed. The document used to convince investors to participate in the buyout is the business plan. This document, as well as financing options, is discussed in the last section on Financing a Worker Buyout.

Table 3

RELEVANT QUESTIONS IN BUYOUT DECISION

	Yes	No
Market Factors		
1) Can you expect continued demand for your products and, if so, approximately how many units can you expect to sell? Number ▭	☐	☐
2) Is it likely that your firm will be able to compete for customers?	☐	☐
3) Is there a means of distribution available to your firm that can be put into place in time to ensure uninterrupted distribution?	☐	☐
4) Can your firm expect to have reliable sources of supply at a competitive price?	☐	☐
Plant Factors		
1) Has the facility been maintained enough to allow continued productive use? Can large capital expenditures be avoided in the next few years?	☐	☐
2) Does your firm have or can it obtain necessary staff and facilities to function independently as soon as a transition is made to a worker-owned firm?	☐	☐
3) Can your firm retain current key suppliers and markets?	☐	☐
4) Does your firm have, and can it continue to keep, the good will of its suppliers and customers?	☐	☐
5) Does your firm have a committed management to lead it?	☐	☐
6) Has your firm historically earned a profits? If not, was it due to causes that can be reversed?	☐	☐
7) Would your firm break even given expected sales volume from the "Market Factors" section, question 1?	☐	☐

8) Can your firm expect to be able to finance its own working capital and some part of its other capital needs after one year of operation? ☐ ☐

Potential Improvements

1) If your firm historically has not earned a profit, can profits be improved through moderate cost reductions or price increases? ☐ ☐

2) Can profits be improved through changing levels of output, mix of products, or introduction of new products? ☐ ☐

3) Can profits be improved through taking better advantage of unique characteristics of your firm? ☐ ☐

4) Can your firm achieve a rate of return sufficient to maintain an efficient facility, repay its lenders and repay employees and investors for their investment? ☐ ☐

205

Appendix D

QUESTIONS AND ANSWERS COMPARING WORKER COOPERATIVES AND CONVENTIONAL CORPORATIONS

BY DAVID ELLERMAN AND PETER PITEGOFF

Introduction

Corporations in the United States are chartered by the states rather than by the federal government, and statutes that authorize corporations exist only at the state level. A corporation is incorporated in one state even though it may do business in many states. Most states authorize a variety of corporate entities, including business corporations, cooperatives, and non-profit corporations.

There are several ways a Mondragon/Industrial Cooperative Association (ICA) worker cooperative may be legally incorporated. One common procedure is to use specialized by-laws such as the ICA Model By-laws within the legal shell of a business corporation. Similarly, one can use special worker co-op by-laws within the legal shell of a generic cooperative, i.e. a corporate entity ordinarily used by farmers' co-ops or consumer co-ops. Thus the company is incorporated either under the normal business corporation statute of the state or under the general cooperative statute of the state. Then the specific by-laws internally restructure the company as a worker cooperative.

At present, five states (Massachusetts, Maine, Connecticut, Vermont, and New York) have enacted special statutes for worker cooperatives. In those states, an enterprise can incorporate directly as a worker co-op under one of these statutes. The worker cooperative corporation laws provide guidance and legal certainty for a corporate entity with worker co-op attributes, such as democratic control by worker-members, return to members based on labor ("patronage") rather than capital investment, and a specialized co-op capital structure of internal accounts. Since these statutes only specify the general characteristics of the worker co-op structure, specific by-laws are still needed to define many of the details of corporate structures, governance, and operation.

Instead of restricting attention to particular states, the generic model of a Mondragon/ICA worker cooperative is compared with a conventional business corporation. It abstracts the minor variations that one might find between the corporate laws of different states. Moreover, although the business corporation laws *and* the worker co-op laws allow for significant variations and hybrid stuctures, the following table will compare the conventional business corporation with the "pure" worker co-op.

1) *How is membership/ownership in the company determined?*

Worker Cooperative: The basic principle is that the membership of the co-op should be the permanent workforce of the firm. Employment in the co-op is a condition of membership so there are no absentee members. After a probationary period, all workers must be accepted into membership or be terminated. Thus, there can be no long-term non-member employees in a working cooperative. The rights of membership carry the obligation to pay a membership fee, often by payroll deductions, which is credited to the member's internal capital account. Voting is always based on the one-person/one-vote principle.

Conventional Corporation: The membership or ownership rights are transferable property rights. Owners are persons who have purchased shares. Many business corporations are "closely held," thus restricting the transfer of ownership to designated persons. Nonetheless, the norm (even in closely held corporations) is that ownership is based on capital investment, that the owner group includes persons who do not necessarily work in the enterprise, that different persons own different amounts of stock shares, and that different persons may have significantly different profit rights and voting power. Voting is based on the one-share/one-vote principle.

2) *Is the interest or capital dividend on the shareholders' capital limited by law?*

Worker Cooperative: Yes. A limitation on the members' return on their capital (as opposed to the labor or "patronage" return) is contained in the federal tax law for cooperatives (Subchapter T of the Internal Revenue Code). A similar limitation is contained in many state statutes. In theory, labor hires capital in a worker co-op so that any return to capital should resemble interest.

Conventional Corporation: No. Capital hires labor. Since equity capital has the residual claimant's role, there is no limitation on the return to capital in the form of capital dividends or capital gains. The return to debt capital would have to be interest-like since it is an expense deductible from taxable corporate income.

209

3) *Is there a limitation on shareholding?*

Worker Cooperative: The usual arrangement in worker cooperatives on the Mondragon/ICA model is for each member to have one and only one share which functions as a non-transferable membership certificate. Multiple shareholding would have no function since two or more membership certificates would confer no more rights than one certificate. The membership share can only be sold back to the cooperative. The members' capital stake in the co-op is not attached to the share but recorded in the members' internal capital account. A member is issued the membership share upon acceptance into membership and fulfillment of the obligations of membership (e.g., payment of the membership fee). Upon termination of work, the membership share is forfeited back to the firm, the member's capital account is closed at the end of the fiscal year, and the balance in the account is paid out over a period of years.

Conventional Corporation: No, except to the extent that owners of a closely held corporation adopt transfer restrictions that limit stock ownership to a defined group.

4) *How are profits allocated and distributed to the members/owners?*

Worker Cooperative: The balance sheet equity, or net worth, of a cooperative is split between the individual capital accounts of the members and one collective account. At the end of each fiscal year, the net income or profit is split in fixed proportions (e.g., 50%-50%) into individual and collective portions. After subtracting any corporate taxes, the remaining collective portion is credited to the collective account. The year's interest (if any) on the individual capital accounts is first subtracted from the individual portion and credited to the members' accounts. That is the return to their capital. The remaining individual portion of the net income is the return to their labor, their patronage dividend. Typically, the patronage allocations are retained in the firm for a certain time period (e.g., 5-7 years) and then paid out in cash. Thus, the patronage allocation is split between the individual account in accordance with each member's patronage (i.e., labor) during the fiscal year. The patronage allocation could be positive or negative, and accordingly it is credited or debited to the members' accounts.

Conventional Corporation: Profits accrue to shareholders in two ways, capital dividends and capital gains. Dividends are declared and paid out in cash (or sometimes stock) after each fiscal year. Earnings retained in the corporation will serve to increase the price of the shares so that value will accrue to the shareholders as capital gains when the shares are sold. Retained losses have the reverse effect.

5) *How does the member/owner ultimately convert the equity into cash?*

Worker Cooperative: The member's equity is the balance in his or her internal capital account. It is paid out in cash in two ways. Retained patronage dividends may be paid out in cash ("rolled over") after the fixed time period (e.g., 5-7 years). A substantial balance (at least the membership fee) should always be retained in a member's account during his or her membership to serve as a "damage deposit," a cushion to absorb retained patronage losses. Upon termination of membership, that remaining balance is paid out quickly or over a period of years depending on the cash position of the cooperative.

Conventional Corporation: By selling the shares, either to another investor or back to the corporation.

6) *What about corporate taxes?*

Worker Cooperative: In coventional corporations, the profits are taxed 'twice', once as corporate profits and once as individual income in the form of dividends or capital gains. Subchapter T of the Internal Revenue Code establishes a norm of single taxation for the patronage- related net income of all cooperatives, including worker co-ops. Any patronage dividends paid out as cash are deductible from taxable corporate income at that time and must be declared as taxable personal income to the individual member who receives the dividend. If the co-op allocates the patronage allocations on paper and retains the cash, then the co-op has the choice of either paying the corporate tax at that time or have the members recognize the non-cash allocation as taxable personal income. If the co-op pays the corporate tax at that time, the cash payment of the dividend to the member at a later date is deductible from corporate taxable income and then the individual pays the personal income tax. Any corporate income *not* allocated to members is subject to corporate tax as in a conventional business corporation.
Conventional Corporation: Standard corporate taxation applies to the net income. A wide range of tax deductions and credits are available to conventional business corporations and to worker co-ops to reduce the net taxable income amount. The shareholders pay the personal income tax on dividends and on the capital gains from the sale of corporate shares.

211

7) *What happens to equity upon dissolution?*

Worker Cooperative: If a worker cooperative is dissolved and the assets are sold, then the outstanding liabilities of the company would have first claim on the proceeds. Any remainder would be used to proportionally pay out the outstanding balances on individual capital accounts. In the unlikely event that all individual account balances could be cashed out fully, the remainder would belong to the collective accounts. There are at least two alternatives for the dispositon of the collective account upon dissolution. One alternative is to treat it like the equity of a non-profit corporation which must be distributed to some charitable cause. The other possibility is to proportionally distribute it to all past and present members in proportion to their patronage. The present members cannot appropriate the collective account as that would divest the past members of their contribution and could provide an untoward incentive to liquidate a profitable cooperative.

Conventional Corporation: After payment of all outstanding liabilities, any remaining proceeds from an asset sale would be proportionally distributed to the shareholders.

8) *How is the company governed?*

Worker Cooperative: The members vote annually, on a one-person/one-vote basis, to elect the board of directors. The board of directors appoints and oversees the chief executive officer and the other members of the management team. The board develops corporate policy, and the managers implement that policy on a day-to-day basis. Managers are not directly elected by the members, unless the company is so small that the board and the membership are essentially the same. Some committees might be committees of the board; some committees might be directly elected by the membership. The judiciary or grievance committee would typically be directly elected. The members would also directly elect officers of any union or legitimate-oppositional structure within the cooperative.

Conventional Corporation: The owners vote, on one-share/one-vote basis, at the annual meeting to elect the board of directors. The board of directors appoints a chief executive officer and other members of management.

9) *Who appoints and has the power to dismiss the chief executive?*

Worker Cooperative: The board of directors. The CEO is accountable to the board and the board is accountable to the membership. The membership could only dismiss the CEO by causing the board to effect the action.

Conventional Corporation: The board of directors.

10) *What are the powers of the members at general membership meetings?*

Worker Cooperative: There must be an annual membership meeting and special meetings of the general membership may be called (e.g., by 10% petition of the members). At the annual meeting, members elect directors to the board and vote on any by-law amendments or resolutions brought before the membership. Board terms may be staggered so only a portion of the directors would be elected each year. The judiciary or grievance committee members and the union or oppositional leaders may also be elected at the annual meetings. The by-laws would typically specify which by-law amendments could not be made by the board and are reserved for the general membership. In general, there is no legal limitation on the agenda topics which may be entertained at the annual or special meetings of the general membership. The by-laws may specify a range of decisions reserved to the members, and the law requires certain major decisions to be voted on by the members.

Conventional Corporation: The principal function of shareholders at the annual meeting is to elect the board of directors and to vote upon any resolutions placed before them. The law requires shareholder voting for certain major issues, such as dissolution, sale of the business, or merger with another corporation.

213

Appendix E

SOURCES OF INFORMATION AND ASSISTANCE

Productivity Centers

Georgia Productivity Center
Georgia Tech Engineering
Experimental Station
Atlanta, Georgia 30332
(404) 894-3404

Manufacturing Productivity Center
ITT Research Center,
10 W. 35th Street
Chicago, Illinois 60616
(312) 567-4800

Maryland Center for Productivity and Quality of Work Life
0121 Tydings Hall
University of Maryland
College Park, Maryland 20742
(301) 454-6688

Oklahoma Productivity Center
322 Engineering North
Oklahoma State University
Stillwater, Oklahoma 74078
(405) 624-6055

Ontario Quality of Working Life Centre
15th Floor, 400 University Avenue
Toronto, Ontario
Canada M7A 1T7
(416) 965-5958

Oregon Productivity Center
100 Merryfield Hall
Department of Industrial Engineering
Oregon State University
Corvallis, Oregon 97331
(503) 754-3249

Pennsylvania Technical Assistance Program
501F J.O. Keller Building
Pennsylvania State University
University Park, Pennsylvania 16803
(814) 865-0427

Productivity Center/ Industrial Engineering Dept.
309 Engineering Building
University of Arkansas
Fayetteville, Arkansas 72701
(501) 575-3156

Productivity Evaluation Center
Virginia Polytechnic Institute and State University
290 Whittemore Hall
Blacksburg, Virginia 24060
(703) 961-4568

Productivity Research and Extension Program
328 Riddick
P.O. Box 5511
North Carolina State University
Raleigh, North Carolina 27607
(919) 737-2362

Texas Center for Productivity and Quality of Working Life
College of Business Administration,
Texas Tech University
Lubbock, Texas 79409
(806) 742-1530

Utah Center for Productivity and Quality of Working Life
Utah State University
Logan, UT 84322-3505
(801) 750-2283

Land Grant College Extension Service Small Business Network

Alabama
Harry B. Strawn
Resource Economist, CES
Auburn University
Extension Cottage
Auburn University, AL 36849
(205) 826-4964

Arizona
David Barkley
University of Arizona
Agricultural Economics
Tucson, AZ 85721

Arkansas
Lee Jones
Cooperative Extension Service
P. O. Box 391
Little Rock, AR 72203
(501) 373-2500

California
George Goldman
University of California-Berkeley
Cooperative Extension Service
324 Giannini Hall
Berkeley, CA 94720
(415) 642-6461

Connecticut
Donald S. Francis
Extension CRD Agent
University of Connecticut
P.O. Box 327
Brooklyn, CT 06234-0327
(203) 774-9600

Delaware
Steve Hastings
University of Delaware
Agricultural Economics
Townsend Hall
Newark, DE 19717-1303
(302) 451-2511

Florida
John Gordon
Extension Economist,
Community Dev.
University of Florida
1167 McCarty Hall
Gainesville, FL 32611
(904) 392-1826

Georgia
Clarence Williams, Jr.
1890 Extension Specialist
Fort Valley State College
Box 4061
Fort Valley, GA 31030
(912) 825-6268

Idaho
Steve Smith
University of Idaho
Agricultural Economics
Moscow, ID 83843

Illinois
David Chicoine
University of Illinois
Agricultural Economics
Mumford Hall
Urbana, IL 61801

Indiana
Jane Weitz
Agricultural Economics
Purdue University
577 Krannert
West Lafayette, IN 47907

Iowa
Kenneth E. Stone
Iowa State University
460 Heady Hall
Ames, IA 50011

Kansas
David L. Darling, Jr.
Kansas State University
115 Umberger Hall
Manhattan, KS 66506
(913) 532-5840

Kentucky
Paul Teague
Community Development Specialist
University of Kentucky
203 Experiment Station Building
Lexington, KY 40546
(606) 257-7190

Louisiana
Sanford Dooley
Extension Economist
Louisiana State University
Room 202T, Knapp Hall
Baton Rouge, LA 70803
(504) 388-2266

Maine
Forest French
Extension Economist
University of Maine
Winslow Hall
Orono, ME 04469
(207) 581-3166

Maryland
Louis C. Thaxton
CRD Specialist
University of Maryland, East. Shore
Room 115 Rigg Hall
Princess Anne, MD 21853-1229
(301) 651-0279

Michigan
Adger Carroll
Agriculture and Natural Resources
Michigan State University
CRD Leader
East Lansing, MI 48824
(517) 355-0118

Minnesota
Jared M. Smally
Program Leader, CRD Program
University of Minnesota
1994 Buford Ave., 146 Classroom
St. Paul, MN 55108
(612) 373-3368

Mississippi
Tom Loftin
State Leader, Community Development
Mississippi State University CES
P.O. Box 5406
Mississippi State, MS 39762
(601) 325-3141

Missouri
Thomas A. Henderson
Director, Business & Industry
Missouri State University
801 Clark Hall
Columbia, MO 65211

Montana
Allen Bjergo
Montana State University
Cooperative Extension Service
238 Wilcos Lane
Corvallis, MT 59828
(406) 961-4538

Nebraska
Don Svobada
University of Nebraska
215 Ag Hall
Lincoln, NE 68583
(402) 472-2967

Nevada
Mike Mooney
University of Nevada at Reno
Agricultural Economics
Reno, NV 89557

New Hampshire
Craig Seymour
University of New Hampshire
McConnell Hall, Room 110, WSBB
Durham, NH 03824
(603) 862-1520

New Mexico
Bob Coppedge
New Mexico State University
Cooperative Extension Service
9301 Indian School Road N.E.
Suite 101
Albuquerque, NM 87112
(505) 292-0097

New York
Stephen D. Brown
Business Development
SUNY
512 Raymond Hall
Potsdam, NY 13676
(315) 267-2131

North Carolina
Bob Dahle
Extension Economist
North Carolina State University
311B Hillsboro Bldg.
Raleigh, NC 27695
(919) 737-2885

North Dakota
Dale Zetocha
Small Business Management Specialist
North Dakota State University
Agricultural Economics
Fargo, ND 58108

Ohio
George Morse
Resource Economist
Ohio State University
2120 Fyffe Road
Columbus, OH 43210
(614) 644-2701

Oklahoma
Gary Holland
Extension Associate
Oklahoma State University
459 Ag Hall
Stillwater, OK 74078
(405) 624-5132

Pennsylvania
William Gillis
Pennsylvania State University
1 Weaver Building
University Park, PA 16802
(865) 854-2561

Rhode Island
Tom Weaver
University of Rhode Island
Resource Economics
Lippitt Hall
Kingston, RI 02881
(401) 847-2470

217

South Carolina
Dan Smith
Project Leader
Clemson University
291 Barre Hall
Clemson, SC 29631
(803) 656-3460

South Dakota
Frank Ketland
South Dakota State University
Cooperative Extension Service
Brookings, SD 57006
(605) 688-4147

Tennessee
Ray Humberd
Professor and Leader, Ag Economics
University of Tennessee
P.O. Box 1071
Knoxville, TN 37901
(615) 947-7271

Texas
Dennis U. Fisher
Economist-Business Development
Texas A & M University
Agriculture Building, Room 12
College Station, TX 77843
(409) 845-4445

Utah
Marion T. Bentley
Utah State University
Department of Economics
UMC 35
Logan, UT 84322
(801) 750-2283

Vermont
Fred Rice
CRD Specialist
University of Vermont, CES
4A Laurette Drive
Burlington, VT 05405

Virginia
J. Douglas McAlister
Director, CRD Programs
Virginia Tech. & State University
233 Smyth hall
Blacksburg, VA 24060
(703) 961-6921

Washington
Garry Smith
Washington State University
Agricultural Economics
Pullman, WA 99164

West Virginia
Robert Moore
West Virginia University
Knapp Hall
Morgantown, WV 26506
(304) 293-5691

Wisconsin
Ayse Somerson
State Program Leader, C&NR
University of Wisconsin
432 N. Lake St., 637 Extension Bldg.
Madison, WI 53706
(608) 263-9260

Innovation Centers

Utah Innovation Center
419 Wakara Way
Suite 206
Salt Lake City, UT 84108
(801) 584-2500

Utah Innovation Center
500 East 1800 North
Logan, UT 84322
(801) 750-2840

Tennessee Innovation Center
P.O. Box 607
Oak Ridge, TN 37830
(615) 576-3436

Small Business Administration Regional Offices

Federal Building and U.S. Courthouse
P.O. Box 36044
San Francisco, CA 94102
(415) 556-7487

Executive Tower Building,
22d Floor
Denver, CO 80202
(303) 837-5763

5 Peachtree Street, NE
5th Floor
Atlanta, GA 30367
(404) 881-4943

838 E. M. Dirksen Federal Building
Chicago, IL 60604
(312) 353-0355

Old Federal Office Building
23d Floor
911 Walnut Street
Kansas City, MO 64106
(816) 374-5288

60 Batterymarch, 10th Floor
Boston, MA 02110
(617) 223-6660

3214 Federal Building
New York, NY 10278
(212) 264-1450

231 St. Asaphs Road, Room 646
Bata Cynwyd, PA 19004
(215) 596-5901

1720 Regal Row, Room 230
Dallas, TX 75235
(214) 767-7643

Dexter Horton Building, 5th Floor
Seattle, WA 98104
(206) 442-567

219

Small Business Development Centers

SBDC Director
University of Alabama in Birmingham
School of Business
1000 South 12th Street, Suite F
Birmingham, AL 35294
(205) 934-7260

SBDC Director
University of Arkansas
1015 West Second Street
Little Rock, AR 72201
(501) 371-5381

SBDC Director
University of Connecticut
School of Business Administration
Box U 41D
Storrs, CT 06268
(203) 468-4135

SBDC Director
Howard University
2361 Sherman Avenue, NW
Washington, DC 20059
(202) 636-7187

SBDC Director
University of Delaware
005 Purnell Hall
Newark, DE 19711
(302) 739-8401

SBDC Director
University of West Florida
137 Hospital Drive, Suite H
Ft. Walton Beach, FL 82548
(904) 243-7624

Acting SBDC Director
University of Georgia
Brooks Hall, Room 348
Athens, GA 30602
(404) 542-4760

SBDC Director
Iowa State University
Center of Industry Research and
Service
Room 205
Ames, IA 50011
(515) 294-3420

SBDC Director
University of Kentucky
College of Business and Economics
Commerce Building, Room 415
Lexington, KY 40506
(606) 257-1751

SBDC Director
University of Massachusetts
School of Business Administration
Amherst, MA 01003
(413) 549-4930 Ext. 304

SBDC Director
University of Southern Maine
246 Deering Avenue
Portland, ME 04102
(207) 780-4423

SBDC Director
St. Louis University
School of Business and
Administration
3674 Lindell Boulevard
St. Louis, MO 63103
(314) 758-3825

SBDC Director
St. Thomas College
2115 Summit Avenue
St. Paul, MN 55105
(612) 647-5840

SBDC Director
University of Mississippi
1855 Eastover Drive, Suite 101
Jackson, MS 39211
(601) 982-6684

SBDC Director
University of Nebraska-Omaha
Omaha, NE 68182
(402) 554-2521

SBDC Director
Rutgers University
180 University Street
Newark, NJ 07102
(201) 648-5627

State Director, SBDC
University of Pennsylvania
The Wharton School
3201 Steinberg Hall
Dietrich Hall/CC
Philadelphia, PA 19104
(215) 898-1219

SBDC Director
Bryant College
Smithfield, RI 02917
(401) 231-1200

SBDC Director
University of South Carolina
College of Business Administration
Columbia, SC 29208
(803) 777-5118

SBDC Director
Utah State University
Logan, UT 84322-3505
(801) 750-2358

SBDC Director
Washington State University
College of Business and Economics
Pullman, WA 99164
(509) 335-1576

SBDC Director
University of Wisconsin
One South Park Street
Madison, WI 53706
(608) 263-7794

SBDC Director
2300 MacCorkle Avenue, SE
Charleston, WV 25304
(304) 346-9471

SBDC Director
Small Business Development
Center of Vermont, Inc.
73 Main Street, Room 7
Montpelier, VT 05602
(802) 862-0200

Appendix F

ICA MODEL BY-LAWS FOR A WORKER COOPERATIVE VERSION II-1983

INDUSTRIAL COOPERATIVE ASSOCIATION
58 DAY STREET, SUITE 200
SOMMERVILLE, MA 02144

Contents   *221*

Article I Corporate Affairs

1) **Name.** The name of the corporation is _____
_____
(hereinafter referred to as the corporation).

2) **Registered Office.** The address of the registered office of the corporation is _____ .

3) **Fiscal Year.** The fiscal year of the corporation shall end on the last day of *(month)* in each year.

4) **Execution of Instruments.** All deeds, leases, transfers, contracts, bonds, notes and other obligations authorized to be executed on behalf of the corporation shall be signed by the President or the Treasurer except as the directors may otherwise determine.

5) **Corporate Records.** Copies of the following documents shall be kept at the principal office of the corporation or at the office of the Clerk, but need not all be kept at the same office: (a) the Articles of Organization and By-laws, (b) records of all meetings of incorporators, directors, and members and (c) the stock and transfer records containing the names of all members and the record address and the stock held by each. These records shall be available to members for inspection at reasonable times and for purposes consistent with good faith exercise of membership rights and responsibilities in corporate affairs.

6) **Article of Organization.** The Articles of Organization are hereby made a part of these By-laws, and the purposes of the corporation shall be as set forth in the Articles of Organization. In the event of any inconsistency between the Articles of Organization and these By-laws, the provisions of the Articles of Organization shall be controlling. All references in these By-laws to the Articles or Articles of Organization shall be construed to mean the Articles of Organization of the corporation as amended from time to time.

Article II Membership and Membership Shares

1) **Membership Organization.** The corporation shall operate on a cooperative basis, with earnings and losses allocated on the basis of patronage in accordance with Article III and with voting by the members in accordance with Article IV.

2) **Eligibility.** Membership shall be limited to natural persons who: (1) patronize the corporation through contributions of their labor on a full-time or part-time basis, (2) have been approved by the Board of Directors or its designees, and (3) have paid or agreed to pay a membership fee in an amount determined by the Board of Directors. Neither the Board nor its designees may discriminate on the basis of race, age, sex, sexual preference, religion, or national origin when considering a person for membership. Except as otherwise determined by the Board, an employee must either be accepted as a member or terminated as an employee within a trial period of _____ months of employment.

3) **Membership Shares & Membership Fee.** The corporation has a single class of common voting stock, hereafter referred to as "membership shares." Each member shall own one and only one membership share, and only members may own such shares. The cost of a membership share shall be determined by the Board of Directors and shall have no preemptive rights to membership shares issued to new members. No capital stock other than membership shares shall be given voting power, except as otherwise provided by law.

4) **Transfer Restrictions.** No membership share or interest therein may be sold, assigned, or otherwise transferred, voluntarily or involuntarily, by operation of law or otherwise, except for a transfer to the corporation.

5) **Membership Termination.** Upon voluntary or involuntary termination of a member's employment by the corporation, except for temporary layoffs or absences, his or her membership shall be terminated and the membership share shall be redeemed by the corporation for consideration determined in accordance with Article III. No member may be terminated involuntarily without written notice and a right to a hearing before a body designated in the Operating Rules.

6) **Certificates for Membership Shares.** Each member is entitled to a certificate representing his or her membership share in such form as prescribed by the Board of Directors. The certificate shall be signed by the President or Vice-President and by the Treasurer or Assistant Treasurer when it is issued. Each membership share shall set forth conspicuously on the face or back of the certificate either: (1) the full text of the restrictions prescribed in section 4, or (2) a statement of the existence of such restrictions and a statement that the corporation will furnish a copy of such restrictions to the holder of such certificate upon written request and without charge. In case of the loss, destruction, or mutilation of a membership certificate, a duplicate certificate may be issued in its place, upon such terms as the Board of Directors may prescribe.

Article III The Internal Capital Accounts

1) **Internal Capital Accounts - Definitions.** The corporation shall have a system of internal capital accounts to reflect its net worth, and to reflect the allocation of the net worth among the members. The following definitions shall apply to terms used in this Article III.

The net worth is the difference between the assets and liabilities on the corporate books (kept according to the Generally Accepted Accounting Principles (GAAP)).

The internal capital accounts consist of the individual capital accounts and the collective account, and may include a start-up losses account. The sum of the (net credit) balances in the internal capital accounts is the net worth of the corporation.

An individual capital account is maintained for each member, and it records the part of the net worth ultimately to be returned to each member.

The collective account is the unindividualized portion of the net worth that is not to be returned to the individual members during the lifetime of the corporation.

The start-up losses account is an optional debit-balance contra-account to the collective account which records the start-up losses to be allocated to the individual capital accounts over an extended period of time. The *start-up period* is the period from the beginning of operations up to but not including the first fiscal year with positive account net income. The *amortization of start-up losses* is the process of transferring debits from the start-up losses account to the individual capital accounts in proportion to patronage over an extended period of time following the years when the start-up losses were incurred.

The accounting net income is the book net income for the fiscal year computed in accordance with the Generally Accepted Accounting Principles. The accounting net income, positive or negative, is divided into the collective net income and individual net income.

The individual net income is fifty percent (50%) of the accounting net income. It is that part which will immediately or ultimately be allocated to the individual members as interest on their individual capital accounts or as patronage allocations.

225

The collective net income is fifty percent (50%) of the accounting net income. It is that part which will only affect the collective account. The collective net income minus the corporate taxes equals the self-insurance allocation.

The corporate taxes to be subtracted from the collective net income are all those taxes including the federal corporate income tax which have not been treated as an expense in determining the accounting net income.

The self-insurance allocation is the collective net income minus the corporate taxes, and it is allocated to the collective account.

The labor patronage of a member or non-member is the total number of hours worked for the corporation during the fiscal year (regardless of the rate of pay). The *members' patronage* is the total number of hours worked by members during the fiscal year, and the *non-members' patronage* is the total number of hours worked during the fiscal year by workers in their trial period. The *total patronage* is the sum of the members' and non-members' patronage.

(Or, if the other definition of "patronage" is used, then the above paragraph is replaced by: "The *labor patronage* member or non-member is the total labor compensation received from the corporation during the fiscal year. The *members' patronage* is the total labor compensation received by members during the fiscal year, and *non-members' patronage* is the total labor compensation received by workers in their trial period. The *total patronage* is the sum of members' and non-members' patronage.")

The patronage dividend is the positive amount of net income that is allocated to the members in proportion to patronage as described in section 1381 of the Internal Revenue Code of 1954 as amended (hereinafter referred to as the IRC). It can take the form of *non-qualified* patronage dividends (as defined in section 1388(d) of the IRC) or *qualified* patronage dividends (as defined in section 1388(c) of the IRC). A *non-qualified* or *qualified written notice of allocation* is the certificate issued to each member specifying the amount of the respective non-qualified or qualified patronage dividend allocated to the member and retained in the corporation.

The negative patronage allocation is the negative amount allocated to the individual capital accounts of the members in proportion to their current labor patronage. A negative patronage allocation may result from current losses or from an allocation to the individual capital accounts from the start-up losses account.

The payment period for a fiscal year is defined as eight and one-half months after the end of a fiscal year. The *patronage calculations and allocations* are to be completed within the *payment period*.

The individual capital account statement is an accounting statement issued to each member during the payment period for a fiscal year which details all the changes in the member's individual capital account for that fiscal year.

The capital contributions to the internal accounts include the membership fee and any additional paid-in capital in excess of the membership fee.

The membership fee is the cost of the membership share. A *redemption* of a written notice of allocation is a distribution of the amount of the notice in cash or other property to the member, ordinarily a fixed number of years after the issuance of the notice.

The termination distribution refers to the distribution of cash and/or notes of indebtedness to an ex-member or an ex-member's estate which is triggered by termination or retirement and which is not a payment in redemption of a written notice of allocation.

The dissolution distribution refers to a distribution, if any, of cash or other property to members and ex-members following the sale, liquidation, or dissolution of the corporation.

1.A) **Individual Capital Accounts.** Each member shall have an individual capital account.

The balance in the individual capital account results from and is increased by: (1) the initial membership fee, plus any other paid-in capital from the member in excess of the membership fee, (2) the accrual of interest on the total balance in the individual capital account at the rate prescribed by these by-laws, or (3) the amount of any written notice of allocation of patronage dividends issued to the member. The balance is decreased by: (1) the application of negative patronage allocations (losses from current operations or, if applicable, losses from the amortization of start-up losses), or (2) the redemption in cash or notes of indebtedness of a written notice of allocation previously issued to the member and recorded in the member's account.

1.B) **The Collective Account.** The balance in the collective account results from and is increased by: (1) the self-insurance allocation, and (2) any gifts or grants to the corporation which are not to be allocated to the individual capital accounts. The balance in the collective account is decreased by negative self-insurance allocations.

(If your cooperative wishes to simplify the By-laws by not having any Start-up Losses Account, then the following section 1.C should be deleted in its entirety — along with references to the Start-up Losses Account elsewhere in the By-laws.)

1.C) **The Startup Losses Account.** The corporation may establish a contra-equity debit-balance account called the "start-up losses account." During the start-up period, the cooperative will allocate only 20% of the current losses, i.e., the individual net income (which is negative during the start-up period) minus the interest on the individual capital accounts, among the individual capital accounts on the basis

227

of labor patronage. The remaining 80% is allocated to the startup losses account. The debit balance in the start-up losses account is increased by such allocations. In each of the four years after such an allocation to the start-up losses account, one-fourth of that loss allocation is distributed to the individual capital accounts on a current patronage basis. The balance in the start-up losses account is decreased by these patronage loss distributions to the individual capital accounts.

2) **Net Income.** The accounting net income of the corporation shall be allocated among the internal capital accounts in accordance with these By-laws.

2.A) **Interest on Individual Capital Accounts.** The individual capital accounts shall accrue interest at an annual rate of _____ percent compounded annually. The interest which accrues on the individual capital accounts for a fiscal year is subtracted from the individual net income to yield the net income allocated according to patronage.

2.B) **Patronage Allocations - General.** In accordance with the law, patronage dividends shall not be declared on non-member patronage, nor shall they exceed the tax-basis net income.

2.B(1) **Positive Patronage Allocations.** If the individual net income, minus the interest accrued during the fiscal year on the individual capital accounts is positive, then the corporation shall declare that patronage net income as a patronage dividend in accordance with section 1381 of the IRC. The patronage dividend is allocated among the members in proportion to their patronage. Each member receives a fraction of the total patronage dividend equal to the ratio of his or her member patronage to the total members' patronage for the fiscal year.

2.B(1a) **Written Notices of Allocation.** In any proportions determined by the Board of Directors, the patronage dividend may be paid in cash, in non-qualified written notices of allocation, and/or in qualified written notices of allocation. During the payment period for the fiscal year, the corporation shall deliver to each member the cash patronage dividend and/or the written notices of allocation showing the amount of any patronage dividend for that fiscal year retained in the corporation and credited to his or her individual capital account. Unless approved by the Board of Directors, the written notices of allocation shall be non-transferable. In the absence of such board approval, any transfer of allocation notices, whether voluntary or involuntary, shall be of no effect against the corporation and shall not entitle the transferee to receive payment from the corporation.

2.B(1b) **Written Notices and Individual Accounts.** The amount of patronage dividends paid to a member in non-qualified or qualified written notices of allocation shall be credited to the member's individual capital account. When allocation notices are redeemed or cancelled, the member's individual capital account shall be accordingly debited. The net income treated as retained patronage dividends credited to the members' accounts may be used for any and all corporate purposes.

(If your cooperative wishes to simplify the By-laws by not providing for the use of qualified (as opposed to non-qualified) written notices of allocation, then the following section 2.B (1c) should be deleted in its entirety — along with the references to "qualified" written notices elsewhere in the By-laws.)

2.B(1c) **Qualified Written Notices of Allocation.** By becoming a member of the corporation, each member shall be deemed to have consented to include in his or her taxable income any qualified written notices of allocation (within the meaning of section 1388 of the IRC) received by him or her at its stated dollar amount, in the manner provided by the section 1385 of the IRC, and to pay the tax thereon. In accordance with section 1388(c) of the IRC, at least twenty percent (20%) of each member's patronage dividend to be paid in cash and qualified written notices of allocation must be paid in cash.

2.B(2) **Negative Patronage Allocations - General.** The individual capital account of each member shall be debited with the fraction of the total negative patronage allocation equal to the ratio of his or her member patronage to the total members' patronage for the fiscal year. If a negative patronage allocation is applied against a portion of an individual capital account represented by a written notice of allocation, the amount of the written notice is accordingly reduced. A written notice is cancelled when its amount is reduced to zero.

(If the cooperative is not using a startup losses account,

then the following sections 2.B(2a) and 2.B(2b) can be deleted.)

2.B(2a) **Startup Losses.** During the start-up period, only twenty percent (20%) of the individual net income, minus the interest on the individual capital accounts, shall be allocated to the individual capital accounts in accordance with patronage. The remaining eighty percent (80%) shall be debited to the start-up losses account. After the start-up period (in the first fiscal year with a positive accounting net income and thereafter), the entire retained individual net income, minus interest on the individual accounts, shall be allocated to the individual capital accounts in accordance with patronage.

2.B(2b) **Amortization of Start-up Losses.** An allocation to the startup losses account shall be amortized on a straight-line basis over a four year (4) period. After each of the four fiscal years following a loss allocation to the start-up losses account, one-quarter (25%) of such an allocation shall be reallocated to the individual capital accounts in accordance with patronage. Five years after the end of the start-up period, the start-up losses account will be empty and may be eliminated from the books of the corporation.

2.B(3) **Individual Capital Account Statements.** During the payment period for a fiscal year and after all the internal account changes which relate to that fiscal year, each member shall be issued an individual capital account statement. This statement shall include the previous balance in the member's account, the accrued interest, the positive and/or negative patronage allocations to the account, the redemptions or distributions from the account, and the resulting current balance in the member's account. If all or part of any written notices of allocation were cancelled by any negative patronage allocations to the account, then the account statement shall specify the notices and amounts cancelled.

2.C) **Collective Net Income - General.** Fifty percent (50%) of the accounting net income (positive or negative) is the collective net income. The collective net income minus the applicable corporate income taxes yields the self-insurance allocation to the collective account.

2.C(1) **Federal Corporate Income Tax.** As described in Sub-chapter T of the IRC, this corporation, as a corporation operative on a cooperative basis, shall deduct from taxable income: (a) any amounts paid during the payment period for the taxable year (eight and one-half months after the end of the fiscal year) as patronage dividends paid in cash, qualified written notices of allocation, or other property (except non-qualified written notices of allocation), and (b) any amounts paid in redemption of non-qualified written notices of alloca-tion. Otherwise, the federal corporate income tax shall be computed as in a corporation not operating on a cooperative basis.

2.C(2) **The Self-Insurance Allocation.** Positive self-insurance allocations shall be credited to the collective account. The net income credited to the collective account may be used for any and all corporate purposes. Negative self-insurance allocations shall be debited from the collective account.

231

3) Capital Contributions and Distributions.

3.A) **Membership Fee.** Each member shall pay to the cor-poration in cash or other property an initial membership fee in an amount determined from time to time by the Board of Directors. The membership fee shall be credited to the member's individual capital account. Any additional capital paid in by a member in excess of the membership fee shall be credited to the member's individual capital account.

3.B) **Redemption of Written Notices of Allocation.** All writ-ten notices of allocation credited to a member's capital ac-count shall be redeemed in cash within five (5) years of their date of issuance unless the Board of Directors determines that a postponement of the redemption is appropriate.

Add if appropriate: The immediately preceding sentence notwithstanding, if a subordination agreement executed by the corporation or the member to whom the notices of alloca-tion were issued requires that the corporation delay or withhold any payment with respect to a written notice of allocation, then such subordination agreement shall govern the timing of payment of such written notices of allocation.

The internal capital account credits, evidenced by writ-ten notices of allocation, shall be paid off in the order of their date of issuance, the oldest allocation notices first, except that the Board may give first priority to the estates of deceased ex-members. In determining the oldest notices, all allocation notices of the same fiscal year shall have the same priority. If any payment is not sufficient to cover all redeemable notices, a proportionate part of the dollar amount of all the redeemable notices shall be paid. When a member's allocation notice is paid off, the member's internal capital account shall be accordingly debited.

3.C) **Termination Distributions.** Upon voluntary or involuntary termination of a member's work in the corporation (excluding temporary layoffs), his or her membership share shall automatically be deemed to have been transferred to the corporation in return for the consideration specified in this paragraph, and the membership share shall be returned to the corporation. The account balance in the terminating person's internal capital account shall be fixed after the adjustment at the end of that fiscal year, and the account shall be closed to any further patronage allocations. The written notices of allocation represented in the account, plus any otherwise unpaid interest, shall be redeemed in accordance with Section 3.B (above). After the year-end adjustments, if the portion of the account not represented by written notices of allocation has a positive balance, then that balance shall be paid to the person in consideration for the membership share in some combination of cash and promissory notes as the Board of Directors shall deem appropriate. The promissory notes issued, if any, shall be payable in full within five (5) years of being issued and shall have such other terms as the Board of Directors shall deem appropriate.

Add if appropriate: The immediately preceding sentence notwithstanding, payment of the notes may be subordinated to the payment of any other obligation and delayed or withheld entirely at any time in accordance with the terms of any subordination agreement to which the cooperative or the payee of the notes, or both, are parties, and the maturity date of the notes may also be extended if the cooperative's Board of Directors determines that the financial condition of the cooperative necessitates such extension.

After the year-end adjustments, if there is no balance in the person's individual capital account which is not represented by written notices, then the membership share shall be returned to the corporation for no consideration.

3.D) **Dissolution Distributions.** On the sale of all the assets, liquidation or dissolution of the corporation, any residual assets left after the payment of all debts and individual capital accounts shall be distributed in proportion to patronage to all the previous and current members, or their heirs; except that no distribution need be made to any person who fails to acknowledge, in a timely manner, receipt of notice of liquidation. It shall be deemed sufficient notice to a current or former member to send notice of liquidation by certified mail, at least 30 days before distribution of any residual assets, to the person's last known business or residence address. Any amounts unclaimed after sufficient notice shall be distributed in proportion to patronage to all previous and current members who acknowledge receipt of notice of liquidation.

(an alternative Section 3.D. is as follows:)

Dissolution Distributions. The capital represented by the collective account is not to be appropriated by any members as individuals. Accordingly, on the sale of all the assets, liquidation or dissolution of the corporation, any residual assets left after the payment of all debts and individual capital accounts shall be distributed to charitable organizations.

233

Article IV Membership Meetings

1) **Annual Meeting.** The annual meeting of the members shall be held on the *(No.) (day)* in *(month)* at *(hour)*. The location of the annual meeting shall be fixed by the Board of Directors or by the President. The annual meeting shall be held for the purpose of electing the Board of Directors, and for any other lawful purposes that are: (1) prescribed by law, by the Articles, or by these By-laws, or (2) specified by the President or by the directors or by at least 10% of the members. If the annual meeting is omitted on the day specified herein, a special meeting may be held in its place and any business transacted shall have the same effect as if transacted at the annual meeting.

2) **Regular Meetings.** Regular meetings of the members may be held without call or formal notice at such places and at such times as the President or a majority of the members may from time to time determine, provided that each member shall be given notice of the determination.

3) **Special Meetings.** Special meetings of the members may be called at any time by the Board or by the President. Upon written application of 10% of the members, a special meeting shall be called by an officer. Special meetings may be called for any lawful purpose.

4) **Notice of Meetings.** A written notice of each annual or special membership meeting stating the time, place, and purpose shall be given by the Clerk or by the officer calling the meeting, at least seven days before the meeting, to each member either: (1) in person, (2) by leaving the notice at the member's residence or usual workplace, or (3) by mailing it to the member's address as shown on the records of the corporation. Notice need not be given to a member if a written waiver of notice, executed before or after the meeting by such member, is filed with the records of the meeting. Each member shall notify the corporation of her or his current mailing address.

5) **Quorum.** A majority of the members at the time of the meeting shall be required to constitute a quorum at any membership meeting.

6) **Voting and Proxies.** Each member of record at the time of the meeting is entitled to one and only one vote on any matter requiring membership voting. Voting by proxy shall not be permitted.

7) **Action at a Meeting.** The President, Chairperson, or other designee, as determined by the Board of Directors, shall preside at membership meetings. When a quorum is present at a membership meeting, a majority of the members present and entitled to vote shall decide any matter to be voted upon by the members, unless a larger vote is required by law or by the Articles or these By-laws. A secret ballot is required if requested by any member present at the meeting. The corporation shall not directly or indirectly vote any share of its stock.

8) **Action Without Meeting.** Any action to be taken by the members may be taken without a meeting if all members entitled to vote on the matter consent to the action in writing. Such written consent shall be filed with the records of the meetings of members, and shall be treated for all purposes as a vote at a meeting.

Article V The Board of Directors

1) **Powers.** The Board of Directors may exercise all the powers of the corporation, including the power to issue stock, except as otherwise provided by law, by the Articles, or by these By-laws. In the event of a vacancy in the Board of Directors, the remaining directors may exercise the powers of the full board until the vacancy is filled except as otherwise provided by law.

2) **Election and Size.** The number of directors shall be determined at the first meeting of the incorporators and thereafter at each annual meeting of the members in accordance with the law and subject to change as provided in section 4 of this Article. The incorporators shall elect the initial directors at their first meeting, and, thereafter the members shall elect the directors at each annual membership meeting or special meeting held in its place. A director need not be a member.

235

3) **Vacancies.** Any vacancy in the Board of Directors, occurring between the annual membership meetings, may be filled at a special meeting of the members or by a majority of the directors then in office.

4) **Enlargement of the Board.** The number constituting the Board of Directors may be increased and one or more additional directors elected at the annual meeting or any special meeting of the members.

5) **Tenure.** Except as otherwise provided by law, by the Articles, or by these By-laws, directors shall hold office until their successors are elected. Any director may resign by delivering his or her written resignation to any officer or to a meeting of the Board of Directors, effective upon receipt or at some later time specified. No director resigning or removed shall have any right to any compensation as such director for any period following his or her resignation or removal, or any right to damages on account of such removal, unless provided by a written agreement or by a resolution of the remaining directors.

6) **Removal.** A director may at any time be removed from office (1) with or without cause by a vote of a majority of the members or (2) for cause by a majority of the directors then in office. A director may be removed for cause only after

reasonable notice and opportunity to be heard before the body proposing to remove the director.

7) **Meetings.** Regular meetings of the Board may be held at such places and times as the Board may from time to time determine. Special meetings of the Board of Directors may be called at any time by the President or by the Clerk at the request of three or more of the directors.

8) **Notice of Meetings.** Notice of the time, place, and purposes of any meeting of the Board shall be given to each director by an officer or by one of the directors calling the meeting. Notice shall be given to each director in person or by telephone or by telegram sent to the director's last known address not less than twenty-four hours before the meeting, or by written notice mailed to such address at least 72 hours before the meeting. Notice need not be given to any director if a written waiver of notice, executed by the director before or after the meeting, is filed with the records of the meeting or to any director who attends the meeting without protesting the lack of notice.

9) **Quorum.** At any meeting of the Board of Directors, a majority of the directors then in office shall constitute a quorum.

10) **Action at a Meeting.** If a quorum is present, a majority of the directors present may take any action on behalf of the Board of Directors, unless a larger number is required by law, by the Articles, or by these By-laws.

11) **Action by Consent.** Any action by the directors may be taken without a meeting if all directors then in office consent to the action in writing and the written consents are filed with the records of the directors' meetings. Such consent shall be treated as a vote of the directors for all purposes.

12) **Committees.** The directors may elect committees and may delegate thereto some or all of their powers except those which they are prohitbited from delegating by the law, by the Articles, or by these By-laws. Except as the directors may otherwise determine, any such committee may make rules for the conduct of its business.

Article VI Officers

1) **Elected Officers.** A President, Treasurer, Clerk, and Chairperson shall be elected annually by the Board of Directors at its first meeting following the annual membership meeting or following a special meeting held in place thereof. Other officers may be elected by the Board of Directors at its discretion.

2) **Qualification.** Each officer shall be a member, and the Chairperson of the Board shall be a director. Any two or more offices may be held by the same person.

3) **Tenure.** Except as otherwise provided by law, by the Articles, or by these By-laws, the term of office of the officer shall be determined by the Board of Directors. Any officer may resign by delivering to any director his or her written resignation, effective upon receipt or at some later time specified. No officer resigning or removed shall have any right to any compensation as such officer for any period following his or her resignation or removal, or any right to damages on account of such removal, unless provided by a written agreement or by a resolution of the directors.

4) **Removal.** The Board of Directors may remove any officers with or without cause. If an officer is removed for cause, he or she is entitled to reasonable notice and an opportunity to be heard by the Board of Directors.

5) **Vacancies.** If any office becomes vacant for any reason, the Board of Directors may elect a successor or successors, who shall hold office for the unexpired term, except as otherwise provided by law, by the Articles, or by these By-laws.

6) **Chairperson of the Board.** The Chairperson of the Board (or, in his or her absence, a temporary chairperson selected by the Board) shall preside at all meetings of the Board and shall have such other duties and powers as determined from time to time by the Board.

7) **President.** The President shall be the chief executive officer of the corporation and shall, subject to the direction of the Board, have general supervision of the business of the corporation. The President shall have such other duties and powers as the Board shall determine from time to time. The

President has the power to enter into contracts in the name of the corporation, and such contracts shall be binding on the corporation and not subject to reversal by the members.

8) **Treasurer.** Subject to the supervision of the directors, the Treasurer shall have: (1) general charge of the finances and custody of the funds of the corporation, (2) power to endorse for deposit or collection all notes, checks, drafts, and other obligations or payments to the corporation and to accept drafts on behalf of the corporation, and (3) shall cause to be kept accurate books of account, which shall be the property of the corporation. If required by the Board of Directors, the Treasurer shall give bond for the faithful performance of duty.

9) **Clerk and Assistant Clerk.** The Clerk shall be a resident of the state of _____ . The clerk shall keep at his or her office or at the principal office of the corporation those documents described in section 5 of Article I and such other documents as the Board of Directors shall determine, and shall have such other duties and powers as determined by the Board. In the absence of the Clerk at a meeting, an Assistant Clerk (if any) or a Temporary Clerk designated by the person presiding at such meeting shall perform the duties of the Clerk.

Article VII Indemnification and Insurance

1) **Indemnification.** The corporation shall indemnify each of its directors and officers against all liabilities and expenses, including amounts paid in satisfaction of judgements, in compromise, or as fines and penalties, and counsel fees reasonably incurred or paid by him or her in connection with the defense or disposition of any action, suit, or other proceeding (whether civil or criminal) in which he or she may be involved, while in office or thereafter, by reason of his or her having been such a director or officer; except with respect to any matter as to which he or she shall have been adjudicated in any proceeding not to have acted in good faith in the reasonable belief that his of her action was in the best interests of the corporation, or with respect to any matter as to which he or she shall agree or be ordered by any court of competent jurisdiction to make payment to the corporation. The right of indemnification herein provided for shall be in addition to any other right which any such person may have or obtain, shall continue

as to any such person who has ceased to be a director or officer, and shall inure to the benefit of the heirs of any such person.

2) **Insurance.** The corporation may purchase insurance to cover any liability or expense reasonably incurred by members, officers, or directors by reason of their having been members, officers, or directors.

Article VIII Amendments

1) **By Members.** The members shall have the power to make, amend, or repeal these By-laws by a vote of a majority of the members present at the membership meeting, provided that the notice for such meeting indicated a change in the By-laws was to be considered.

2) **By Directors.** The Board of Directors shall have the power to make, amend, or repeal these By-laws by a vote of a majority of directors, provided that:

a) The Board may not make, amend, or repeal any provision of these By-laws which by the law, by the Articles, or by these By-laws requires an action by the membership;

b) The Board may not make, amend, or repeal any provision of these By-laws which alters the procedure for making, amending, or repealing the By-laws or which alters the provisions for removal of directors;

c) Not later than the time of giving notice of the membership meeting next following the adoption, amendment, or repeal by the directors of any By-law provision, notice thereof stating the substance of such adoption, amendment, or repeal shall be given to all members.

Article IX Operating Rules

1) **Operating Rules.** Written rules, separate from these By-laws, may be established by the members or by the Board of Directors. These Operating Rules may be added to, amended, or repealed at any meeting of the members or the Board, by a majority of the quorum. The Operating Rules shall be

239

binding on all members and directors, unless inconsistent with the law, the Articles, or these By-laws. A current copy of the Operating Rules shall be maintained by the Clerk, and a copy shall be available to any member requesting a copy.

Appendix G

EDUCATIONAL NEEDS ASSESSMENT FOR WORKER-OWNED COOPERATIVES

The following questions should be filled out by members of the cooperative. The completed surveys can then be tabulated and a report prepared. The report will provide a basis for completing an educational plan, and for obtaining needed education and training for worker-members.

	Yes	*No*
A) Are you a member of your co-op's board of directors?	☐	☐
B) Are you a manager or supervisor?	☐	☐
C) Do you serve on any committees?	☐	☐
D) If you do not hold an elected office now, do you want to hold an office in the future?	☐	☐

E) How long have been a shareholder?

_____
Months / Years

F) Assuming there was no cost to you, how much of your time would you be willing to spend (during any one year) at workshops learning skills in the following areas?

Governance

1) How to develop or improve
co-op by-laws. *None 4 Hours 1 Day 2 Days 2+ Days*

2) How to govern your co-op. *None 4 Hours 1 Day 2 Days 2+ Days*

3) Your rights and respon-
sibilities as a co-op member. *None 4 Hours 1 Day 2 Days 2+ Days*

4) How to hold an election. *None 4 Hours 1 Day 2 Days 2+ Days*

5) How to protect your rights. *None 4 Hours 1 Day 2 Days 2+ Days*

Decision-Making

6) How to improve the
decision-making process in
your co-op. *None 4 Hours 1 Day 2 Days 2+ Days*

7) How to be a more effective
member of your
organization. *None 4 Hours 1 Day 2 Days 2+ Days*

8) How to chair a meeting. *None 4 Hours 1 Day 2 Days 2+ Days*

9) How to be a board member. *None 4 Hours 1 Day 2 Days 2+ Days*

10) How to be a more effective
supervisor. *None 4 Hours 1 Day 2 Days 2+ Days*

11) How to be a more effective
leader. *None 4 Hours 1 Day 2 Days 2+ Days*

12) How to get your ideas about
running the business made
into policy. *None 4 Hours 1 Day 2 Days 2+ Days*

13) How to help committees
reach decisions about your
co-op. *None 4 Hours 1 Day 2 Days 2+ Days*

14) How to give and take
criticism. *None 4 Hours 1 Day 2 Days 2+ Days*

15) How to resolve conflicts in a group.   *None   4 Hours   1 Day   2 Days   2+ Days*

16) How to listen to fellow workers.   *None   4 Hours   1 Day   2 Days   2+ Days*

17) How to be a member of a standing committee such as planning or finance.   *None   4 Hours   1 Day   2 Days   2+ Days*

Communications

18) How to write letters and reports.   *None   4 Hours   1 Day   2 Days   2+ Days*

19) How to improve your knowledge as a worker-owner of what happens daily and weekly in your business.   *None   4 Hours   1 Day   2 Days   2+ Days*

243

20) How to produce a newsletter for your co-op.   *None   4 Hours   1 Day   2 Days   2+ Days*

21) How to write songs and plays about working and cooperative life.   *None   4 Hours   1 Day   2 Days   2+ Days*

Legal Issues

22) What are the tax laws in your state.   *None   4 Hours   1 Day   2 Days   2+ Days*

23) How to lower your taxes.   *None   4 Hours   1 Day   2 Days   2+ Days*

24) How laws help or hurt worker-owned businesses.   *None   4 Hours   1 Day   2 Days   2+ Days*

25) How to approach legal issues facing your cooperative.   *None   4 Hours   1 Day   2 Days   2+ Days*

26) How to change those laws affecting worker-owned businesses.   *None   4 Hours   1 Day   2 Days   2+ Days*

Outside Help

27) How to use consultants.	*None*	*4 Hours*	*1 Day*	*2 Days*	*2+ Days*
28) How to use an accountant.	*None*	*4 Hours*	*1 Day*	*2 Days*	*2+ Days*
29) How to use a tax specialist.	*None*	*4 Hours*	*1 Day*	*2 Days*	*2+ Days*

Financial Management

30) How to read and understand your co-op's financial statement.	*None*	*4 Hours*	*1 Day*	*2 Days*	*2+ Days*
31) How to keep the co-op's books.	*None*	*4 Hours*	*1 Day*	*2 Days*	*2+ Days*
32) How to collect overdue accounts.	*None*	*4 Hours*	*1 Day*	*2 Days*	*2+ Days*
33) How to negotiate a contract.	*None*	*4 Hours*	*1 Day*	*2 Days*	*2+ Days*
34) How to distribute co-op profits.	*None*	*4 Hours*	*1 Day*	*2 Days*	*2+ Days*
35) How to compute your co-op's cash flow.	*None*	*4 Hours*	*1 Day*	*2 Days*	*2+ Days*
36) How to get the credit your business needs.	*None*	*4 Hours*	*1 Day*	*2 Days*	*2+ Days*

Productivity

37) How to collect information you need to make a decision.	*None*	*4 Hours*	*1 Day*	*2 Days*	*2+ Days*
38) How to figure how productive you are every day.	*None*	*4 Hours*	*1 Day*	*2 Days*	*2+ Days*
39) How to figure how productivity affects profits.	*None*	*4 Hours*	*1 Day*	*2 Days*	*2+ Days*
40) How to improve and control the quality of your products or services.	*None*	*4 Hours*	*1 Day*	*2 Days*	*2+ Days*

41) How to lower production
    costs. *None 4 Hours 1 Day 2 Days 2+ Days*

42) How to plan for new pro-
    ducts and services for your
    cooperative. *None 4 Hours 1 Day 2 Days 2+ Days*

43) How to develop and/or
    understand your co-op's
    business plan. *None 4 Hours 1 Day 2 Days 2+ Days*

Sales and Marketing

44) How to sell your co-op's
    product. *None 4 Hours 1 Day 2 Days 2+ Days*

45) How to deal with
    customer/client complaints. *None 4 Hours 1 Day 2 Days 2+ Days*

46) Where your co-op fits into
    the business market. *None 4 Hours 1 Day 2 Days 2+ Days*

Personnel Management

47) How to handle grievances. *None 4 Hours 1 Day 2 Days 2+ Days*

48) How to hire new members. *None 4 Hours 1 Day 2 Days 2+ Days*

49) How to fire members. *None 4 Hours 1 Day 2 Days 2+ Days*

50) How to establish sick leave
    and other personnel benefits. *None 4 Hours 1 Day 2 Days 2+ Days*

51) How to deal with
    discrimination and prejudice
    in your co-op (i.e. sexism,
    racism, ageism, etc.) *None 4 Hours 1 Day 2 Days 2+ Days*

52) How to establish a proba-
    tionary period policy for
    new employees. *None 4 Hours 1 Day 2 Days 2+ Days*

53) How to establish co-op pro-
    cedures for buying back the
    shares of worker-owners at
    retirement or termination. *None 4 Hours 1 Day 2 Days 2+ Days*

245

General

54) How to use a computer or a microcomputer. *None 4 Hours 1 Day 2 Days 2+ Days*

55) How to meet the special needs of certain groups (e.g. women) within your business. *None 4 Hours 1 Day 2 Days 2+ Days*

56) How to teach other members of your co-op new skills. *None 4 Hours 1 Day 2 Days 2+ Days*

57) How to organize and run a day care center in your co-op. *None 4 Hours 1 Day 2 Days 2+ Days*

58) How to change work in your co-op so that work usually done by women only can be done by men and vice versa. *None 4 Hours 1 Day 2 Days 2+ Days*

59) How to improve your management practices. *None 4 Hours 1 Day 2 Days 2+ Days*

60) What are the differences between a worker-owned business and one owned only by a few people. *None 4 Hours 1 Day 2 Days 2+ Days*

61) How co-ops got started: their success and failures. *None 4 Hours 1 Day 2 Days 2+ Days*

62) How worker-owners from other countries run their businesses. *None 4 Hours 1 Day 2 Days 2+ Days*

63) How worker-owners from other countries do the same job as you. *None 4 Hours 1 Day 2 Days 2+ Days*

64) How to make worker-owned businesses strong politically in your town or state. *None 4 Hours 1 Day 2 Days 2+ Days*

65) Why some co-ops failed.   *None   4 Hours   1 Day   2 Days   2+ Days*

66) How to start a new worker-
    owned business.   *None   4 Hours   1 Day   2 Days   2+ Days*

67) How to convert an existing
    business to
    worker-ownerships.   *None   4 Hours   1 Day   2 Days   2+ Days*

G) If you personally would
   need to pay for these
   courses, what is the most
   you would pay to attend a
   one-day workshop on your
   favorite issue?   *$5 $10 $11-25 $26-50 $50-100   over $10*

	Yes	*No*

H) (Assuming they were free) would you travel
   out of *city, state,* for six weeks to take 3 or
   4 of these courses at *college?*   ☐   ☐

I) Would you attend meetings with co-op
   members from other towns who do the same
   job as you?   ☐   ☐

J) Should your co-op's board of directors
   schedule time every 3 months for you to
   learn a new skill from one of your fellow
   members?   ☐   ☐

K) Should your cooperative plan to hold on-site
   classes?

	Yes	No
yearly	☐	☐
quarterly	☐	☐
monthly	☐	☐
every two weeks	☐	☐
weekly	☐	☐
daily	☐	☐

L) What should be the maximum length of educational
   workshop sessions?   *1hr   4hrs   1day   2 days   1week   2 weeks*

	Yes	No

M) Should these educational
workshops be taught by:

Some member of the
cooperative who knows the
subject?

A student from a college
who is studying the subject?

Some other expert outside of
your business?

Appendix H

A SAMPLE BUSINESS PLAN

This Appendix is a continuation of Chapter Four. It is an illustration of a business plan, suggesting, but only suggesting, one way to organize and present such a document. The organization, language, and appearance of the business plan reflects its authors' abilities while providing potential lenders insights into the firm's probable success.

Each business plan should consist of four elements: a cover designating that the document is a business plan; a table of contents; the sectional summaries along with supporting data or tables; and an appendix. Each content section should be limited to a short summary statement no longer than a single, double-spaced page. Data presented in each sectional summary should be kept at a minimum with detailed documentation presented in the appendix, or withheld until requested.

Business Plan

THE WORKER-OWNED COOPERATIVE

Prepared By
The Worker-Owned Cooperative
With Technical Assistance By
Workplace Democracy, Inc.

December 15, 1985

Contents

253

Section 1 General Overview
of the Business Opportunity

The Worker-Owned Cooperative is a new corporation established under the laws of North Carolina to manufacture Wham-doodles, a key component necessary to upgrade Clear-Copy Corporation's X930 copy machines, a system with 22 million units sold in five years since its introduction in 1980. Wham-Doodles are electronic data storage devices, and are key parts in the new ClearCopy X930. Additionally, Wham-doodles are being designed into copy machines being planned by ClearCopy competitors, and no change in technology is expected until at least 1997. Exclusive license to manufacture Wham-Doodles, and to use the name Wham-Doodle, has been secured by The Worker-Owned Cooperative.

1) Wham-Doodles are a proven product with respect to engineering.

2) Wham-Doodles are known in the electronic copying marketplace as the single most important innovation in a decade.

3) Demand for Wham-Doodles is projected to reach 1.5 million units annually within five years. Contracts with ClearCopy Corporation for 250,000 Wham-Doodles the first year can be signed within five days after completion of all necessary capital loans. This figure will expand by 10 percent annually for four years.

The Worker-Owned Cooperative, to be located at 3989 West Mulberry Drive, River City Industrial Park, will initially provide 35 persons the unique opportunity to own and manage a high technology business with significant growth potential. Most of the 35 persons seeking to found this business are presently unemployed, having recently lost their jobs when Ever Moving Flashlights relocated to Haiti.

Revenues generated by the new business are expected to total $1,250,000 in 1986, and increase by 19 percent each year thereafter for five years. Total capital required to start the Wham-Doodle Cooperative is $500,000, with the 35 worker-owners supplying $175,000, or $5,000 per person.

Section 2   Product Plan

Wham-Doodles are miniaturized electronic data processing devices essential to the production of ClearCopy Corporation's X930 model office copy machine. ClearCopy is currently the leading copy machine manufacturer in the world, and currently holds 32 percent of the U.S. market for office copiers. It is also the leading supplier of these machines in the European market. The proposed products are called Wham-Doodles because they resemble the child's toy made for years by Appalachian mountain families to entertain children. Wham-Doodles were longish sticks with notches cut onto one side. A small propeller was then fastened with a nail to the end. By rubbing a smooth stick along the ribbed notches, the propeller turned, giving children many hours of imaginative play. Today's electronic Wham-Doodle is also a rod, but made of plastic. Rather than being notched, tiny electronic data pulsers are attached to the 10 centimeter long rod. These pulsers control signals to the copy machine's printer, alternating signals according to pre-set rates. The result is a substantial increase in the accuracy, efficiency and speed of the printing process. The eleven-pulser Wham-Doodle was invented by Harvey Mindset of Brocton, N.C., who holds all patent rights. No other applications have yet been found for the Wham Doodle; but Mr. Mindset is devoting considerable energy searching for new applications. He has signed a contract with The Worker-Owned Cooperative giving the company exclusive rights to manufacture and market the product, and specifying that any production modification, or new products emerging from his research will be licensed to The Worker-Owned Cooperative for manufacture and marketing.

255

Section 3   Market Plan

Initially, between start-up and the end of the second year, The Worker-Owned Cooperative's entire production yield will be purchased by ClearCopy Corporation. At the end of the second year, 85 percent of the 323,500 units produced will be sold direct to ClearCopy. The remainder will be available for sale by The Worker-Owned Cooperative to a potential market among ClearCopy competitors. Because of licensing restrictions, no other firm can manufacture Wham-Doodles for 10 years after production starts. The projected market overview for the years from 1986 to 1990 is summarized in Exhibit 5.

Section 4 Raw Materials Plan

The 7-gauge, triple strength polymer plastic rods which form one basic component of the Wham-Doodle will be purchased under a renewable, five-year contract with StuPont Chemical of Moneyington, Delaware. Electronic pulsers will be imported by Wewon Imports, a subsidiary of Nippon International, of Osaka, Japan, also under a five-year renewable contract. Additionally, The Worker-Owned Cooperative has arranged with Wewon Imports for shipments of 20,800 units per month, as a means to reduce storage costs. Metal brackets will be manufactured on site, from aluminum obtained from Dynamic Metal, Inc. Rivets, screws, and wiring will be obtained from Deuce Hardware and Wire Manufacturing. Purchase contracts at favorable prices have been negotiated with both suppliers. All raw materials will be delivered to the plant by truck.

Since Wham-Doodle's demand is very predictive, a form of JIT (just-in-time) inventory reordering system would be profitable to the firm. JIT inventory ordering and production concepts have been pioneered and successfully used by Japanese manufacturing firms to significantly reduce inventory holding costs. The concept of JIT inventory is to buy inventory as it is needed; not just in case it is needed. It is important for The Worker-Owned Cooperative to set up reliable relationships with suppliers so that inventory can be ordered in advance to arrive at the right time to begin production. With the predictive contract set up with ClearCopy Corporation, this inventory model can be used.

Section 5 Personnel Plan

As has been mentioned, the 35 persons seeking to found The Worker-Owned Cooperative previously worked for Ever Moving Flashlight. Six members of the new firm have extensive management experience, both with Ever Moving or with other mid-sized firms. On average, the 35 founders had worked for Ever Moving slightly more than fourteen years each. Among the group there are three individuals with engineering training and extensive experience in setting up and operating a production line. Overall, this is an experienced, stable workforce committed to the success of the enterprise—as demonstrated by their personal financial investment in The Worker-Owned Cooperative.

The members of The Worker-Owned Cooperative have democratically elected a six-member Board of Directors, three of whom have management experience and three with extensive production skills. The Board of Directors, in turn, has named Winifred (Winnie) Winston, manager, delegating to her day- to-day policy implementation, authority over production, administration, budget, and fiscal control. Ms. Winston began her career with the now- departed Ever Moving Flashlight in 1962 as a production supervisor upon graduation from Appalachian State University with a degree in mechanical engineering. In 1964, Ms. Winston returned to Piedmont State and completed a Master of Business Administration degree. After returning to Ever Moving in 1965 she was promoted to various other positions in the company, eventually being named general manager in 1978, a position she held when it was relocated out of the country.

Worker members have also elected a six-member Social Council, which will assist the general manager and Board of Directors in developing all personnel procedures, assist in grievance and dispute resolution, and formulate suggestions from the entire membership on social governance policy for consideration by the Board of Directors.

Finally, the membership has decided to develop a job rotation system to enable workers to learn new job skills and expand their knowledge base. Once a worker has mastered his or her job assignment, he or she may request the opportunity to learn a new job or to take specialized training in areas needed by the firm. Once trained in the new skill, the workers may rotate jobs periodically in harmony with the efficient operations and workforce needs of the firm. Managers will also rotate during a five-year cycle, seeking through this policy to insure a supply of broadly trained managers for future growth of the business. The management rotation plan, as the policy is called, works as follows: An assistant general manager is elected for a one-year probationary term of office. During the year, the elected person will work with supervisors in each department of the firm, and will take appropriate courses at Piedmont State University. Upon completion of the first year probationary period, if approved by the general manager and Board of Directors, the assistant general manager will serve a three-year term as assistant to the general manager. The assistant general manager will replace the general manager during the fifth year, with the outgoing general manager serving as a consultant during the fifth year, and assuming new responsibilities for the firm, but outside direct management.

Section 6) Financial Plan

Financing will be obtained to begin the company by asking each of the 35 worker-owners to contribute $5,000, totaling $175,000, by mortgaging the plant for $200,000, by securing a term loan for $25,000, and by securing a revolving credit line from the bank for $100,000. The sources and applications of financing are illustrated in Exhibit 1.

The total assets for The Worker-Owned Cooperative will be $500,000 at the time of startup. The beginning balance sheet for the cooperative is presented as Exhibit 2.

The revolving $100,000 loan must be completely revolved once a year. Its purpose is to provide a buffer for inventory because of cyclical demand fluctuations. The sales forecast in Exhibit 4 illustrates a higher demand for Wham-Doodles at the end of the year because more copiers are purchased to take advantage of the tax advantages allowable under the investment tax credit. It is projected that the sales price of $5.00 for Wham-Doodles will increase each year by a 10% inflation rate. Growth of sales to ClearCopy are projected to grow at an annual rate of 10% and the growth of other sales are projected to be 20% after the second year. Exhibit 5 provides projected sales for the five-year period from 1986 to 1990.

The equipment necessary to begin operations is set out in Exhibit 3. This equipment will allow the company to produce at 80% capacity. In order to expand capacity to meet additional demand, $80,000 is budgeted in 1987, and $75,000 in 1988 for the purchase of new equipment.

Seventy-five thousand dollars as allocated for working capital and prepaid expenses to begin operations and to secure favorable credit relations and contracts with suppliers.

The cash budget (Exhibits 6, 7, 8) reflects the cash flow of the company for the years 1986, 1987, and 1988. Sales revenue is collected on the terms of net 30 days. Accounts payable are also paid on a net 30 day agreement. Wages are projected at an average rate of $10.50 a hour to be paid every two weeks. In January, 25 workers will be on payroll; this number will increase to 29 in July to increase production. Every year the number of worker-members will be increased to keep up with the increase in demand. Salaries will be paid out beginning at $2,300 a month to managers. The mortgage will be paid over 40 years at 11.5% interest. The term loan will be paid over 3 years at 12% interest. The revolving credit line will be charged at 12% interest. The revolving credit line will be paid at $9,000 per month. During July, August, and

September the loan will be renewed to ensure at least a $5,000 beginning cash balance for the month.

The pro-forma income statements in Exhibit 9 show that about 75% of revenues are allocated to inventory costs. About 16% of the revenues are allocated to operating expenses. About 7% of the revenues are allocated to interest and taxes and 3.17% of revenues is left over for net profit after taxes. The plan shows an increase in profit margin from 3 to 4.7% in 1988. Pro-forma balance sheets for January 1, 1987, 1988 & 1989 are provided in Exhibit 10.

The straight-line depreciation election was taken to determine the depreciation expense. The equipment is being depreciated over 10 years and the truck is being depreciated over 5 years.

With the present sales price of $5.00, fixed costs of $19,770, and variable costs of $4.68 per unit, a break even quantity of 61,351 units is desired at a dollar volume of $286,984. (See Exhibit 11).

259

Section 7 Taxation Plan

Income tax for The Worker-Owned Cooperative has been calculated at 28% for 1986, 30% for 1987 and 35% for 1988. This rate has been applied after itemization and investment and energy tax credits have been taken. The amount estimated will be paid in quarterly installments, using Corporate Estimated Tax Form 503. Exhibit 12 outlines the Federal Tax Calendar which is applicable to business firms (and individuals). Any differences from the estimated amount listed in the pro-forma income statements (Exhibits 9 and 10) will be charged to a deferred income tax account.

The Worker-Owned Cooperative will seek to qualify as a cooperative for federal tax purposes, under the provisions of Subchapter T. If and when this approval is granted by the Internal Revenue Service, it should reduce the tax liability on the company and improve the balance sheet. However, since approval has not been granted yet, the data on which income taxes have been figured is based on the corporate provisions of the tax code.

Section 8 Charter and Summary of By-Laws

The Worker-Owned Cooperative has been incorporated as a for-profit corporation in Delaware, and is qualified by the United States Internal Revenue Service as a Subchapter T enterprise, meaning that:

☐ Members control the firm through the democratic principle of one person, one vote, with the entire membership electing a Board of Directors, or other governance committees which, in turn, appoint management.

☐ The right to profits, or net income, is vested only with members, and must be distributed in the form of patronage refunds rather than traditional stock dividends.

☐ Should the corporation dissolve, any remaining assets must be distributed to the members, or former members, on the basis of labor patronage over the life of the cooperative.

☐ At least 50 percent of the persons employed must be members.

260

A copy of the firm's charter, articles of incorporation, and by-laws are included in the appendix of this document.

Section 9 Governance Plan

The Worker-Owned Cooperative, being a worker-owned and managed production enterprise, has established an internal governance plan which sets forth areas of responsibility for the entire membership, the Board of Directors, and the social council, thus assuring clear lines of authority, decision-making and accountability, as well as grievance procedures. Specific details of the governance plan have yet to be fashioned by the founding workforce. But, in general, the membership bears ultimate responsibility and authority for policies and decisions which affect the character of the firm, and its profitability. The Board of Directors, elected by the membership, bears the legal responsibilities of the firm with regard to customers, creditors, suppliers, and for internal administration, and have fiduciary duty. The Board of Directors may appoint as many standing or temporary committees as it deems necessary to manage the firm. The social council is responsible for the protection of individual member's rights, may hear any grievance brought to it, recommend policies to the Board of Directors or membership, and may be consulted by the Board or managers with regard to personnel policies and membership rights. An organization chart of The Worker-Owned Cooperative is included as Exhibit 13.

Section 10 Social Audit Plan

Cooperatives normally balance financial objectives with social objectives, unlike many firms which gauge success only in terms of profits. The social utility of The Worker-Owned Cooperative will be measured four ways systematically over time: analysis of cost-benefit ratios between contributions made by the firm to the worker-members, or surrounding community, (assets) and determinants to the same as a result of the firm's actions (liabilities); by measuring the outlays for social purposes within the firm and outside; by measuring the value of the productive capabilities of members; and, finally, by a social performance audit to gauge how the firm's activities affect democracy at home and abroad. The purpose of the social audit is threefold: (1) to assure members of a regular assessment of their democratic control of the firm; (2) to identify the costs the cooperative imposes on the community; and (3) to serve as a means to gauge the extent to which the cooperative fulfills its own stated objectives.

261

Section 11 Education and Training Plan

The aim of education and training in The Worker-Owned Cooperative is to insure that all members may develop those skills or capabilities which increase their control over and responsibility for corporate decisions, resources, and outcomes. The opportunity to participate in educational activities, or to learn any job in the cooperative is open to any full- vested member regardless of race, sex, creed, national origin, educational attainment level, or political values.

Workplace Democracy, Inc., has been contracted to help design a training program for staff of the cooperative, focusing on the fundamentals of worker-ownership and cooperative decision-making. In addition, as the first step toward implementing the Personnel Policy outlined in Section 5, two key staff members have been identified to take a special financial management course at the local college, and a third individual will enroll in a special manufacturing engineering short course at North Carolina State. They will commence their studies on January 5, 1986.

Section 12 Financial Exhibits

The following financial exhibits illustrate the worker-owned cooperative business plan.

Exhibit 2

THE WORKER-OWNED COOPERATIVE
SOURCES AND APPLICATIONS OF FINANCING

SOURCES

Worker Owners:

1) $5,000.00	13) $5,000.00	25) $5,000.00
2) 5,000.00	14) 5,000.00	26) 5,000.00
3) 5,000.00	15) 5,000.00	27) 5,000.00
4) 5,000.00	16) 5,000.00	28) 5,000.00
5) 5,000.00	17) 5,000.00	29) 5,000.00
6) 5,000.00	18) 5,000.00	30) 5,000.00
7) 5,000.00	19) 5,000.00	31) 5,000.00
8) 5,000.00	20) 5,000.00	32) 5,000.00
9) 5,000.00	21) 5,000.00	33) 5,000.00
10) 5,000.00	22) 5,000.00	34) 5,000.00
11) 5,000.00	23) 5,000.00	35) 5,000.00
12) 5,000.00	24) 5,000.00	

Total Worker-Owners $175,000.00

Bank Loans:

Mortgage Loan   200,000.00
Term Loan   25,000.00
Revolving 12-
 Month Loan   100,000.00

Total all Sources $500,000.00

APPLICATIONS

Purchase Factory   250,000.00
Equipment   100,000.00
Inventory   75,000.00
Working Capital   45,000.00
Reserve for Contingencies   30,000.00

Total $500,000.00

Exhibit 3

THE WORKER-OWNED COOPERATIVE
CAPITAL EQUIPMENT LIST

Equipment	Model	Cost or List Price (Lower)
Research & Development:		
Electron Microscope	SUB-1000	$2,000.00
Hewlett Packard Cad-Cam Computer	31-CZ	15,000.00
Dayton All-Purpose Tooling Machine	XL-800	2,346.00
Subtotal		$19,346.00
Manufacturing:		
Copyjapan Robotics Inc. Silicon Tooler	CCAT-1	49,000.00
Qualifree Inc. Electonic Surveyor	A1000	2,965.00
Assemblies-Made-Easy Inc. Conveyor Belt	ABC123	1,234.56
Joe's Job Shop Co., Molds & Dies		999.00
Miscellaneous Tools and Microscopes		456.00
Subtotal		$54,654.56
Selling:		
1 Ford Delivery Truck	FIX-999	13,000.00
Cash Register		382.00
Subtotal		$13,382.00
Administrative:		
Office Furniture		1,797.39
Safe		456.90
2 IBM XT Personal Computers	ROSE-3	6,666.66
Clear Copy Copy Machine	X930	2,806.49
Telephone & Communications Equipment		890.00
Subtotal		$12,617.44
Total		$100,000.00

263

Exhibit 4
_____

THE WORKER-OWNED COOPERATIVE
PRO-FORMA INCOME STATEMENTS FOR THE YEARS 1986-1988
_____

	1986	1987	1988
Net Sales Revenue	$1,150,000.00	$1,779,250.00	$2,182,23.00
Cost of Goods Sold			
Beginning Inventory	100,000.00	129,056.10	161,070.14
Cost of Goods Manufactured	887,812.80	1,436,206.18	1,752,630.41
Less Ending Inventory	129,056.10	161,070.14	196,299.00
Total	$858,756.70	$1,404,192.14	$1,717,401.55
Gross Margin	$291,243.30	$375,057.86	$464,833.45
Operating Expenses			
Indirect Supplies	10,000.00	20,000.00	23,334.00
Office Supplies	2,000.00	4,000.00	5,32.00
Utilities	8,400.00	8,400.00	9,000.00
Administrative Salaries	126,500.00	138,000.00	165,600.00
Insurance and Bonding	5,0000	10,000.00	11,000.00
Legal & Accounting	2,500.00	5,500.00	5,500.00
Telephone	1,365.00	2,155.00	2,155.00
Miscellaneous	13,550.00	12,000.00	15,000.00
Depreciation	11,300.00	14,633.33	17,758.33
Total	$180,615.00	$214,688.33	$254,679.33
Income before Interest & Taxes	$110,628.30	$160,369.53	$210,154.12
Interest	$60,000.00	$58,000.00	$52,500.00
Taxes	$14,175.92	$30,710.86	$55,178.94
Net Income	$36,452.38	$71,658.67	$102,475.18
Net Profit Margin	3.17%	4.03%	4.70%

Exhibit 5

THE WORKER-OWNED COOPERATIVE
PRO-FORMA BALANCE SHEETS January 1, 1987, 1988, 1989

ASSETS	1987	1988	1989
Current Assets:			
Cash	$82,788.86	$97,036.94	$142,720.53
Marketable Securities	19,240.74	19,240.74	79,000.00
Accounts Receivable	126,090.00	237,088.04	311,48.00
Inventory	129,053.37	161,070.14	365,159.74
Prepaid Supplies	5,433.00	7,555.67	7,555.67
Prepaid Expenses	7,500.00	8,000.00	8,000.00
Subtotal	$370,105.97	$529,991.53	$913,919.94
Fixed Assets:			
Land & Factory	250,000.00	250,000.00	250,000.00
Equipment (net)	78,300.00	69,600.00	60,900.00
Truck (net)	10,400.00	7,800.00	7,800.00
Subtotal	$338,700.00	$327,400.00	$318,700.00
Total Assets	$708,805.97	$857,391.53	$1,232,619.94

265

LIABILITIES & WORKER-OWNER ASSETS

Current Liabilities:	1987	1988	1989
Notes Payable (revolving)	$68,000.00	$57,000.00	$10,000.00
Accounts Payable	141,542.38	80,678.98	101,000.00
Accrued Expenses	0.00	73,729.90	143,000.00
Payroll Payable	58,796.00	58,951.00	72,072.00
Taxes Payable	14,175.92	$30,710.86	55,178.94
Subtotal	$282,514.30	$301,070.74	$381,250.55
Long-Term Liabilities			
Term Loan Payable	16,666.67	8,333.33	0.00
Mortgage Payable	195,000.00	190,000.00	185,000.00
Worker-Owners' Equity:	211,452.38	246,658.67	277,475.18
Worker-Owner Investment	175,000.00	175,000.00	175,000.00
Internal Accounts	19,812.50	55,664.39	106,946.91
Reserves	15,850.00	44,531.51	85,557.53
Education	3,962.50	11,132.88	21,389.38

Subtotal	$637,744.05	$731,320.78	$851,369.00

TOTAL LIABILITIES & ASSETS

	$920,258.35	$1,032,391.52	$1,232,619.94

Exhibit 6

THE WORKER-OWNED COOPERATIVE
BREAK-EVEN ANALYSIS

Fixed Costs:

Administrative Salaries	$126,500.00
Legal & Accounting	5,500.00
Telephone	1,365.00
Depreciation	11,300.00
Utilities	8,400.00
Insurance & Bonding	10,000.00
Interest	60,000.00
Taxes	14,175.92

Total Fixed Costs per month	$19,770.08

Variable Costs:

Materials	$1.67
Labor	2.80
Factory Overhead	0.10
Supplies	0.05
Miscelaneous	0.06

Total Variable Costs	$4.68
Selling Price	$5.00
Break-Even Quantity	*61351*
Break-Even Dollar Volume	$286,983.98

Exhibit 7

THE WORKER-OWNED COOPERATIVE
CUMULATIVE VALUE OF MEMBER INTERNAL ACCOUNTS 1986-1990

	1986 $	1987 $	1988 $	1989 $	1990 $
Sales	1,250,000	1,779,000	2,182,000	2,679,000	3,293,000
Sales Growth	—	42%	23%	23%	23%
Profit Percentage	0.03	0.04	0.05	0.08	0.08
Net Profit	39,625	71,704	102,565	200,943	246,975

Allocation of Profits in Total for 35 workers

267

	1986	1987	1988	1989	1990
Internal Accounts @ 50%	19,812	35,809	51,163	100,243	123,044
Reserves @ 40%	15,850	28,682	41,026	80,377	98,790
Education @ 10%	3,962	7,170	10,256	20,094	24,698

Allocation of Profits by Worker/owner

	1986	1987	1988	1989	1990
Internal Accounts per worker per year	566	1,023	1,462	2,864	
Cumulative Internal Accounts	566	1,589	3,051	5,915	9,430

NOTE: Interest of 7.5% on previous year's internal accounts is subtracted from the total (50 percent) profit allocation to workers before distribution.

Exhibit 8

THE WORKER-OWNED COOPERATIVE
CUMULATIVE VALUE OF INTERNAL ACCOUNTS 1986 TO 2005

	1986-1990	1991-1995	1986-2000	2001-2005
Allocation of Profits				
Net Profit	$661,812	$2,026,888	$3,965,100	$6,320,990
50% to Internal Accounts less 7.5% interest on prior year's worker allocation	$330,072	$1,006,261	$1,960,844	$3,112,840
Allocation of Internal Accounts per Worker-Owner				
5-year allocation	$9,431	$28,750	$56,024	$88,938
Cummulative balance	$9,431	$38,181	$94,205	$183,143

Exhibit 9

THE WORKER-OWNED COOPERATIVE
BEGINNING BALANCE SHEET December 15, 1985

ASSETS

Current Assets:

Cash	$43,000.00	
Marketable Securities	6,500.00	
Accounts Receivable	0.00	
Inventory	75,000.00	
Prepaid Supplies	12,000.00	
Prepaid Expenses	13,500.00	
Subtotal		$150,000.00

Fixed Assets:

Land & Factory	250,000.00	
Equipment (net)	87,000.00	
Truck (net)	13,000.00	
Reserves	0.00	
Education	0.00	
Subtotal		$350,000.00
Total Assets		$500,000.00

LIABILITIES & WORKERS' EQUITY

Current Liabilities:

Notes payable	$100,000.00	
Accounts Payable	0.00	
Unearned Revenues	0.00	
Subtotal		$100,000.00

Long-Term Liabilities

Term Loan Payable	25,000.00	
Mortgage Payable	200,000.00	
Worker-Owners' Equity:	175,000.00	
Internal Accounts	0.00	
Subtotal		$400,000.00
Total Liabilities & Equity		$500,000.00

269

Exhibit 10

**THE WORKER-OWNED COOPERATIVE
SALES FORECAST FOR THE YEAR 1986**

1st & 2nd Quarters

	January	February	March	April	May	June
Market Size:						
Clear Copy	15000	15000	15000	15000	15000	15000
Other	0	0	0	0	0	0
Total	15000	15000	15000	15000	15000	15000
	$	$	$	$	$	$
Average Unit Price	5.00	5.00	5.00	5.00	5.00	5.00
Sales:						
Clear Copy	75,000.00	75,000.00	75,000.00	75,000.00	75,000.00	75,000.00
Others	0.00	0.00	0.00	0.00	0.00	0.00
Total	75,000.00	75,000.00	75,000.00	75,000.00	75,000.00	75,000.00

Assumptions: *$5.00 unit price negotiated for a full year.
Clear Copy's demand for Wham Doodles is highest in 4th qtr. because of ITC tax advantage.
Wham Doodles will not be introduced to other buyers until 1987.*

Exhibit 10

THE WORKER-OWNED COOPERATIVE
SALES FORECAST FOR THE YEAR 1986
3rd & 4th Quarters

	July	August	September	October	November	December
Market Size:						
Clear Copy	15000	20000	35000	40000	30000	20000
Other	0	0	0	0	0	0
Total	15000	20000	35000	40000	30000	20000
	$	$	$	$	$	$
Average Unit Price	5.00	5.00	5.00	5.00	5.00	5.00
Sales:						
Clear Copy	75,000.00	100,000.00	175,000.00	200,000.00	150,000.00	100,000.00
Others	0.00	0.00	0.00	0.00	0.00	0.00
Total	75,000.00	100,000.00	175,000.00	200,000.00	150,000.00	100,000.00

Assumptions: $5.00 unit price negotiated for a full year.
Clear Copy's demand for Wham Doodles is highest in 4th qtr. because of ITC tax advantage.
Wham Doodles will not be introduced to other buyers until 1987.

271

Exhibit 11

THE WORKER-OWNED COOPERATIVE
CASH BUDGET FOR THE YEAR 1986

1st & 2nd Quarters

	January $	February $	March $	April $	May $	June $
Beginning Cash Balance:	43,000.00	17,300.00	26,490.00	32,946.67	36,603.33	19,260.00
Plus Cash Receipts (30 day payment lag)						
Sales from Clear Copy	0.00	75,000.00	75,000.00	75,000.00	75,000.00	75,000.00
Sales from Others	0.00	0.00	0.00	0.00	0.00	0.00
Total Cash Receipts	43,000.00	92,300.00	101,490.00	107,946.67	111,603.33	94,260.00
Cash Disbursements:						
Material Purchases	0.00	0.00	0.00	0.00	25,000.00	25,000.00
Direct Labor	21,000.00	42,000.00	42,000.00	42,000.00	42,000.00	42,000.00
Indirect Supplies	0.00	0.00	0.00	0.00	0.00	0.00
Factory Overhead	1,500.00	1,500.00	1,500.00	1,500.00	1,500.00	1,500.00
Office Supplies	0.00	0.00	0.00	0.00	0.00	0.00
Utilities	700.00	700.00	700.00	700.00	700.00	700.00
Administrative Salaries	0.00	11,500.00	11,500.00	11,500.00	11,500.00	11,500.00
Insurance and Bonding	0.00	0.00	0.00	0.00	0.00	0.00
Legal and Accounting	0.00	0.00	0.00	0.00	0.00	0.00
Telephone	0.00	260.00	60.00	60.00	60.00	145.00
Miscellaneous	2,500.00	600.00	1,700.00	4,500.00	500.00	500.00
Mortgage Payment	0.00	0.00	1,833.33	1,833.33	1,833.33	1,833.33
Term Loan Payment	0.00	250.00	250.00	250.00	250.00	250.00
Revolving Loan Payment	0.00	9,000.00	9,000.00	9,000.00	9,000.00	9,000.00
Total Cash Disbursement	25,700.00	65,810.00	68,543.33	71,343.33	92,343.33	92,428.33
New Cash Balance	17,300.00	26,490.00	32,946.67	36,603.33	19,260.00	1,831.67
Loan from Rev. Credit Line	0.00	0.00	0.00	0.00	0.00	4,000.00
New Beginning Cash Balance min. of $5,000	17,300.00	26,490.00	32,946.67	36,603.33	19,260.00	5,831.67

Exhibit 11

THE WORKER-OWNED COOPERATIVE
CASH BUDGET FOR THE YEAR 1986

3rd & 4th Quarters

	July $	August $	September $	October $	November $	December $
Beginning Cash Balance:	5,831.67	5,898.33	5,245.00	5,891.67	40,241.44	85,758.30
Plus Cash Receipts (30 day payment lag)						
Sales from Clear Copy	75,000.00	75,000.00	100,000.00	175,000.00	200,000.00	150,000.00
Sales from Others	0.00	0.00	0.00	0.00	0.00	0.00
Total Cash Receipts	80,831.67	80,898.33	105,245.00	180,891.67	240,241.44	235,758.30
Cash Disbursements:						
Material Purchases	25,000.00	25,000.00	33,000.00	60,296.89	80,079.81	78,586.10
Direct Labor	42,000.00	48,720.00	48,720.00	48,720.00	48,720.00	48,720.00
Indirect Supplies	5,000.00	0.00	0.00	5,000.00	0.00	0.00
Factory Overhead	1,500.00	1,750.00	1,750.00	1,750.00	1,750.00	1,750.00
Office Supplies	1,000.00	0.00	0.00	1,000.00	0.00	0.00
Utilities	700.00	700.00	700.00	700.00	700.00	700.00
Administrative Salaries	11,500.00	11,500.00	11,500.00	11,500.00	11,500.00	11,500.00
Insurance and Bonding	5,000.00	0.00	0.00	0.00	0.00	0.00
Legal and Accounting	2,500.00	0.00	0.00	0.00	0.00	0.00
Telephone	150.00	150.00	100.00	100.00	150.00	130.00
Miscellaneous	500.00	750.00	500.00	500.00	500.00	500.00
Mortgage Payment	1,833.33	1,833.33	1,833.33	1,833.33	1,833.33	1,833.33
Term Loan Payment	250.00	250.00	250.00	250.00	250.00	250.00
Revolving Loan Payment	9,000.00	9,000.00	9,000.00	9,000.00	9,000.00	9,000.00
Total Cash Disbursement	105,933.33	99,653.33	107,353.33	140,650.23	154,483.14	152,969.43
New Cash Balance	(25,101.67)	(18,755.00)	(2,108.33)	40,241.44	85,758.30	82,788.86
Loan from Rev. Credit Line	31,000.00	24,000.00	8,000.00	0.00	0.00	0.00
New Beginning Cash Balance min. of $5,000	5,898.33	5,245.00	5,891.67	40,241.44	85,758.30	82,788.86

Exhibit 12

THE WORKER-OWNED COOPERATIVE
CASH BUDGET FOR THE YEAR 1987

1st & 2nd Quarters

	January $	February $	March $	April $	May $	June $
Beginning Cash Balance:	70,048.12	26,313.42	11,925.28	5,059.85	5,249.57	7,992.71
Plus Cash Receipts						
(30-day payment lag)						
Sales from Clear Copy	103,000.00	103,000.00	103,000.00	103,000.00	103,000.00	103,000.00
Sales from Others	5,000.00	10,000.00	12,500.00	15,000.00	25,000.00	25,000.00
Total Cash Receipts	178,048.12	139,313.42	127,425.28	123,059.85	133,249.57	135,992.71
Cash Disbursements:						
Material Purchases	59,349.37	46,437.81	42,475.09	41,019.95	44,416.52	45,330.90
Direct Labor	53,592.00	53,592.00	53,592.00	53,592.00	53,592.00	53,592.00
Indirect Supplies	5,000.00	0.00	0.00	5,000.00	0.00	0.00
Factory Overhead	1,815.00	1,815.00	1,815.00	1,815.00	1,815.00	1,815.00
Office Supplies	0.00	1,000.00	0.00	0.00	1,000.00	0.00
Utilities	700.00	700.00	700.00	700.00	700.00	700.00
Administrative Salaries	11,500.00	11,500.00	11,500.00	11,500.00	11,500.00	11,500.00
Insurance and Bonding	5,000.00	0.00	0.00	0.00	0.00	0.00
Legal and Accounting	2,500.00	0.00	0.00	0.00	0.00	0.00
Telephone	195.00	260.00	200.00	100.00	150.00	145.00
Miscellaneous	1,000.00	1,000.00	1,000.00	1,000.00	1,000.00	1,000.00
Additional Capital Equipment	0.00	0.00	0.00	0.00	0.00	0.00
Mortgage Payment	1,833.33	1,833.33	1,833.33	1,833.33	1,833.33	1,833.33
Term Loan Payment	250.00	250.00	250.00	250.00	250.00	250.00
Revolving Loan Payment	9,000.00	9,000.00	9,000.00	9,000.00	9,000.00	9,000.00
Total Cash Disbursement	151,734.71	127,388.14	122,365.43	125,810.28	125,256.86	125,166.24
New Cash Balance	26,313.42	11,925.28	5,059.85	(2,750.43)	7,992.71	10,826.47
Loan from Rev. Credit Line	0.00	0.00	0.00	8,000.00	0.00	0.00
New Beginning Cash Balance min. of $5,000	26,313.42	11,925.28	5,059.85	5,249.57	7,992.71	10,826.47

Exhibit 12

THE WORKER-OWNED COOPERATIVE CASH BUDGET FOR THE YEAR 1987

3rd & 4th Quarters

	July $	August $	September $	October $	November $	December $
Beginning Cash Balance:	10,826.47	7,993.98	5,607.66	25,758.44	67,525.62	118,320.42
Plus Cash Receipts (30-day payment lag)						
Sales from Clear Copy	103,000.00	103,000.00	140,000.00	190,000.00	218,500.00	140,000.00
Sales from Others	30,000.00	30,000.00	30,000.00	30,000.00	30,000.00	24,250.00
Total Cash Receipts	143,826.47	140,993.98	175,607.66	245,758.44	316,025.62	282,570.42
Cash Disbursements:						
Material Purchases	47,942.16	46,997.99	58,535.89	81,919.48	105,341.87	94,190.14
Direct Labor	53,592.00	64,680.00	64,680.00	64,680.00	64,680.00	64,680.00
Indirect Supplies	5,000.00	0.00	0.00	5,000.00	0.00	0.00
Factory Overhead	1,815.00	2,200.00	2,200.00	2,200.00	2,200.00	2,200.00
Office Supplies	0.00	1,000.00	0.00	0.00	1,000.00	0.00
Utilities	700.00	700.00	700.00	700.00	700.00	700.00
Administrative Salaries	11,500.00	11,500.00	11,500.00	11,500.00	11,500.00	11,500.00
Insurance and Bonding	5,000.00	0.00	0.00	0.00	0.00	0.00
Legal and Accounting	3,000.00	0.00	0.00	0.00	0.00	0.00
Telephone	200.00	225.00	150.00	150.00	200.00	180.00
Miscellaneous	1,000.00	1,000.00	1,000.00	1,000.00	1,000.00	1,000.00
Additional Capital Equipment	0.00	80,000.00	0.00	0.00	0.00	0.00
Mortgage Payment	1,833.33	1,833.33	1,833.33	1,833.33	1,833.33	1,833.33
Term Loan Payment	250.00	250.00	250.00	250.00	250.00	250.00
Revolving Loan Payment	9,000.00	9,000.00	9,000.00	9,000.00	9,000.00	9,000.00
Total Cash Disbursement	140,832.49	219,386.33	149,849.22	178,232.81	197,705.21	185,533.47
New Cash Balance	2,993.98	(78,392.34)	25,758.44	67,525.62	118,320.42	97,036.94
Loan from Rev. Credit Line	5,000.00	84,000.00	0.00	0.00	0.00	0.00
New Beginning Cash Balance min. of $5,000	7,993.98	5,607.66	25,758.44	67,525.62	118,320.42	97,036.94

Exhibit 13

THE WORKER-OWNED COOPERATIVE
CASH BUDGET FOR THE YEAR 1988

1st & 2nd Quarters

	January $	February $	March $	April $	May $	June $
Beginning Cash Balance:	97,036.94	58,461.43	46,013.42	40,774.41	34,048.41	34,848.07
Plus Cash Receipts (30-day payment lag)						
Sales from Clear Copy	125,000.00	125,000.00	125,000.00	125,000.00	125,000.00	125,000.00
Sales from Others	20,000.00	20,000.00	22,500.00	25,000.00	27,500.00	30,000.00
Total Cash Receipts	242,036.94	203,461.43	193,513.42	190,774.41	186,548.41	189,848.07
Cash Disbursements:						
Material Purchases	80,678.98	67,820.48	64,504.47	63,591.47	62,182.80	63,282.69
Direct Labor	58,951.20	58,951.20	58,951.20	58,951.20	58,951.20	58,951.20
Indirect Supplies	6,667.00	0.00	0.00	5,000.00	0.00	0.00
Factory Overhead	2,200.00	2,200.00	2,200.00	2,200.00	2,200.00	2,200.00
Office Supplies	0.00	1,333.00	0.00	0.00	1,333.00	0.00
Utilities	750.00	750.00	750.00	750.00	750.00	750.00
Administrative Salaries	13,800.00	13,800.00	13,800.00	13,800.00	13,800.00	13,800.00
Insurance and Bonding	5,500.00	0.00	0.00	0.00	0.00	0.00
Legal and Accounting*	2,500.00	0.00	0.00	0.00	0.00	0.00
Telephone	195.00	260.00	200.00	100.00	150.00	145.00
Miscellaneous	1,250.00	1,250.00	1,250.00	1,250.00	1,250.00	1,250.00
Additional Capital Equipment	0.00	0.00	0.00	0.00	0.00	0.00
Mortgage Payment	1,833.33	1,833.33	1,833.33	1,833.33	1,833.33	1,833.33
Term Loan Payment	250.00	250.00	250.00	250.00	250.00	250.00
Revolving Loan Payment	9,000.00	9,000.00	9,000.00	9,000.00	9,000.00	9,000.00
Total Cash Disbursement	183,575.51	157,448.01	152,739.01	156,726.00	151,700.34	151,462.22
New Cash Balance	58,461.43	46,013.42	40,774.41	34,048.41	34,848.07	38,385.85
Loan from Rev. Credit Line	0.00	0.00	0.00	0.00	0.00	0.00
New Beginning Cash Balance min. of 5,000	58,461.43	46,013.42	40,774.41	34,048.41	34,848.07	38,385.85

Exhibit 13

THE WORKER-OWNED COOPERATIVE
CASH BUDGET FOR THE YEAR 1988

3rd & 4th Quarters

	July $	August $	September $	October $	November $	December $
Beginning Cash Balance: Plus Cash Receipts (30-day payment lag)	38,385.85	25,522.37	5,301.58	42,229.05	100,180.70	154,598.80
Sales from Clear Copy	125,000.00	125,000.00	175,000.00	225,000.00	250,000.00	180,125.00
Sales from Others	30,000.00	32,500.00	35,000.00	42,500.00	35,750.00	31,360.00
Total Cash Receipts	193,385.85	183,022.37	215,301.58	309,729.05	385,930.70	366,083.80
Cash Disbursements:						
Material Purchases	64,461.95	61,007.46	71,767.19	103,243.02	128,643.57	122,027.93
Direct Labor	58,951.20	72,072.00	72,072.00	72,072.00	72,072.00	72,072.00
Indirect Supplies	6,667.00	0.00	0.00	5,000.00	0.00	0.00
Factory Overhead	2,200.00	2,200.00	2,200.00	2,200.00	2,200.00	2,200.00
Office Supplies	0.00	1,333.00	0.00	0.00	1,333.00	0.00
Utilities	750.00	750.00	750.00	750.00	750.00	750.00
Administrative Salaries	13,800.00	13,800.00	13,800.00	13,800.00	13,800.00	13,800.00
Insurance and Bonding	5,500.00	0.00	0.00	0.00	0.00	0.00
Legal and Accounting	3,000.00	0.00	0.00	0.00	0.00	0.00
Telephone	200.00	225.00	150.00	150.00	200.00	180.00
Miscellaneous	1,250.00	1,250.00	1,250.00	1,250.00	1,250.00	1,250.00
Additional Capital Equipment	0.00	75,000.00	0.00	0.00	0.00	0.00
Mortgage Payment	1,833.33	1,833.33	1,833.33	1,833.33	1,833.33	1,833.33
Term Loan Payment	250.00	250.00	250.00	250.00	250.00	250.00
Revolving Loan Payment	9,000.00	9,000.00	9,000.00	9,000.00	9,000.00	9,000.00
Total Cash Disbursement	167,863.48	238,720.79	173,072.53	209,548.35	231,331.90	223,363.27
New Cash Balance	25,522.37	(55,698.42)	42,229.05	100,180.70	154,498.80	142,720.53
Loan from Rev. Credit Line	0.00	61,000.00	0.00	0.00	0.00	0.00
New Beginning Cash Balance min. of $5,000	25,522.37	5,301.58	42,229.05	100,180.70	154,598.80	142,720.53

Exhibit 14

FEDERAL TAX CALENDAR

	Jan	Feb	Mar	April	May	June	July	Aug	Sept	Oct	Nov	Dec
Individual Income Tax				**15th** return and tax due								
Individual Estimated Tax	**17th** Voucher 4 balance of 1982 estimated tax due			**17th** Voucher 1 1/4 of 1983 estimated tax due		**15th** Voucher 2 1/4 of 1983 estimated tax due			**15th** Voucher 3 1/4 of 1983 estimated tax due			
Partnership Income				**15th** return due								
Corporate Income Tax			**15th** return and deposit 1/2 of tax due			**15th** deposit balance of tax due						

Individual Income Tax/ Return (Form 1040), together with balance of tax, due by 15th day of 4th month following end of year. Automatic extension of time to file for 4 months may be obtained by filing jForm 4868 by sme date. Additional extension may be requested on form 2688.

Individual Estimated Tax / Form 1040-ES and 1/4 of tax due on 15th day of 4th, 6th and 9th months of year and 1st month following end of year.

Partnership Income/ Return (Form 1065) due by 15th day of 4th month following end of year. Extension of time to file may be requested on Form 2758. Partnership pays no tax since income is reported on partners' returns due by same date.

Corporate Income Tax/ Return (Form 1120) due by 15th day of 3rd month following end of year. Application for automatic extension of time to file (Form 7004) also due by same date. Additional extension may be requested on Form 7005. Payment of tax per return due in equal installments by 15th day of 3rd and 6th months following end of year; payment to be made to authorized depository on Form 503.

Exhibit 14 (Cont.)

FEDERAL TAX CALENDAR

	Jan	Feb	Mar	April	May	June	July	Aug	Sept	Oct	Nov	Dec
Corporate Estimated Tax/ Form 503 used for deposit of estimated tax. Deposits due in equal quarterly installments on 15th day of 4th, 6th, 9th, and 12th monts of year.				15th deposit 1/4 of tax due		15th deposit 1/4 of tax due			15th deposit 1/4 of tax due			15th deposit 1/4 of tax due
Small Business Corporation/ Return (Form 1120S) due by 15th day of 3rd month following end of year. Application for automatic extension of time to file (Form 7004) also due by same date. Additional Extension may be requested on Form 7005. Payment of tax per return due in equal installments by 15th day of 3rd and 6th months following end of year; payment to be made to authorized depository on Form 503.			15th return and deposit 1/2 of tax due			15th deposit balance of tax due						
Payroll Taxes/ Quarterly return (Form 941) of combined withheld income, employer's and employee's social security taxes (FICA) due April 30, July 31, Oct. 31, and Jan. 31. Pay tax with return unless required to make deposits to authorized depository. If all deposits are made timely, quarterly return is postponed 10 days.	31st 4th quarter 1982			2nd 1st quarter			1st 2nd quarter			31st 3rd quarter		
(A) If cumulative combined withholding taxes at the end of any month of the calendar quarter exceed $500, but not as much as $3,000 or more at the end of any eighth monthly period (see B below), deposit by 15th of next month must be made on Form 501.	17th Dec. 1982 dep. due	15th Jan. dep. due	15th Feb. dep. due	15th Mar. dep. due	16th April dep. due	15th May dep. due	15th June dep. due	15th July dep. due	15th Aug. dep. due	17th Sept. dep. due	15th Oct. dep. due	15th Nov. dep. due

Exhibit 14 (Cont.)

FEDERAL TAX CALENDAR

FEDERAL TAX CALENDAR	Jan	Feb	Mar	April	May	June	July	Aug	Sept	Oct	Nov	Dec
(B) If cumulative combined withholding taxes at the end of any calendar quarter do not exceed $500, payment is due by the end of the following month. Payment may be made with the quarterly Form 941 or with Form 501.	**31st** 4th qtr. 1982 deposit due				**2nd** deposit due			**1st** deposit due		**31st** deposit due		
Individual withholding (Form W-2) and reconciliation statements (Form W-3) are due the last day of February. Employers must furnish employees with Form W-2 by January 31st.	**31st** W-2 to employees	**28th** statements due										
Unemployment Insurance (FUTA)/ Return (Form 940) for calendar year due January 31st. Quarterly deposits with Form 508 required if FUTA tax for quarter plus previously undeposited amount exceeds $100. If all deposits made on time, return postponed 10 days.	**31st** 1982 return and tax due				**2nd** deposit 1st qtr. FUTA due			**1st** deposit 2nd qtr. FUTA due		**31st** deposit 3rd qtr. FUTA due		
Information Returns/ Every person, including a nonprofit organization, who makes payments of commissions not covered by withholding must file an information return (Form 1099, Form 1087, etc.). Copy must be sent to payee by January 31st. Form 1099, etc. with summary on Form 1096 must be filed with government by February 28th.	**31st** copy to payee	**28th** return due										

280

Source: *"Tax 1983 Calendar", Price Waterhouse, Copyright 1982.*

Exhibit 15

ORGANIZATION AND STRUCTURE OF THE WORKER-OWNED COOPERATIVE

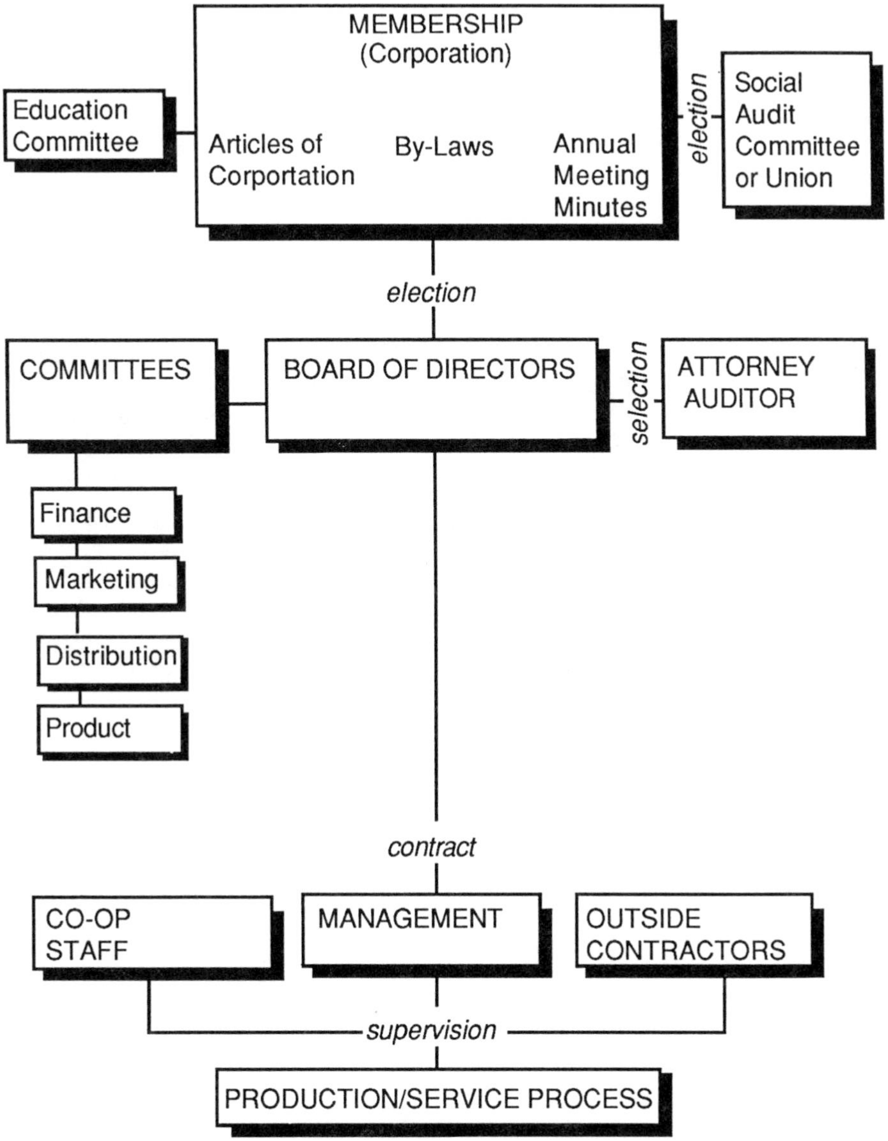

FOOTNOTES

Introduction

283

1. E.F. Schumacher, **Good Work,** London: Abacus, 1980.

2. Robert Oakshott, **The Case for Workers' Coops,** London: 1978; Greater London Enterprise Board, **A Strategy for Co-operation: Worker Co-ops in London,** London: nd,; **Cooperation and Job Creation in Wales: A Feasibility Study,** Wales T.U.C., August 1981.

3. "Employee Ownership and Corporate Performance," compiled by the National Center for Employee Ownership, **Employee Ownership,** Vol V February 1985, p. 3.

4. Keith Bradley and Alan Gelb, **Share Ownership For Employees,** London: Public Policy Centre, 1986, pp. xxiii-xiv.

5. Ibid., pp. 67.

6. Ibid.

7. Alain Cote, "Ten Thousand Quebec Workers Try Another Way," **Worker Co-Ops,** Vol. 6 Summer 1986, pp. 8-9; Claude Carbonneau, "Worker Co-ops Witness Remarkable Growth in Quebec," **Worker Co-Ops,** Vol 4 Fall 1984, pp. 1.

8. Ibid.

9. Ibid.

10. Ibid.

11. Adapted from Grant Ingle, "How to tell what's hot and what's not in workplace innovation," **Workplace Democracy,** No. 53 Summer 1986, pp. 16-17.

Chapter One

1) T.W. Mercer, **Co-operation's Prophet: The Life and Letters of Dr. William King of Brighton with a Reprint of The Co-operator, 1828-1830.** Manchester: Cooperative Union, 1947, pp. 65-66.

2) As quoted in Paul Lambert, **Studies in The Social Philosophy of Cooperation**, Manchester: The Cooperative Union, 1963, pp. 53-54.

3) As quoted in Joseph G. Knapp, **The Rise of American Cooperative Enterprise: 1620-1920**, Danville, Ill.: Interstate Printers & Publishers, 1969, p. 31.

4) As quoted in Knapp, p. 34.

5) As quoted in Knapp, p. 33.

6) As quoted by John R. Commons and John B. Andrews, **A Documentary History of American Industrial Society**, Vol. IX, p. 138.

7) As quoted in Knapp, pp. 36-37.

8) As quoted in Commons and Andrews, p. 139.

9) Derek C. Jones and Donald J. Schneider, "Self-Help Production Cooperatives: Government-Administered Cooperatives During the Depression," in Robert Jackall and Henry M. Levin, **Worker Cooperatives in America**, Berkeley: U. of California Press, 1984, pp. 57-84.

10) Ana Gutierrez-Johnson, "The Mondragon Cooperative Model," **Changing Work**, Vol. 1, 1984, p. 40.

284

Chapter 2

1) There is a good deal of confusion about the definition and use of the term "worker-owned firm." Stewart E. Perry and Hunt C. Davis have sought to specify what is meant by the term. They have set forth a provisional definition: "A worker-owned enterprise (firm) is a formal organization designed with the ultimate goal of earning at least a threshold level of income for its members, largely by producing goods and/or services within one of three general organizational forms: (1) a worker- owned *partnership*; (2) a worker-owned *operating corporation*; and (3) a worker-owned *holding corporation*." Using the Perry-Davis definition, the worker-owned firm outlined in this book comes under the second category—the worker-owned operating corporation—which is "a chartered joint stock, cooperative, or other for-profit firm engaged directly in production in which more than 50 percent of the workers have more than 50 percent of both active ownership and passive ownership rights." Stewart E. Perry and Hunt C. Davis, "The Worker-Owned Firm: The Idea and Its Conceptual Limits," **Economic and Industrial Democracy**, Vol. 6 (August 1985), pp. 275-296.

2) In the typical leveraged buyout, a group of investors buys out a company's shareholders by leveraging, or borrowing heavily against, the target company. These investors put up between 1 and 10 percent of the total purchase price in cash. Executives of the target company often contribute some of the money. The rest of the purchase price, up to 95 percent in some cases, is financed by layers of loans from banks and insurance companies. The usual strategy is to use the company's cash on hand, its cash flow or the sale of some assets to reduce the debt.

3) Susan R.A. Honeyman, "Largest ESOP in Nation Comes into Being in Seymour," **Connecticut Business Journal**, June 18, 1985; Deborah Hallberg, "When the Workers Own the Company," East Hartford **Business Times**, July 1985.

4) "Do ESOP's Really Broaden the Ownership of Wealth?" **Employee Ownership**, Vol. V October 1985, p. 1.

5) International Cooperative Alliance, 1966.

6) Paul Bernstein, **Workplace Democratization: Its Internal Dynamics**, New Brunswick, N.J.: Transaction Books, 1976.

7) David P. Ellerman, "ESOPs & CO-OPs: Worker Capitalism & Worker Democracy," **Labor Research Review**, Vol 1, Spring 1985, pp. 56-57.

8) Ibid, p. 60.

9) Dale Feuer, "A World Without Layoffs: Wouldn't It Be Lovely," **Training**, August 1985, pp 23-31; Jocelyn F. Gutchess, "Employment Security and Productivity? It Can be Done," **National Productivity Review**, Summer 1985, pp 275-286; Gary B. Hansen, "Preventing Layoffs: Developing an Effective Job Security and Economic Adjustment Program," **Employee Relations Law Journal**, Vol. 11 Autumn 1985, pp. 239-268.

10) David P. Ellerman, **Management Planning With Labor as a Fixed Cost: The Mondragon annual Business Plan Manual**, Somerville, Mass.: Industrial Cooperative Association, July 1984, pp. 5-13.

11) Ibid., p. 6.

12) Interview with founder-members of Mondragon, as quoted in Keith Bradley and Alan Gelb, **Cooperation at Work: The Mondragon Experience**, London: Heinemann Educational Books, Ltd., 1983, p. 75.

13) Corey Rosen, Katherine J. Klein, and Karen M. Young, **Employee Stock Ownership in America: The Equity Solution**, Boston: Lexington Books, 1986, pp. 193-194.

14) Ibid., pp. 194-195.

15) John A. Welsh and Jerry F. White, **Entrepreneurship: Practical Tips or How To Survive in a Room Full of Entrepreneurs**, Dallas: Caruth Institute of Owner-Managed Business, Edwin L. Cox School of Business, Southern Methodist University, 1985, p. 1.

16) Garth A. Hanson, **Entrepreneurship: A Career Alternative**, Columbus: The National Center for Research in Vocational Education, 1984.

17) "The Entrepreneurial Mystique," **INC**, October 1985, p.35.

18) Ibid.

19) Ibid.

20) Clair E. Hein, **Starting Your Business**, Ames: Cooperative Extension Service, Iowa State University, September 1984., p. 2.

Chapter 3

1) Charles Turner, "Goals of the Education Program in the Organizing Phase of a Democratically-Owned Firm," **Proceedings of the National Employee-Ownership and Participation Conference, October 12-14, 1984, Greensboro, North Carolina**, pp. 441-448.

2) Quoted in J. Carruthers, "The Emergence of Worker Co-operatives in New South Wales," **Work and People**, Vol. 7, No. 3, 1981.

3) Meredith, Geoffrey G., Nelson, Robert E. and Neck, Philip A., **The Practice of Entrepreneurship**. Geneva: International Labour Office, 1982, p. 33.

4) Much of the material in this section has been adapted from **Buyout: A Guide For Workers Facing Plant Closings**, published by the Department of Economic and Business Development, State of California, Second Printing, September 1983, pp. 27-34.

5) Frank Lindenfeld, "O & O Markets: The Labor and Cooperative Movements Get Together," **Changing Work**, Vol. 1, 1984, p. 45; Noel Weyrich, "Changing the Pace," **New Age Journal**, November 1984.

6) Clark, Dennis and Guben, Merry. **Future Bread: How Retail Workers Ransomed Their Jobs and Lives**. Philadelphia, O & O Investment Fund, 1983, p. 84; Cherlyn S. Granrose, Eileen Applebaum, and Virenda Singh, "Saving Jobs Through Worker Buyouts: Economic and Qualitative Outcomes for Workers in Worker-Owned, QWL, and Non-QWL Supermarkets," **IRRA: Proceedings of the Thirty-Eighth Annual Meeting, New York, December 28-30, 1985**, pp. 196-204.

7) Jeremy Brecher, "If All People are Banded Together," *Labor Research Review*, Vol. V No. 2, Fall 1986, pp. 3-6.

286

Chapter 4

1) Frank Lindenfeld, "O & O Markets: The Labor and Cooperative Movements Get Together," **Changing Work**, Vol. 1, 1984, p. 45.

2) Jack Cheevers, "It's All Over for Workers at Rainbow," **The Tribune**, June 3, 1986.

Chapter 5

1) David Ellerman, "What Is a Workers' Cooperative?" Somerville, Mass.: Industrial Cooperative Association, n.d., p.8.

2) Janet Howley, **Financing Worker Cooperatives: Short Directory of Sources**, Somerville, Mass.: Industrial Cooperative Association, August 1982.

3) Lynn Asinof, "Small Town Decides Best Way to Lure High-Tech Firms Is to Invest in Them," **Wall Street Journal**, August 7, 1985.

Chapter 7

1) Peter J. Honigsberg et al., **We Own It**, Laytonville, Cal.: Bell Springs Publishing, 1982, p. 54.

2) Ibid.

3) Ana Gutierrez-Johnson, "The Mondragon Model of Cooperative Enterprise: Considerations Concerning Its Success and Transferability," **Changing Work**, Vol. 1 Fall 1984, p. 41.

4) U.S. Department of Agriculture, **Director Liability in Agriculture Cooperatives**, Cooperative Information Report No. 34. Washington, D.C., 1984.

5) David Ellerman, "ESOPs & CO-OPs: Worker Capitalism & Worker Democracy," **Labor Research Review**, Vol 6 Spring 1985, pp. 64-65.

6) Ibid.

7) Ibid.

8) Corey Rosen, "U.S. Tax Law Encourages Employee Ownership," *Worker Co-ops* Winter 1987, p. 7.

9) David Ellerman, "The Co-op/ESOP Debater" *Worker Co-ops*, Winter 1987, p. 9.

Chapter 8

1) Branko Horvat, "The Organizational Theory of Workers' Management," in **International Yearbook of Organizational Democracy** Vol. 1, edited by Colin Crouch and Frank A. Heller. New York: John Wiley Sons, 1983. pp.279- 300.

2) Caja Laboral Popular, **The Mondragon Experiment**, Mondragon: n.d., pp. 6-7.

3) David Ellerman, "The Legitimate Opposition at Work: The Union's Role in Large Democratic Firms," Somerville, Mass.: Industrial Cooperative Association, September 1985.

4) J. Richard Hackman, Edward E. Lawler III, and Lyman W. Porter, **Perspectives on Behavior in Organizations**. New York: McGraw-Hill, 1983.

5) Susan J. Fowler and Rachel A. Willis, "What is So Special About Space Builders, Anyway?" **Workplace Democracy**, Vol. XII (Spring/Summer 1985), pp. 6, 10.

6) George Lassere, **Co-operative Enterprises** Manchester, the Co-operative Union, 1959. Trans. by Anne Lamming. p. 84.

7) "Cloudy Days for Solar Center," **Workplace Democracy**, Volume XII (Fall 1985), p.23.

8) As quoted in Corey Rosen, et.al., **Employee Ownership in America: the Equity Solution**, Boston: D.C. Heath & Company, 1986, pp. 177-178.

9) Ewell Paul Roy, **Cooperatives: Development, Principles and Management**. Danville, Ill.: Interstate Printers Publishers, 1981. p. 448.

Chapter 9

1) Jaroslav Vanek, "Education For the Practice of Self-Management in the United States," (Ithaca, New York: 1977), mimeo, p. 1.

2) Susan J. Fowler and Rachel A. Willis, "Democratic Management and Learning: A Case Study of a Small Enterprise," **Proceedings of the National Employee-Ownership and Participation Conference**, Greensboro, N.C., October 12-14, 1984, pp. 294.

3) Art Danforth, "Dashed Hopes, Broken Dreams," 1980. Mimeo, p. 8. See also Robert Jackall and Henry M. Levin, eds., **Worker Cooperatives in America**. Berkeley: U. of California Press, 1984, p. 82.

4) George Burt, **A Report on the Third Year's Activities, The Scottish Adult Basic Education Unit-SABEU**, Edinburgh: Atholl House, 1983, p. 21.

5) "Rainbow Workers Cooperative," **Workplace Democracy**, Vol. 12 (Fall 1985), p.23.

6) John S. Rausch, "At Dungannon: The Struggle Continues," **Workplace Democracy**, Vol. 12 Fall 1985, p. 8, 19.

7) Ibid.

8) Keith Bradley and Alan Gelb, **Cooperative at Work: The Mondragon Experience**, London: Heinemann Educational Books, 1983, p. 70.

288

ADDITIONAL READING

Introduction

Bluestone, Barry, and Harrison, Bennett. **The Deindustrialization of America**. New York: Basic Books, 1982.

Bowles, Samuel, and Gintas, Herbert. **Democracy & Capitalism**. New York: Basic Books, 1986.

Bradley, Keith and Gelb, Alan. **Worker Capitalism: The New Industrial Relations**. Cambridge, Mass.: MIT Press, 1983.

Bradley, Keith, and Gelb, Alan. **Share Ownership For Employees**. London: Public Policy Centre, 1986.

"Deindustrialization: Restructuring the Economy," **The Annals of the American Academy of Political and Social Science.** Vol. 475 September 1984.

"Economic Justice for All: Catholic Social Teaching and the U.S. Economy," **Origins: NC Documentary Service**, Vol. 16, No. 24 November 27, 1986, pp. 409-455.

Kennedy, Donald, ed. **Labor and Reindustrialization: Workers and Social Change**. Dept. of Labor Studies, The Pennsylvania State University, 1984.

Rosen, Corey, Klein, Katherine J., and Young, Karen M. **Employee Ownership in America: The Equity Solution**. Boston: D.C. Heath & Co., 1986.

Surpin, Rick. **Enterprise Development and Worker Ownership**. New York: Community Service Society, 1984.

Woodworth, Warner, Meek, Christopher, and Whyte, William F. **Industrial Democracy: Strategies for Community Revitalization**. Beverly Hills: Sage Publications, 1985.

Chapter 1

Bonner, Arnold. **British Co-operation**. Manchester: Co-operative Union. Rev. Ed. 1970.

Curl, John. **History of Work Cooperation in America**. Berkeley: Homeward Press, 1980.

Gutierrez-Johnson, Ana. **Industrial Democracy in Action: The Cooperative Complex of Mondragon**. (Ph.D. Dissertation, Cornell University, 1982.) Ann Arbor: University Microfilms, 1982.

Jackall, Robert and Levin, Henry M. **Worker Cooperatives in America**. Berkeley: University of California Press. 1984.

Jones, Derek Charles. **The Economics of British Producer Cooperatives**. (Ph.D. Dissertation, Cornell University, 1974.) Ann Arbor: University Microfilms, 1974. Especially Chapter 1.

Linehan, Mary and Vincent Tucker. **Workers' Co-operatives: Potential and Problems**. Cork: U.C.C. Bank of Ireland Centre for Co-operative Studies, 1983. Especially Part One.

Oakeshott, Robert. **The Case for Workers' Co-ops**. London: Routledge & Kegan Paul, 1978.

Chapter 2

Bernstein, Paul. **Workplace Democratization: Its Internal Dynamics**. New Brunswick, N.J.: Transaction Books, 1976.

Bradley, Keith, and Gelb, Alan. **Share Ownership for Employees**. London: Public Policy Centre, 1986.

Employment Security in a Free Economy: A Work in America Institute Policy Study. New York: Pergamon Press, 1984.

Gunn, Christopher E. **Workers' Self-Management in the United States**. Ithaca: Cornell University Press, 1985.

Gutchess, Jocelyn F. **Employment Security in Action: Strategies That Work**. New York: Pergamon Press, 1985.

Hanson, Garth A. **Entrepreneurship: A Career Alternative**. Columbus: The National Center for Research in Vocational Education, 1984.

Lambert, Paul. **Studies in the Social Philosophy of Co-Operation**. Manchester: Co-operative Union, 1963.

Mason, Ronald. **Participatory and Workplace Democracy: A Theoretical Critique of Liberalism**. Carbondale: Southern Illinois University Press, 1982.

Rosen, Corey, Katherine J. Klein and Karen M. Young. **Employee Ownership in America: The Equity Solution**. Boston: D.C. Heath & Co., 1986.

Russell, Raymond. **Sharing Ownership in the Workplace**. Albany: State University of New York Press, 1984.

Chapter 3

A Guide for Communities Facing Major Layoffs or Plant Shutdowns. Washington, D.C.: U.S. Department of Labor, 1980.

Clark, Dennis and Guben, Merry. **Future Bread: How Retail Workers Ransomed Their Jobs and Lives**. Philadelphia: O&O Investment Fund. 1983.

Early Warning Manual. Chicago: Midwest Center for Labor Research, 1986.

Hansen, Gary B., and Bentley, M. T., **Problems and Solutions in a Plant Shutdown: A Handbook for Community Involvement**. Logan: Utah Center for Productivity and Quality of Working Life, Utah State Univ., 1981.

Hanson, Garth A. **Entrepreneurship: A Career Alternative**. Columbus: National Center for Research in Vocational Education, 1984.

Hargraves, Richard. **Starting a Business**. North Pomfret, Vt.: David Charles. 1982.

How to Organize a Worker Buyout. Somerville, Mass.: Industrial Cooperative Association.

Kanawaty, George. **Managing and Developing New Forms of Work Organization**. Geneva: International Labour Office. 2nd. ed. 1984.

Parzen, Julia, Catherine Squire and Michael Kieschnick. **Buyout: A Guide For Workers Facing Plant Closings**. 2nd Printing. Sacramento: State of California, Department of Economic and Business Development. September 1983.

Kieschnick, Michael; Parzen, Julia; Rosen, Cory; and Squire, Catherine. **Employee Buyout Handbook**. Arlington, Va.: National Center for Employee Ownership. Revised 1985.

Manitoba Employee Ownership Handbook. Winnipeg: Manitoba Business Development and Tourism. 1985.

Schweke, William, and Stares, Rodney. **Sewing the Seeds of Economic Renewal: A Manual for Dislocated Communities**. Washington, D.C.: Center for Enterprise Development, 1986.

Chapter 4

Bangs, David H. and Osgood, William R. **Business Planning Guide**. Dover, NH.: Upstart Publishing Co. 2nd. ed., 1983.

Balogh, Judy, et. al. **Beyond a Dream: An Instructors Guide For Small Business Exploration**. Columbus, Oh.: The National Center for Research in Vocational Education, 1985.

Fisher, Dennis U. **Fundamentals of Business: An Instructor's Guide to Providing Business Management Training for Operators of Small Independently Owned Businesses**. Mississippi State U.: Southern Rural Development Center, Mississippi State University, June 1985. (This publication is available from any of the four regional rural development centers located at Cornell, Iowa State, Mississippi State, and Oregon State universities.)

Saglio, Janet, and Hackman, J. Richard. **The Design of Governance Systems for Small Worker Cooperatives.** Somerville, Mass.: Industrial Cooperative Association, 1982.

Smith, Robert M. **Helping Adults Learn How To Learn.** San Francisco: Jossey-Bass, Inc., Publishers, 1983.

Spreckley, Freer. **Social Audit: A Management Tool For Co-Operative Training.** Leeds: Beechwood College Publications. n.d.

Chapter 5

Peggy Butkereit. "Capital Ideas," in **Moving Food**, October-November 1981, pp. 39-42.

Small Business Financing. American Bankers Association, 1120 Connecticut Avenue, NW, Washington, D.C. 20036

The 1982 Users Guide to Government Resources for Economic Development. Northeast-Midwest Institute, P.O. Box 37209, Washington, D.C.

Economic Development. Economic Development Administration, Washington, D.C., 20013.

Financing Employee Ownership. National Center for Employee Ownership, 426 17th Street, Suite 650, Oakland, CA 94612

Handbook of Small Business Finance. Superintendent of Documents, U.S. Government Printing Office, Washington, D.C. 20402

Larry P. Kostroski, **Financing For Your Small Business.** Madison: University of Wisconsin—Small Business Development Center, 1986.

Chapter 7

Employee Ownership: A Reader. Oakland, CA: National Center for Employee Ownership. 1985.

Honigsberg, Peter J.; Kamoroff, Bernard; and Beatty, Jim. **We Own It.** Laytonville, Ca.: Bell Springs Publishing, 1982.

Kieschnick, Michael, et. al. **Employee Buyout Handbook.** Revised. ed. Oakland, CA: National Center for Employee Ownership. 1985.

Pitegoff, Peter. **The Democratic ESOP.** Somerville, Mass.: Industrial Cooperative Association, June 1986.

Rasmussen, A. E. **Financial Management in Cooperative Enterprises.** 4th ed. Saskatoon, SK.: Co-operative College of Canada. 1981.

Chapter 8

Bradley, Keith, and Gelb, Alan, **Cooperation at Work: The Mondragon Experience**. London: Heineman Educational Books, 1983.

Ouchi, William G., **Theory Z**. New York: Avon Books, 1982.

Saglio, Janet H., and Hackman, J. Richard. **The Design of Governance Systems for Small Worker Cooperatives**. Somerville, Mass.: Industrial Cooperative Association, 1982.

Chapter 9

Cohen-Rosenthal, Edward. "Orienting Labor-Management Cooperation Toward Revenue and Growth," **National Productivity Review**, Vol 4 Autumn 1985, pp. 385-396.

Eccles, Tony. **Under New Management**. London: Pan Books, 1981.

Lazes, Peter and Costanza, Tony. "Cutting Costs Without Layoffs Through Union-Management Collaboration," **National Productivity Review**, Vol. 2 Autumn 1983, pp. 362-370.

Nightingale, Donald V. **Workplace Democracy: An Inquiry Into Employee Participation in Canadian Work Organizations**. Toronto: University of Toronto Press. 1982.

Parker, Mike. **Inside the Circle, A Union Guide to QWL**. Boston, Southend Press, 1985.

Participative Problem-solving Workbook. Baltimore: ECR Associates, 1984.

Perspectives on Labor-Management Cooperation. Washington, D.C.: U.S. Department of Labor, Bureau of Labor-Management Cooperative Programs, 1983.

QWL: Buzzword or Breakthrough. Baltimore: ECR Associates, 1985.

QWL/EI. Lansing: Lansing Area Joint Labor-Management Committee, Inc., 1983.

Schuller, Tom. "The Democratization of Work: Educational Implications," in T. Schuller and Jacquetta Megarry (eds.) **Recurrent Education and Life- long Learning**. London: Kogan Page, 1979.

Simmons, John, and Mares, William. **Working Together**. New York: Knopf, 1983.

Sims, Henry P., Jr., and Manz, Charles C. "Conversations Within Self-Managed Work Groups," **National Productivity Review**, Vol 1 Summer 1982, pp. 261-269.

293

INDEX

296